Producing We

Producing Welfare

A Modern Agenda

Chris Miller

Consultant editor
Jo Campling

First published 2004 by
PALGRAVE MACMILLAN
Houndmills, Basingstoke, Hampshire RG21 6XS and
175 Fifth Avenue, New York, N.Y. 10010
Companies and representatives throughout the world

PALGRAVE MACMILLAN is the global academic imprint of the Palgrave Macmillan division of St. Martin's Press, LLC and of Palgrave Macmillan Ltd. Macmillan® is a registered trademark in the United States, United Kingdom and other countries. Palgrave is a registered trademark in the European Union and other countries.

ISBN 0–333–96092–0   hardback
ISBN 0–333–96093–9   paperback

This book is printed on paper suitable for recycling and made from fully managed and sustained forest sources.

A catalogue record for this book is available from the British Library.

A catalog record for this book is available from the Library of Congress.

10   9   8   7   6   5   4   3   2   1
13   12   11   10   09   08   07   06   05   04

Printed in China

119821

For my father Jan Miszewski (1906–2001)

Contents

Acknowledgements

I would like to take this opportunity to thank a number of people who have offered support, ideas and feedback in the writing of this book. Colleagues and students on the MSc programme, Leadership and Organisation for Public Services, at the University of the West of England have been influential in shaping the book's overall focus and structure through their engagement with the issues. Particular thanks go to my colleagues at UWE especially Mike Broussine, Jane Dalrymple, Harry Ferguson, Matthew Jones, Judy Orme and Pat Taylor, all of whom along with Mavis Zutshi read and commented upon at least one of the draft chapters. An earlier version of Chapter 7 first appeared in the *International Journal of Sociology and Social Policy* Vol. 20 No. 5/6, 2000 as a jointly authored piece by myself and Yusuf Ahmad, entitled, 'Collaboration and partnership: An effective response to complexity and fragmentation or solution built on sand?' I am grateful to Yusuf for the opportunity to draw upon this article and also for personal benefits derived from the numerous collaborative and sometimes competitive initiatives we have shared together. I owe a considerable debt to my old friend Jon Davies who worked his way through the whole of the draft manuscript while still managing to produce stimulating and challenging comments.

Finally, embarking upon the production of a book demands a commitment from those closest to the author, although they are not always aware of the consequences and don't have an equal say in the matter. Inevitably, this book would not have been completed without the support of Mavis and Laurie and their willingness to tolerate my absences for lengthy periods of time 'downstairs in the study'. For them no simple 'thanks' is adequate.

Introduction

The UK welfare settlement that was established after the Second World War (1939–45) is undergoing its second transformation. The first attempt to radically alter the British welfare system took place between 1979 and 1997, under the New Right governments of Margaret Thatcher and John Major. The second began with the Labour Party's 1997 election victory under the leadership of Tony Blair. This book is concerned with the emergent features associated with the organisation, instruments and relationships of social welfare that will characterise the forthcoming period in how Britain responds to collective needs.

The relationships between the 'organisational' and 'social' welfare settlements and their impact on policy outcomes have been a neglected area in the policy literature and in practice. Greater attention has been given to the function, aims, detail and impact of specific policies and the function of social welfare in advanced capitalism. This is an attempt to help redress the balance. Matters of organisation, process and social relationships have always been important to those in receipt of services. Individual service users have long complained about the nature and quality of welfare relationships they must endure and, by implication, what this signals in terms of their own social status, and the impact this has on self-perception. Such concerns have typically focused on the nature of the welfare product, the status of the welfare subject and the role adopted by the service provider.

In relation to the welfare product, grievances have highlighted:

- the lack of choice in provision;
- inequities in access to and distribution of services;
- inflexibility in response to individual need and circumstances;
- the drab service uniformity and poor, second rate, standards of provision;
- the disproportionate amount of time spent on 'needs assessment' rather than the provision of services;

- the physical design and lack of care given to public buildings in which welfare transactions take place.

The stigmatised status of the welfare subject has been all too evident in:

- the experience of being shunted between one agency to another, having to constantly repeat the same information with nobody appearing to take responsibility for providing a response to the overall circumstances;
- being excluded from the decision-making processes concerned with current or future provision;
- the perception that decisions made in respect of individual needs are based, at least in part, on the social category or personal life style of the user;
- the sense that successful, valued and socially contributing citizens do not need to engage with public provision;
- being 'spoken about' rather than 'spoken to' or engaged in dialogue by professionals;
- the overwhelming sense that public services are to be approached as a supplicant rather than a citizen.

Finally, the role adopted by the professionals responsible for the assessment and delivery of welfare services has been a particular cause for concern especially in relation to:

- a lack of coordination and failure to communicate between provider agencies;
- a failure to develop effective and sustainable collaborative inter-professional relationships;
- a failure, indeed refusal, to consult service users or provide sufficient information so that informed decisions can be made;
- a lack of local accountability for how services are provided;
- a lack of transparency in relation to either the assessment of needs or the services then offered or denied;
- a dismissal of local or 'common sense' knowledge and a failure to 'listen' to users, against the unjustified elevation of untested or unproven professional 'knowledge' and 'judgement'.

Individual service users and user organisations have made complaints, voiced their protest, or lodged an appeal against specific decisions or actions and campaigned for a better service. Local community-based organisations have for many years campaigned to change aspects of service delivery and organisation with a view to increasing, improving or redesigning the material aspects of policy. A minority of welfare professionals has likewise expressed concern about relationships with service users and the way services are organised, but this has had little impact on mainstream provision or professional behaviour. Many service users have expressed their frustration in other, less socially acceptable but sometimes more effective ways. Both types of reaction can elicit the label of a 'difficult' user. Others have withdrawn from the service either through frustration or a sense that they would no longer endure the personal indignities required to secure a desired but often inadequate service. The majority has kept complaints and frustrations private for fear of jeopardising the chances of securing what is needed.

A central tenet of this book is that how policies are perceived, constructed and delivered at the local, even micro, level is critical to their effectiveness and that, by implication, there exists considerable flexibility for the shaping of policies by local actors. It is, therefore, concerned with those organisations, their cultures and practices, charged with the delivery of social policies. Crucially, it is concerned with the evolving relationships and processes between welfare providers, those who either directly or indirectly receive services, and the wider citizenry and its political representatives. Central to the argument is that in a modern welfare system service users should be neither dependent on a state dominant model nor the chaotic functioning of the market. What is required is a welfare state that is active and enabling, in which the welfare subject is at the centre of provision. As the Commission on Social Justice argued,

> the welfare state must not only look after people when they cannot look after themselves, it must also enable them to achieve self-improvement and self-support ... a hand-up rather than a hand-out (1994: 223–4).

The 1997 election of a Labour Government after nearly eighteen years of neo-liberal Conservative rule provided an opportunity to revisit the fundamentals of how social needs are met through an organised system of welfare. The Conservatives, first under Margaret Thatcher and then John Major, had maintained an ideological

onslaught on the principles and practice enunciated in the creation
of the post-war 'classic' welfare state. For most of the post-war
period this state-dominant model generated sufficient agreement
across the political spectrum for writers to think in terms of a British
consensus. Yet, during the eighteen years in office, successive
Conservative governments had made substantial and damaging
inroads into what appeared to be firmly established structures and
instruments of welfare. Free market competitive and managerial
practices were injected into all areas of policy. The state's virtual
monopoly over the provision of services and the identification of
social issues worthy of a collective response was broken and a
significant mixed economy of providers created. Local democratic
institutions were systematically undermined and marginalised by
the creation of unaccountable bodies, the removal of local government's tax raising capacity, the centralisation of strategic policy
and its implementation through a detailed audit process judged
against a background of performance targets. All of this was
conducted supposedly in the name of providing service users or
consumers, with greater choice.

Welfare professionals were vilified either as entirely self-
interested empire builders concerned to turn everyone into a client
or busy-body do-gooders unable to distinguish a hard luck story
from a genuine case, and constantly taken advantage of by scheming
and deceptive 'scroungers'. Professional interventions were seen
either as oppressive or ineffective. Their representative bodies were
shunned and attacked. Those who were in receipt of welfare services were projected as feckless and undeserving, and the nation
generally castigated their pathological-like dependence on the
state (Murray, 1990). Increasingly the New Right attempted to isolate
particular social groups, such as single parents, as exploiters of
Britain's welfare impulse and in particular pointed to post-war
immigration as a drain on resources. The growing proportion of
expenditure on welfare was identified as a major cause of Britain's
lack of economic investment and its post-war failure to compete
successfully in global markets (Barry *et al.*, 1984). The state was
presented as an over-protective 'nanny' that had displaced the role of
the family, undermined the moral fibre of the country, and promoted
and legitimised ever-new forms of deviancy (Harris and Seldon,
1979; Friedman, 1980). By the time Labour was elected, Britain was
a more fragmented and divided society with some of the highest
levels of inequality in the world and consistently behind all other

major advanced countries on a wide range of indices used to judge both prosperity and well-being.

The overwhelming defeat of the Conservatives and rejection of the outcomes they had pursued presented Labour with a real opportunity to introduce radical measures. It also faced some significant challenges, not least of which was repairing the damage to the social fabric instituted by the previous government and reasserting the role and significance of public service values and practices in sustaining both social and individual well-being. Further there was enough evidence to suggest that the New Right critique of state welfare resonated with the public. A number of the neo-liberal reforms, such as the purchaser/provider split, had also brought demonstrable improvements. The New Right had done a comprehensive job in identifying earlier Labour governments as profligate 'tax and spend' bodies, in the pocket of narrow, self-interested trade unions, undermining individual freedom of choice, stifling any entrepreneurial spirit, overwhelming it with red tape, and the champion of ineffective state monopolies. The incoming Labour government felt compelled to distance itself from such associations.

The New Right had not been alone in its criticism of the post-war welfare state. Much of the mounting criticism during the 1970s had emanated from service users, community organisations, those on the political left and from front-line welfare professionals (Bolger *et al.*, 1981; Langan and Lee, 1989). If there was a dominant message from such critics it was that whilst it was appropriate for the state to provide services, the way in which they were provided was unacceptable (CSE State Group, 1979; Cockburn, 1980; London Edinburgh Weekend Return Group, 1980). Moreover, what it did was often inappropriate, ineffective and insufficient. Too many of the challenging social and economic issues remained, and in some cases had become worse, despite a variety of initiatives over many years. In short, there could be no easy return to pre-Thatcherite welfare. There had been no 'golden period' beyond the immediate post-war sense of achievement at the construction of comprehensive collective provision. Things had changed in other respects, too. The nature of British society was profoundly different in the late twentieth century from what it had been fifty years earlier. It was internally more diverse, complex, fragmented and divided, less deferential and more uncertain of itself and in its relationships to what was a new global order.

Labour's return to office came, despite its huge majority, without the energy of any grass-roots movement. Labour brought with it a new younger group of politicians – many surprised to be elected – and a small army of political advisors. They came with energy and fresh ideas but not the connections with socialist politics. Indeed, they were the children of Thatcherism and influenced by the politics of the time. There were high expectations of change, and such delight and relief at the sheer scale of the Tory defeat but this had not been achieved on the basis of a well-organised infrastructure outside the Labour Party that had skillfully crafted together an alternative set of policies.

The impact of Tory strategy, successive election defeats and disappointment with the outcomes of radical reform within Labour-held local authorities in the early 1980s had ensured that the broad extra-parliamentary opposition remained demoralised and cautious. Events elsewhere, such as the collapse of the Soviet and East European bloc, and the electoral success of the political right across Europe added to this sense of caution. Within academia and from left intellectuals there had been critical texts and popular journals, such as *Marxism Today* (closed in 1991), on the politics and impact of Thatcherism, but few that addressed the detail of what might be the policy alternatives (Brown and Sparks, 1989; Loney *et al.*, 1991; Cloke, 1992; Flynn, 1993; Clarke and Newman, 1997). Innovative approaches such as those presented by Hoggett (2000a) and Williams (2000) arrived too late. Reports such as *Faith in the City* (1985) and the *Commission on Social Justice* (1994) set out the arguments for change and, in the latter case, distinguished between different political responses to the issues and argued for a 'third way' between free markets and state collectivism. It identified the 'deregulators' and the 'levellers' as two tendencies trapped by the past and contrasted them with the 'investors' who accept the interdependence of market and collective provision. The 'investors',

> combine an ethical commitment to equality of opportunity…a vision of the good society, and a compelling analysis of how modern capitalism works – as well as how it can be changed (1994: 94).

If Labour entered office in less than ideal circumstances, despite its majority, its subsequent actions have been less than reassuring to those seeking radical social reform. From the outset, it was concerned that a second term of office would be needed and sought to avoid defeat through fiscal imprudence throughout its first term. Yet it was also ambitious for immediate success, a formula designed for 'wheeling and dealing' opportunism. Labour's caution over how to position itself plus its determination to hold on to office fuelled the suspicion that it was primarily concerned with holding on to power for its own sake rather than challenging powerful market interests or substantially raising welfare expenditures. The decision to work for the first two years in office within Tory-determined financial expenditure projections was a huge disappointment to its supporters, as was the dilution of pre-election pledges, such as on the level of minimum wage.

Labour has also been over-eager to get close to big business, along with the other defenders of privilege and authority, the monarchy and the establishment, while distancing itself from its own traditional loyal supporters. The belief that it should and can work with private business has not been matched by clarity around the conditions for such collaboration or its expectations of the market. Meanwhile, it has not demonstrated the same unconditional approach in working with other sectors. Its preference for the politics of America, domestic and foreign, rather than the more inclusive approaches of its social democratic European partners has further alienated it from left-of-centre support. It has been impatient for short-term success and has all too easily assumed an authoritarian stance when faced with resistance from 'entrenched interests' to its proposals for change. Following the success of Margaret Thatcher's leadership, Labour has been determined to demonstrate that it too is a 'strong' government that won't be sidetracked. Despite its rhetoric of greater public engagement and working collaboratively in partnership with all stakeholders, it quickly developed a reputation for arrogance and centralised control freakery.

At the heart of the problem lies Labour's attempt to separate the reform of welfare from a commitment to eradicating social and economic inequities. Despite much rhetoric about the 'vision' of 'social inclusion' and a plethora of targets, Labour has been unable to project a convincing story of how the 'new' Britain will make a substantial difference for those at the bottom of the economic and social ladder. It has drowned the public sector in policy initiatives and adopted radical measures in the organisation and delivery of social welfare, many of which have been long supported by

progressive policy theorists and activists. A lot hangs on the success
of these changes for the future of progressive collectivist welfare. To
succeed, Labour needs the support of those responsible for their
implementation. It has so far failed to convince those on the centre-
left and many ordinary supporters working in front-line public
services, that it has a political strategy for which it is worth making
the changes to practice that would be required.

Book outline

The purpose of this book is to focus on some of the most significant changes in relation to the organisation and delivery of social
welfare initiated by Labour. Such changes provide the initial ingre-
dients for progressive welfare practice. There is still much to be
done to refine and promote them. My aim is to explore some of the
as yet unresolved associated dilemmas. Ultimately, any reform of
organisational structures, processes and ways of working will
remain vulnerable to dissipation and sabotage unless grounded in a
wider political strategy. My hope is that in the absence of such a
worthwhile strategy the progressive features emerging from the new
organisational framework will not be lost. Despite many reservations
about Labour's strategy, there is mileage to be gained in engaging
positively with core features of the organisational package and not
being overwhelmed by cynicism.

The book's first two chapters review the organisational arrangements of the post-war period, the restructuring under the New
Right and Labour's overall vision. Chapter 3 explores the implications of the ongoing institutionalisation of the mixed economy of
welfare with a particular focus on the public–private partnership and
the multitude of relationships entered into by service users, while
Chapter 4 considers the implications of the increased role of the
non-profit sector. Chapter 5 examines the shifting emphasis away
from managerialism to leadership and the need to develop a culture
of learning within and between public service organisations.
Chapter 6 focuses on the impact of the 'quality agenda' and is
followed in Chapter 7 by an examination of collaborative working
across agencies, professions and sectoral boundaries. Chapter 8 is
devoted to the now taken-for-granted need to involve service users
more directly in the planning and implementation of services both
at a personal and collective level. Chapter 9 explores the revival in

the importance given to 'community' as both the object and basis of policy, raising questions about the concept's durability. Finally, Chapter 10 examines the meaning and potential implications of Labour's declared commitment to greater public engagement and capacity building. Each chapter has its own internal coherence, but the book's focus is such that it necessarily involves some considerable but sign-posted cross-referencing, since some policy issues can best be explored through different lenses.

1

Organising and Delivering Welfare

The organisation of welfare services and their mode of delivery were not sharply contested issues during the construction of the UK post-war welfare state. The key features of the new welfare services did reflect deeply held assumptions about the relations between government and citizen, and the management and organisation of society. Nevertheless, there were other priorities and more contentious issues. What received greatest attention throughout the 1945–79 period were the specific details of particular policy interventions and their outcomes, and the related questions of the basis of entitlement, differential access and the overall impact of provision. Similarly, considerable attention has been given to systemic issues as in the purposes and functions of welfare within a market economy, the impact of welfare reform on economic and social transformation and structural inequalities, the policy-making process and the theory-implementation gap.

Undoubtedly, these are all crucial concerns at the heart of any welfare strategy. However, the way in which social welfare is organised and the processes by which it is delivered is the glue that binds a welfare system together and expresses its core values. Mounting protests from service users, community activists and social movements during the late 1960s and 1970s, much of which focused on the experience of being a service user, generated technical 'fix-it' solutions rather than a radical re-examination of the relationship between service provider and service user. It was only after the 1979 election of the first New Right government of Margaret Thatcher, ironically committed to the residualisation and de-legitimisation of public services, that new forms of welfare organisation began to emerge. With Labour's 1997 election victory, restructuring the social relations of welfare and the organisational framework in which they are contained has become a priority. The importance of such issues has been underlined by stubborn resistance to change, for example, in relation to inter-professional work, despite the almost universal agreement on the need to do so.

This chapter briefly considers the organisational arrangements and social relations for the delivery of social welfare during 1945–79, which is acknowledged as the 'classic welfare state'. It then highlights the profound changes introduced during the eighteen years of neo-right Conservative government 1979–97, during which public service organisations were subjected to a process of marketisation. The contemporary period, since 1997, and the changes introduced by the new Labour Government is the subject of the next chapter. This chapter begins by arguing that while matters of organisation and process have not featured as prominently as other aspects of concern, they are central to the effectiveness of social policies and to the experience of the service user.

The means and ends of social welfare

The ways in which social welfare is organised and delivered have much to tell us about ourselves as a society including:

- the priority we ascribe to formal welfare systems as against market or informal transactions;
- our sense of citizenship, identity, belonging and risk-sharing;
- our commitment to social justice and a collective intolerance of unacceptable inequities;
- our commitment to the equal worth of all, our inter-subjectivity, capacity for self-actualisation and the democratisation of social life;
- the relationship between social rights and responsibilities or duties;
- our approach to dependency, inter-dependency and the place of caring;
- our perceptions of the service user as both a universal and differentiated category.

It has long been assumed that welfare outcomes can be achieved without having to pay too much attention to the processes that deliver them. Whenever organisational shortcomings are identified, the quest is to find the 'right' policy or make technical adjustments, rather than examine the deeper processes and meanings embodied within the organisation itself. This lack of attention given to matters of organisation and process should not be surprising. A powerful organisational paradigm, characterised by hierarchy, deference to authority and expertise, emerged at the end of the nineteenth century and has until recently dominated all spheres of activity – governmental, commercial, militaristic, political and even social life (Hoggett, 1990).

Welfare policies, embodying values, goals and objectives, as well as specific service outputs are filtered through organisations and are altered in the process. The transformative possibilities between policy intentions and implementation within the 'black box' of the policy process has long been recognised (Hill, 1997). The role of front-line welfare professionals, operating at the service provider/ user interface and responsible for the actual delivery of services, has been significant in the management of demand and service rationing (Lipsky, 1980). However, the organisation and delivery mechanisms of social welfare are not simply an obstruction that 'get in the way' of policy goals and therefore demands our some-what reluctant attention. Rather, it is central to the meaning of welfare, as it is in any project of social and political transformation. The means and ends of welfare are inextricably bound together, each reflecting the other. It is not simply a question of the 'means' having been neglected and split off from the ends of welfare. It is rather that this analytical absence has been a direct consequence of the social democratic Labourist vision underpinning the post-war welfare system since 1945 (Hoggett and McGill, 1988).

For many service users, the 'means' of welfare are the personifica-tion or embodiment of the service. The direct experience of a social welfare agency, its employees, how it conducts its business, its effectiveness in relating to the user as a person-citizen and in responding to the specific need that brought them to it, defines the reality and meaning of welfare. There can be real differences in the experience of various service user categories – patient, claimant, tenant or client – and for different subcategories within these – single parent or pensioner claimant, child abuser or potential foster parent – or for different social groups within each subcategory – young black male 'schizophrenic' or 'depressed' middle-class mental health patient (Saraga, 1998). Nevertheless, there are a number of features within the organisation and delivery of social welfare that apply to all categories and operate within all core services. Such core features have contributed to the emergence and persistence of differential experiences for different groups of service users. By paying close attention to the core components in the organisation and delivery – the 'how we go about doing what we want to achieve' – it becomes easier to root out dysfunctional or unacceptable processes, procedures and organisational forms.

The organisation of the post-war welfare state

Four welfare 'settlements' are commonly associated with the post-war construction of the UK's welfare state, of which the 'organisational' is one alongside the 'political', 'social' and 'economic' (Hoggett, 1994; Clarke and Newman, 1997; Hughes, 1998). Hughes refers to such settlements as,

> ... a kind of framing consensus ... a set of positions negotiated by the key or most powerful groups ... (that) create a temporary period of stability or equilibrium, even while they remain complex, contested and fragile (1998: 4).

The post-war organisational settlement, for what was an ambitious programme of social reconstruction, was hardly a matter of deep contestation. It emerged from an understanding of 'sound administration' developed in the late nineteenth century and practised in the civil service, the military and economic life as the basis by which to organise and coordinate (Hoggett, 1987). This organisational form, an essentially progressive or 'modern' development, had been reinforced by the 1939–45 wartime experience in which state-controlled centralised planning and coordination had been essential. Post-war reconstruction and meeting emergent labour market requirements for a better trained, more sophisticated workforce were pressing issues, as was responding to rising political and economic expectations and the fear of social unrest with the European advancement of Soviet communism. Yet, the post-war ambitions were not simply driven by necessity. The Liberal William Beveridge captured the spirit of the times in his 1942 *Social Insurance and Allied Services* report (Beveridge, 1942) in which he called for the abolition of the five giants of 'Want', 'Idleness', 'Ignorance',

'Squalor' and 'Disease', that plagued economic and social development and threatened the social order. Labour's social reform
programme would not only harness the solidarity and collectivism
spawned by the war, through enhanced citizenship, but would
provide the basis for Britain's ambitions to retain its superiority as
a moral world power (Clarke and Langan, 1993).

A planned, coordinated, systematic, properly resourced programme, backed by a determined political will was assumed to be
the only desirable option, and the state, the only body capable of
providing this (Chamberlayne, 1992). State management and control would ensure that the pre-war vagaries of the market, that
had brought mass unemployment and deepening social divisions
throughout the inter-war period, would be avoided and that chance,
fate or predilection would no longer determine individual life-
chances. Further, the arbitrary, uneven, moralising and bitterly
resented activities of those charities engaged in the management
of the poor would also become a thing of the past.

The classic welfare state model, a step on the road to socialism
for some of its proponents, was and continues to be constructed
with the market economy at its core. Paid employment was the
primary source of personal income and the satisfaction of need,
while the levels of state financial benefits were determined by the
wage structure. The model contained an unproblematic acceptance
of the then dominant nuclear family, economically supported by
a male breadwinner. Other family forms were either treated as
a minority status, undesired and unfortunate, or simply ignored
(Woodward, 1997; Langan, 1998). Further, it had quite misplaced
nationalistic and imperialistic overtones, along with a restricted and
essentially passive view of citizenship (Hughes, 1998; Saraga, 1998).
An awareness of such limitations is essential in setting the context
to the post-war consensus and constructing a contemporary agenda
for change. Yet, it is important to recognise that within the politics
of the time, the reconstruction package represented a major transformation and one that has shaped domestic politics since. The
popular enthusiasm that greeted the Beveridge Report, and swept
Labour to power was not based upon a delusion, even if the subsequent enactment of the reforms created barriers to change and
became an obstacle in the acceptance of new social conditions
(Timmins, 1995).

The organisational arrangements for the state-orchestrated
programme centred on the twin concepts of bureaucracy and

professionalism, constituting what Newman and Clarke (1994) describe as the 'organizational architecture of the welfare state' (p. 23). This was a profoundly hierarchical and elitist structure based upon a belief, well expressed by the influential Fabians, in an enlightened neutral state. By enlisting the 'best minds' able to apply their scientific knowledge, gained through extensive training, the state could identify and resolve social and economic issues (O'Brien and Penna, 1998). It would be prepared to ration resources and, if necessary, to discipline those unwilling to act on the basis of such expertise marshalled to meet their 'own best interests' and those of the nation state. Those unable to respond through no fault of their own but posing a risk either to themselves or others would be offered a form of economic or social protection.

This combination of expert power, central planning and complex provision left little room for active citizenship. Fabianism was deeply suspicious of the citizen and whilst advocating social reform saw this as a task requiring careful management and guidance by experts who knew better, particularly in the area of moral behaviour. Service users were to be the passive recipients of state provision. A certain degree of gratitude was to be expected, complaining was not, and user self-doubt and deference towards those in authority could be exploited, to determine whether they were sufficiently 'deserving'. Outside of local and national elections, communities or service constituencies were rarely consulted about policy changes or involved in service evaluation. With some notable exceptions, as in Bevan's housing programme, service quality or individual choice was considered to be less important than ensuring universal basic provision, while outside of urgent health care the particular life circumstances of the individual service user had little influence over the timing of any service. Nevertheless, for many recipients such services provided a lifeline in the struggle to make ends meet and enhanced the quality of life.

Only the state is capable of ensuring that basic services are available to all at the point of need and, by guaranteeing social rights and benefits, enabling those at the bottom of the social and economic ladder to achieve the standards deemed to be 'essential' for active citizenship and personhood. Yet, as with any top-down initiative, the concept of equality embedded within citizenship is tempered by a lingering sense of the recipient as inferior or inadequate. While securing citizenship and providing for individual and collective security was at the heart of the reform agenda, establishing both the necessary institutional frameworks and educative processes was essential to a successful outcome and could not be left to chance. Moreover the welfare package was crucially concerned with ensuring that all those able to work did so, that benefits did not undermine labour markets, and that those who were ineligible did not secure them on a false basis. Further, by identifying desirable or necessary levels of, for example, healthcare, education, child-rearing or social behaviour, the state is obliged both to encourage the pursuit of such beneficial practices and ensure that consequent responsibilities and obligations are fulfilled.

Bureaucratic forms of organisation

Bureaucratic forms of organisation were viewed by sociologists such as Max Weber (1864–1920) or administrators such as Henri Fayol (1841–1925) as an inevitable feature of modern capitalism, the most rational, technically superior of systems (Weber, 1948). Bureaucracy offered an authority and legitimacy linked to legality and expertise thereby challenging the legitimacy and power of the elected politician (Weber, 1947). For Weber, bureaucracy, a human creation, threatened to ensnare and dominate its creators, destroying our humanity, within an almost indestructible 'iron cage'. This web of rules, regulations and procedures would transform the structures designed as a means to an end to become an end in themselves crushing the subject's spontaneity (Clegg, 1990; Morgan, 1997). In their sociologically 'ideal' form, rarely to be found in reality, bureaucracies were characterised by:

- the investment of authority in an impersonal order;
- a hierarchical division of labour with functional specialisms;
- a comprehensive body of rules and procedures;
- a precise definition of the authority and responsibilities contained within each role;
- a system of recruitment and promotion based on merit and qualification;
- a salaried staff employed in posts that constitute their primary form of employment and offering a predictable career structure;
- staff who are subject to a code of discipline and unable to appropriate their position.

As a distinctly modern form of organisation, the 'ideal' rational bureaucracy offered efficiency, stability, continuity and certainty. It would provide reliable, objective, fair and equitable treatment of individuals based on a set of objective rules and procedures. Much of the subsequent literature has been concerned to identify the shortcomings or failures of the bureaucratic 'ideal' (Blau and Scott, 1963; Crozier 1964; Silverman, 1970; Burrell and Morgan, 1979).

A bureaucratic structure combined with professional expertise promises a regulated approach based on impartial standardised principles and practices that can both assess eligibility and ensure that designated benefits flow to those entitled, whilst allowing some room for individual discretion. The inherent tensions between bureaucratic and professional forms of organisation, whilst not immediately apparent, increased as the state broadened the scope of its interventions into virtually all aspects of social and personal life. As means-tested and discretionary benefits were extended, or other forms of conditionality and rationing were introduced, especially those concerned with measuring the degree or urgency of need, greater emphasis had to be placed upon the judgements of front-line professional staff.

The application of bureaucratic regulation to social welfare did not automatically mean that uniform provision existed between or within those state departments concerned with similar policy issues or service user group. For example, the mechanisms by which referrals were received into the post-1971 social service departments created, following the Seebohm Report, and converted into 'cases' varied considerably. Some operated a weekly referral allocation system involving all social workers with case distribution dependent on a loose sense of individual expertise, current workloads, and the previous professional and organisational divisions between childcare, mental illness and services for the elderly. Others made an initial distribution based on geographically located teams followed by a team-based workload related system. In either case, allocations might be either made as part of a full team meeting or decided by a senior professional. Some agencies established specialist 'intake teams' or 'duty officers' operating on a rotation basis. These designated workers handled all referrals and worked with them for a specified period before a decision was taken as to whether they were to become long-term cases.

Such variations were to be found across all locally administered services and reflected the diverse responses to managing demand, prioritising urgency or need, ensuring fairness and maximising available expertise. Rather than being imposed from above, the allocation systems were determined usually by the front-line professionals and once successfully established became department policy. Such working practices were rarely evaluated and continuity relied on the judgements of the professionals. Beyond the requests for additional financial resources and the collation of case data there was little management or bureaucratic interference in either the organisation of the work or the professional practice of the front-line workers.

The process of defining individual service user needs and identifying appropriate responses is time consuming and involves well-developed inter-personal skills. Bureaucracies operate to predictable and formulaic procedures alongside an almost obsessive adherence to the rules. Large cumbersome bureaucratic structures struggle to respond quickly and effectively in a changing and unstable environment. Bureaucratic codification and organisation are poorly suited to those who work with complex individual dilemmas, where the relationship between service provider and service user is at the heart of both a successful engagement and specific outcomes of that process. Vulnerable users such as the mentally-ill, the distressed, abused, those with special learning needs, or lacking in self-esteem, may require a prolonged relationship with an individual professional before they are able to identify and specify their needs. Only then can these be matched against what might be possible or translated into a request for a specific service or additional provision.

Social interventions provoke competing and multiple interpretations of reality and interests for which skilled judgements are required. Complex problems rarely relate to bureaucratically determined organisational configurations. However, a 'silo-mentality' has prevailed within departments responsible for particular policy areas (DETR, 2000a). Departmental size has been a signifier of importance in the inter-departmental battles for resources. Territory has been jealously guarded. Bureaucratic regulation and professional elitism has combined in a mutually reinforcing process to 'manage the client experience'. Each department and the professionals employed therein have differed from each other over values and ethics, qualifications, accountability, allegiances, management styles, self-perception and ways of interacting. Operating within what was an insular and parochial culture, individual departments developed their own cultures containing restrictive perceptions and practices in relation to service users, and subsequently have found themselves locked in conflict with colleagues from other departments over the response to particular problems.

It was not until the 1980s, in parallel with shifting practices in the private sector, that a number of organisational changes, such as local authority decentralisation, began to challenge the dominant bureaucratic paradigm (Peters and Waterman, 1982; Boddy and Fudge, 1984; Hambleton and Hoggett, 1987; Hall and Jacques, 1989). These emergent practices have drawn upon three related disciplines – the sociological understanding of globalisation and labour market patterns (Crook *et al.*, 1992); organisational and human resource development (Morgan, 1988; Senge, 1990); and the Tavistock-based Klienian psycho-dynamic tradition (Hirschorn, 1988). Central to this new paradigm is the concept of flexibility in job roles and functions, employment levels, patterns and security. Flexibility is proffered as the only viable response to environmental change (Pollert, 1988). In contrast to the bureaucratic form such post-modern organisations are characterised by:

- continuous change and renewal through creativity and innovation;
- strong leadership and increased employee autonomy;
- an engaged and visible management, concerned as much with strategic vision as with operational direction;
- flatter hierarchies, greater use of team working, and decentralised structures with centralised strategic direction and localised operational control;
- outward-looking, network-based and people-focused approach, in relation to customers and employees;
- recognition of the emotional aspects to organisational life;
- the centrality of human capital in organisational success with high levels of employee participation;
- an organisational culture conducive to creativity, change and learning.

Whilst such ideas were beginning to find their way into public sector organisations through the 1980s and early 1990s and were occasionally embraced enthusiastically, they remained peripheral at this time. Much more dramatic and significant was the introduction of a New Right managerialist philosophy, marking a return to ideas and systems reminiscent of private sector 'Taylorism', so influential in the shift to mass production in the early part of the twentieth century. Before examining these developments in more detail we turn our attention to the role of professionals in shaping post-war welfare.

Public service professionalism

At the heart of professionalism, and in contrast to bureaucracy, is the concept of individual judgement and discretion. Such autonomy is granted on the basis of certified training, expertise in a systematic and complex body of knowledge, continuous professional development, adherence to an ethical code of practice, and peer group accountability (Friedson, 1976; Wilding, 1982). Professionals are authorised to exercise discretionary power and in so doing stress the complexity, uncertainty and specificity of the circumstances they encounter. The possession of scarce and socially desirable knowledge, validated by qualifications, sometimes shrouded in mystifying language, and protected by the power to regulate access to recognised training, has ensured a powerful labour market bargaining position. For the well-organised professions, this has secured a protected, privileged and well-rewarded position amongst the social and economic elite. Reinforced by a lack of public accountability, this relative autonomy – power, privilege – underpinned by claims of an ethical practice and self-sacrificing altruistic motivation, allegedly absent from other occupations, has too easily been translated into an over-inflated sense of self-importance. More significantly, it lead to the creation of restrictive practices, detrimental to service users denied access to skills and expertise because of professional boundary demarcations. Greater complexity and less ethical certainty have diminished the capacity of any single profession to respond effectively to individual and social problems. This is reflected in the current emphasis on inter-professionalism, greater flexibility and the redefinition of roles and boundaries for welfare professionals (DoH, 1998a; DETR, 2000a; DoH, 2001a).

The capacity to control and restrict access to a privileged market position is not granted as a consequence of some inherent characteristics, but is secured and maintained through conscious and determined efforts sustained over time by well-organised bodies (Johnson, 1972; Parry and Parry, 1976; Larson, 1977). To be a professional, territory has first to be claimed, mechanisms of access constructed and regulated, and a knowledge base developed and protected. Further, those involved must behave as if they are professionals both by asserting their assumed superiority and regulating their own behaviour. Fournier (1999), following Friedman (1977), argues that current appeals to the 'professionalism' of an occupational group can equally be a strategy deployed by the state to control the indeterminate and flexible nature of practice. However, recent governments have expressed less confidence in self-regulation (Foster and Wilding, 2000) and more direct controlling mechanisms have been introduced. These have included target setting and performance measurements for policy implementation, external audits and internal appraisal mechanisms, fostering competition within and between agencies, and 'naming and shaming' poor performance through the publication of league tables. The growth of the generic managers, and their increased authority, alongside the emphasis on professional accountability to service users have reinforced these changes.

When employed within large bureaucratic organisations, professional autonomy is constrained by formal rules, procedures, and the tendency towards codification and classification. In public service organisations they are further constrained by state mediation over the nature of the client group, the determination of the goals and limits of intervention, the size of the workforce, and the resources available to fulfil the role. Such dependency on the nature of the work, the size and existence of the client base, and the organisational structures within which it is performed, undermines the very basis of a claim to professionalism and restricts the room for manoeuvrability. Consequently, public service professionals have struggled to secure full professional recognition, and the concomitant rewards, from either the public or their political masters. This has been especially so for professions created as a direct consequence of state expansion within social welfare and health, and who are vulnerable to political decisions to reduce or withdraw provision. Only medicine, the one well-established and powerful body prior to state expansion, has been able to retain its professional status. Yet, this too has been under attack as a consequence of its resistance to managerialism, high profile medical failures, a more knowledgeable and assertive public and demands for greater public accountability.

Other public service occupations have at best secured a rather tentative and weak position as 'semi-professions' (Etzioni, 1969) in which their 'professionalism' is often reduced to a more popular definition of 'a job done well' and thus not dissimilar from other occupations. Rather than being able to claim expert knowledge, public service professionals are constantly challenged by competing sources of legitimation, especially from political parties and service users (Friedson, 1994). Despite such reservations and limitations on their capacities and status, public service professionals still retain some limited power and autonomy, derived from the state's need for an educated workforce to intervene in social life, thereby creating a tension with the bureaucratic impulse. Wilding (1982) highlighted the capacity of the public service professional to:

- define needs and problems and the nature of any response;
- control individual access to public services;
- deny or remove individual rights and freedoms;
- control the distribution of scarce resources both within and between different service user groups; and
- influence or create changes in strategic policy.

As a reflection on the post-war period Wilding's assessment is more a statement of potential rather than a description of what was practised in the immediate post-war period. This was not the daily experience of individual front-line professionals employed as housing officers, youth workers or education welfare officers (the 'School Board man'), in pre-Seebohm departments as childcare, welfare or mental health officers, or in healthcare as health visitors, school, district or ward nurses. Significantly, for those employed within local government, in childcare, welfare, housing, education, public health or planning, they were referred to not as professionals but as 'officers'. They were officials, subalterns, administrators, subordinates employed in carrying out the requirements of others. Service users referred to them not in the same deferential tones as they might do doctors but with the more contemptuous and demeaning 'him/her from the welfare'. The 'power' that could be exercised was not experienced as that derived from a professional judgement but rather that of the petty-minded official who might equally be a stickler for the rules or be swayed by an emotional appeal. The adherence to rules was also no doubt a source of defensive security in the light of what until the 1970s were low levels of education and the virtual absence of formal qualifications for all but a few state welfare workers.

Foster and Wilding (2000) suggest that a professional vision was confined to a 'golden age' of the 1950s and 1960s. Since then the well-meaning professional claims have floundered. During the subsequent two decades, beginning with the Wilson government, attempts were made to define a more proactive and responsive professional agenda. Frustration amongst the better educated entrants with the limitations of the state in the drive for social reform, and restricted career advancement, led to a more radical agenda that then became the subject of further attack (Langan and Lee, 1989). Any ambition for professional recognition was further undermined by a lack of conviction amongst a significant proportion of public sector employees, who rejected the implicit elitism of professionalism and opted instead for a trade union identity. This was reinforced by poor leadership from within the emergent professional bodies (Miller, 1996). For the left, professionalism represented a conservative force acting oppressively as agent of a capitalist and patriarchal state, and in pursuit of its own self-interest. While radicals within the public sector challenged the elitist and conservative aspirations of those claiming professional status and criticised bureaucratic restrictions and insensitivities, the New Right attacked its supposed power.

Welfare professionals stood accused by Thatcherism of having captured the welfare agenda in order to extend their role and swell their ranks. They were charged with being both unresponsive to user needs and of engineering a relationship of client dependency, and of being resistant to political change. A series of professional failures exposed them to charges from all parties of incompetence. Labour process writers such as Braverman, have argued that all professionals face a process of proletarianisation, as their labour is stripped of its complexity and mystery through routinisation, standardisation and bureaucratisation, thereby rendering professional labour more susceptible to managerial control (Braverman, 1974; see Friedman 1977 for a dissenting view). The current demands for greater flexibility, functionality in multi-skilling, task integration and devolved responsibilities add similar pressures (Crook *et al.*, 1992). The combined attack on bureaucracy and professionalism undermined the post-war faith in the power of the dispassionate and expert professional to resolve individual and social problems and left it exposed to the efforts of the New Right to introduce private sector features through a process of marketisation.

Welfare professionals have not lost the capacity to respond to service users as individuals facing complex and unique circumstances with their own particular understandings and reflexive capacity. There continue to be opportunities to apply their knowledge and experience, to make a considered judgement arrived at in collaboration with others, to identify the most appropriate response, represent these within the agency and, when necessary, pressurise it to adapt its procedures accordingly. In so doing, they define new priorities, open up new areas of activity and demand more resources. When agencies prove unresponsive or ineffective, welfare professionals are able to support users to organise in other ways to pressurise for state recognition of their needs. The challenge facing welfare professionals lies in disentangling the relationship between discretion and knowledge on the one hand and elitism and reward on the other. Public recognition of the value of professional judgement is more likely to be forthcoming if welfare professionals acknowledge what they do not know as much as what they claim to know, and demonstrate a willingness to a process of co-learning alongside service users. To do so they need the skills and aptitude to work collaboratively rather than seeking to protect professional roles and territorial boundaries, value other knowledge bases including the experiential knowledge of the service user, and behave as contributing partners in addressing complexity and uncertainty.

The New Right and organisational reform

The New Right under Margaret Thatcher was little concerned with identifying the most effective form of public sector organisation. Rather, it was preoccupied by what it perceived as government 'over-load', having succumbed to organisational, professional and electoral pressure. Successive post-war governments had not only over-extended themselves but had helped create the illusion that the state could identify and respond effectively to human need. Ambitious promises had been made but not fulfilled, leading to frustration and a further crisis of legitimation. State provision had created a culture of dependency that undermined individual independence and sapped entrepreneurialism, thereby restricting economic growth and damaging competitiveness, removing the incentives to be autonomous and to accept the responsibility to care for dependents.

Insufficient attention had been given, so it was argued, to the costs of welfare. These were predicted to increase, as so much provision was demand-led with service entitlement going automatically to those occupying particular social categories. It was asserted that the rising proportion of the gross domestic product allocated to welfare provision placed an unbearable burden on the taxpayer. The near monopoly position enjoyed by state professionals gave little incentive to be efficient or to explore alternative forms of provision. Instead they had a vested interest in service expansion or 'bureau-maximisation', and ensuring that their role was designated as indispensable. Well-organised provider interest groups, in the form of trade union and professional bodies, were said to have exploited the situation to ensure that member interests, rather than service recipient needs, took precedence. Moreover, service users did not always welcome the interventions of state officials, but were alienated and powerless in the face of professional arrogance and dissatisfied with the methods employed. The system was not only incomprehensible to use or administer but was also open to abuse, while for those in 'real need' it could be experienced as degrading and mean.

The New Right, whose concerns but not solutions often echoed those of the political left, sought fewer public services. They were determined to lower welfare costs by reducing service quality, imposing greater restrictions on entitlement, and increasing and stigmatising the hurdles placed in the way of those who find themselves a 'client'.

> It is time to change the approach to what governments can do for people and to what people can do for themselves: time to shake off the self-doubt induced by decades of dependence on the state as master not as servant (Margaret Thatcher, 1979).

Public services were to be restructured in the image of free market private enterprise, through what was a phased process of 'marketisation'. This was uneven and variable, according to the nature of each service, and diverse in form, shifting between 1979 and 1987 from incremental pragmatism to a more strategic approach (Farnham and Horton, 1999). Clarke and Newman (1997) argue that the effect of marketisation was not that of the state shedding its responsibilities but rather one of 'dispersal' that created complex sets of new relationships. This broadened and increased state power while simultaneously opened up new opportunities for others to challenge or influence the state.

First, marketisation involved breaking up the near monopoly position enjoyed by the state through the formalisation of a mixed economy of welfare. This was to be achieved by:

- Direct privatisation of public services, sub-contracting out to private for-profit companies, and the introduction of charges for particular services.
- Private sector investment and involvement in public provision was actively encouraged.
- Community and non-profit organisations, alongside market sector bodies, were offered an expanded role. This was paralleled by attempts to revive charitable giving and informal care in the delivery of services.
- Service users were encouraged to utilise private services to meet personal needs. Particular groups were actively discouraged from accessing services by stigmatising them as inadequate, irresponsible or scrounging. All forms of 'dependency' were denigrated and the independent, self-reliant, competitive, and ultimately self-interested individual elevated.

Within public sector organisations marketisation included:

- The creation of competitive contract driven 'quasi' markets through the separation of provider and purchaser functions previously combined within single state agencies, into distinct organisational entities and the introduction of other trading relationships.
- The transformation of public service language through the introduction of free enterprise concepts such as 'entrepreneur-ialism', 'value for money' and 'efficiency', 'consumers', 'customers' and 'product choice'.
- Increased internal competition and regulation including the use of 'league tables', target setting, output controls and performance management.
- The introduction of a layer of generic managers, wherever possible drawn from the market sector or else through the conversion of professionals.

- Market-based managerial principles, language and practices, promoted by market 'experts' recruited as consultants, were adopted within welfare organisations and became evident within the drafting of policy documents.
- The introduction of greater labour 'flexibility' and job insecurity while undermining the status of welfare professionals and their representative bodies.

A culture of managerialism focused on meeting targets and, underpinned by a reassertion of the 'right to manage', was defined as the core to all public service organisations, irrespective of their sectoral location, and as a means of controlling bureaucrats, professionals and wayward local politicians. 'Authority' was decentralised to local managers, as a form of 'remote control' (Hoggett, 1994), to act in ways that achieved the set targets. State regulation was maintained through the introduction of an external audit regime, centrally determined service targets and the imperative to work within the three 'E's of economy, efficiency and effectiveness. Centralised and detailed requirements were introduced over the nature and content of what could be delivered, to whom, under what circumstances and at what cost.

Quangos (quasi-non-governmental organisations) or non-governmental departmental organisations, appointed by and accountable to government ministers, grew considerably. These were removed from local political, citizen or user control and accountability but had responsibility for specific areas of service delivery. Local authority discretion was reduced or eliminated through the expansion of ring-fenced budgets and cuts in the amount of general funding. Some aspects of marketisation, introduced by Thatcher, were subsequently modified during Major's term of office. For example, in the early 1990s the culture of provider fragmentation and competition was gradually replaced by a more collaborative approach. Similarly, professionals were less vilified and service users were again spoken of in terms of the 'rights', albeit still primarily as consumers, through the introduction of a series of 'charters'.

Labour has continued to modify New Right policies. Thus, it has retained the purchaser–provider split, which was perhaps the most significant organisational change under Thatcher, although services are now 'commissioned' and collaboration rather than competition is to define organisational and professional relationships. It has continued to extend a mixed economy of welfare, promote service user choice, and has retained a deeply ambiguous attitude towards welfare professionals. It has continued to impose change, rather than seek prior professional endorsement, but has increasingly found it necessary to recognise the pivotal role of the professional in ensuring successful implementation. Ultimately, it has paid far greater attention to increasing service user and public engagement and ensuring greater professional accountability.

Labour continues to be enamoured of the market and has stressed the need for private finance and a partnership with the private sector to underpin public sector growth while expecting public sector organisations to learn from private sector best practice. While accepting that a pure market form is inappropriate for public provision, it is adamant that there can be no return to a pre-1979 era dominated by a state monopoly of welfare and bureau–professional power.

2

Labour, Modernisation and the Third Way

In 1997, after eighteen years of being exiled to the opposition benches, the Labour Party regained office. It entered government, committed to the modernisation of welfare provision, and determined that having gained power it would not lose it through incautious behaviour or by pursuing policies associated with 'old' Labour socialism (Levitas, 1998). In its desire to distance itself from its predecessors, it re-branded itself as 'new' Labour. After five years in office and the day-to-day business of government, but with a second general election victory secured, the sense of being 'new' has faded. Nevertheless, re-election was an opportunity to remind the voters of Labour's vision:

> We favour true equality: equal worth and equal opportunity, not a crude equality of outcome focused on incomes alone. Strong public services – universal but personalised – are fundamental to this vision of a fairer, more prosperous society (Blair, 2002: 2).

As noted at the end of the previous chapter there have been a number of continuities in Labour's approach and that of its Conservative predecessor. The government has often appeared more concerned to distinguish itself from earlier Labour governments as it has from the New Right. However, its belief in an 'inclusive society' is an important distinction between it and Thatcherism. This chapter provides an overview of the broad themes and key ideas within Labour's 'Third Way'. Core features of the approach as they apply to the organisation and delivery of social welfare are the subject of the remaining parts of the book.

The vision

Prior to his election as prime minister, Tony Blair defined the task in terms of, 'how the enduring values of 1945 can be applied to the very different world of today', and demanded nothing less than a process of national renewal (Blair, 1996). Six years on and it was necessary to reiterate the same point

> It is time to acknowledge that the 1945 settlement was a product of its time and we must not be a prisoner to it (Blair, 2002: iv).

Blair had called for 'a new settlement...where opportunity and responsibility go together' (Blair, 1996: 16), requiring a 'new language of social justice' (p. 22). On behalf of the Party, he pledged 'a nation at work, not on benefit' (p. 38). Both the Labour Party and the nation were diagnosed as in need of 'modernisation', as 'the force of change outside the country is driving the need for change within it' (p. 23). Again in 2002, the message was repeated

> Our task is to give modern expression to our values in a time of unprecedented aspirations, declining deference and increasing choice, of diverse needs and greater personal autonomy (Blair, 2002: 9).

Blair has argued consistently that the left has 'undervalued' the concept of responsibility. In presenting such arguments, Blair has drawn heavily from two earlier reports – Faith in the City (1985) and the Commission on Social Justice (1994), the latter having been commissioned by the deceased former party leader John Smith. Blair maintained that the way ahead lay in constructing a cohesive stakeholder society built on opportunity, responsibility, fairness and trust (Deacon, 1997). This was the one 'big idea left in politics' and he promised

> a new social order...based on merit, commitment, and inclusion...a true community of citizens...based on rights and responsibilities together (Blair, 1996: vii–viii).

Driver and Martell (1998) argue that Blair skilfully exploited the contradiction of Thatcher's jingoism and nationalism while overseeing economic and social decline to inspire and conjure up a post-Thatcherite response to global forces,

> People want to be proud of Britain, but they have lost confidence...
> they are losing an identity without finding or developing a new one...
> its best times lie ahead, fired with ambition but improved by idealism,
> compassion and justice...We cannot afford the costs of mass unemploy-
> ment and poverty...We live as one nation, and must act as one
> too...Social justice, the extension to all of a stake in a fair society is the
> partner of economic efficiency and not its enemy (Blair, 1996: v–vi).

With almost missionary zeal Blair described his generation as
one, '...frightened for our future and unsure of our soul' (p. 45).
Driver and Martell (1997) argue that Labour's 'Third Way' represents politics 'after Thatcher', which believes that the competitive
individualism of neo-liberal policies is insufficient to create a successful economy. A new post-Thatcherite consensus has emerged,
similar to the earlier one of the immediate post-war period, that
private enterprise alone cannot attend to societal welfare. The
relentless pursuit of market individualism and the denigration of the
state and intermediary bodies within civil society had substantially
undermined social cohesion. To that extent Labour's modernisation
project is one of recovery, an attempt to put back what has been
undone by Thatcherism but without denying the need for a far-
reaching reform initiative, a view articulated in the outspoken
rejection of pre-Thatcherite 'old' Labour policies (Labour Party,
1997).

Labour's complaint is less about the objectives of Thatcherism,
especially its emphasis on an entrepreneurial culture and need for
greater efficiency, and more with the lack of balance in its approach.
It continues to prioritise and pursue a successful market economy
in which enterprise is rewarded but one in which anyone making
an effort can feel a part. Further, if 'making an effort' produces
cohesion, inclusiveness and reward then it is not too unreasonable
to first pressurise and then penalise those who refuse to meet such
normal obligations whilst still expecting social and economic
protection. Equally, it is legitimate to confront those within the
public services that resist or undermine the modernisation agenda.
As Blair stated:

> We expect high standards of professional engagement. We seek a new
> flexibility in the professions that break down old working practices, old
> demarcations. (Blair, 2002: 27).

A modernised public sector

On returning to office, the Labour government quickly identified a modern welfare service as,

> active in its efficiency, its support, its transparency, in tailoring its service to individual needs, in its use of information technology to co-ordinate the different sectors; it will also reclaim and reshape an ethos of public service (DETR, 1998a: 71–8).

Modernised public services were needed in order

> to create better government to make life better for people… We will modernize our system of government so that it brings services to the people, is more accountable and brings more power to local communities (Cabinet Office, Executive Summary, 1999).

Giddens (1998) describes Blair as the 'archetypal moderniser' sustained by the view that:

> Britain lags behind other industrial societies in various key respects… crusty old institutions which have lost their relevance to the modern world (p. 31).

Blair has continued to make the same point that,

> Let us start with a blunt truth. Our public services, despite the heroic efforts of dedicated public servants and some outstanding successes, are not of the quality a nation like Britain needs (Blair, 2002: 1).

Labour seeks to achieve a balance between rejecting a New Right philosophy but not all its objectives or specific policies, while reassuring those on the right of the political centre that it is not a 'tax and spend' government. For much of its first term of office, obsessed with the desire to secure a record-breaking second term, the Blair government paid considerable attention to the political right. Following the election and another resounding victory, and with the continuing weakness of the opposition, Labour has appeared more able to address its own constituency. Here the balance is to maintain the loyalty of its own traditional voter base while increasing its support through an appeal to a new centre-left coalition. Consequently, it rejects both a return to the Beveridgean solutions of the post-war period and to the Conservative free market strategies that dominated the 1980s, described by Blair as the

> most feckless, irresponsible group of incompetents ever to be let loose on the government of Britain (Blair, 1996: 28).

Free market strategies, with their emphasis on self-reliance and possessive individualism along with the denial of the 'social', created a more divided society with what became unacceptable levels of social and economic inequality. The scale of Labour's 1997 victory, reinforced by the 2001 election, has forced the Conservatives to abandon their Thatcherite approach and move closer to the same centre ground now occupied by Labour and thereby creating the possibility for a new consensus (Powell and Hewitt, 1998). Labour's appeal is increasingly to the centre-left to take the opportunity to shape the destiny of the country by rehabilitating public services through 'bold' reforms after twenty years of such neglect (Blair, 2002). At the heart of such a reform process is the rejection of the post-war Fabian inspired professional and bureaucratic model of welfare. This bureau–professional model had already been fatally undermined by long-standing criticisms, from both left and right. It was already too closely identified with welfare dependency, the denial of personal choice and agency, an overemphasis on social rights rather than responsibilities, and a drain on productive investment. Moreover, times have changed and post-war practices and structures do not meet the requirements of a more socially diverse and less deferential society. There is greater diversity in employment patterns and family arrangements, and shifting demographic structures. Citizens are more assertive and have a greater sense of their individuality, from which new needs are identified. New strategies are required that acknowledge both global markets and widespread social and environmental concerns.

Looking to the future by learning from the past

Labour has placed considerable stress on the importance of learning from previous policies and politics (SEU, 1998; DSS, 1999). This evidence-based approach was subsequently adapted into a more pragmatic emphasis on 'what works is what counts'. One strand of analysis focused on counting the cost of Thatcherism. For example, work on disadvantaged neighbourhoods highlighted the growing divide between those that were poor, in which there was a concentration of social and economic problems, and the rest. Specifically, it demonstrated widening health inequalities, growing unemployment in areas already badly affected, a doubling in the proportion of those living in low-income households between the end of the 1970s and early 1990s, a tripling of child poverty between 1979 and 1995–96, a rise in family breakdowns, and a significant skills shortage. Key areas which previous government policies had failed to tackle were highlighted in what was seen as a vicious cycle of decline. A lack of leadership, failure to work collaboratively through 'joined-up' policies, a failure to engage with local communities and service users, inadequate dissemination, or poor use of knowledge, information and best practice were all highlighted as matters for urgent concern. This was essentially a mapping exercise to review the success of previous efforts to secure desired outcomes and take stock of current issues and challenges that were then linked to future targets.

Labour has drawn inspiration from a number of theoretical positions, such as Beck (1992), Giddens (1994), Putnam (1995) and Etzioni (1995). These have focused on the changing social, economic and political patterns that require quite different solutions to those advanced in the previous fifty years. Giddens has argued old divisions based on social class are no longer the central dynamism for change. The working class had been reshaped by new technologies and multiple divisions of labour, its collective strength undermined by economic globalisation, government policy, and the shift from an industrial to a knowledge and service economy. He dismisses the relevance of any structural determinants in mapping individual and collective choices and capacities (Hoggett, 2000a). Beck describes this as the 'risk society', characterised by 'diversity, unclarity and insecurity in people's work and life' (2000: 1). A more socially complex world had emerged in which new personal identities were constantly being defined and new allegiances formed. Giddens (1994) speaks of the need for 'positive welfare', a 'generative politics' concerned 'to allow individuals and groups to make things happen, rather than have things happen to them' (p. 15).

The influence of social capitalist theorists, such as Putnam (1995) is also evident. Putnam identified what he saw as a decline in social capital that threatened American democracy. Social capital was defined in terms of the levels of trust, reciprocity, shared norms, behaviour, and sense of belonging alongside formal and informal networks within a neighbourhood. It is the 'glue' that binds communities together. Putnam took its most visible signs as the level of engagement in local activities and organisations and argued that social capital could be used to act as a resource to lever in resources to strengthen communities. Etizoni's communitarianism more straightforwardly highlighted what he saw as the negative consequences of the new social order on families, collective responsibility and ethical behaviour. The communitarian crisis rests on the apparent imbalance between 'rights' and 'responsibilities', and urges the government to strengthen its moral agenda (Etzioni, 1995).

Labour's subsequent approach is an attempt to translate these theoretical strands into coherent policy. The emphasis has been on individual responsibility within a socially inclusive society. It seeks preventive policies, designed to avoid the necessity of welfare benefits, with a more limited commitment that 'those in genuine need will always get help and support...' (Blair, 1998). Labour's vision is of a society in which 'active' and 'responsible' citizens are fully engaged in the labour market, in their communities and in the democratic processes. Writers such as Beck would suggest that such broad objectives conceal the nature and product of such engagement. Although Labour's vision is of an inclusive society, and thus distinctive from the New Right, it is explicit about the expectations of membership and willing to impose regulatory measures in respect of those who are unwilling to meet those expectations.

A new organisational framework

Labour offered a pragmatic 'modern' welfare package, a 'new deal' (Powell, 2000; Lister, 2001). In arguing for a 'Third Way', distinctive from both old Labour and the New Right, Blair called upon the left to abandon its intellectual pessimism and address the practical politics of 'what is possible' (Showstack, 1996). Public services would need to modernise in order to compete within a global free market capitalism. Further, during the first two years of office this was to be secured within the spending plans of the previous Conservative administration. Labour's commitment to reform was matched by its determination to secure a second electoral victory (Rawnsley, 2000) and to this end the modernisation agenda unfolded during the first four years of Blair's premiership. Some common themes emerged applicable across public provision including:

- increased coordination, through 'joined-up' policy, strategic thinking and professional practice;
- a plurality of service providers working in partnership and coordinating strategic responses to complex problems;
- service user and public involvement in the planning, delivery and monitoring of policy;
- efficiency and accountability through national service standards and targeting of provision on identifiable, vulnerable or challenging groups, such as rough sleepers, the unemployed, looked-after children, high-risk mental-health service users, teenage mothers, or those in need of basic skills education;
- an emphasis on service quality, continuous improvement, performance management, and the identification and dissemination of good practice;
- evidence-based practice, combined with the adoption of 'common sense' pragmatism;
- strong leadership and good public sector management;
- a revival of public sector professionalism and ethos.

Early in his second term, Blair (2002) summarised what he now defined as four key principles of reform. These reflected both the outcomes of four years of reform but also a shift in emphasis following accusations of an over-centralised approach. He now emphasised:

1. a national framework of standards with minimum floor targets;
2. an increase in devolved power, or 'earned autonomy', to those providers who have demonstrated their capacity to meet national targets allowing for greater local diversity and more effective consumer pressure at the front-line of service delivery;
3. a reform of public service professionals;
4. greater choice between service providers and within each service.

These features are at the core of this book. The importance of the broader economic, political and social context in which the reforms are embedded is not denied. Nor is it assumed that Labour's response is the most appropriate. However, there is merit in examining the robustness of the emergent framework, its constituent elements and impact on policy outcomes. Labour's modernisation of the organisation and delivery of public provision has not been a by-product of a larger strategy to create a residual system of welfare. It also reflects a long-standing critique of previous delivery mechanisms from service users, community-based organisations, professionals and academics (Williams, 2001). The characteristics of a modern public service as identified above pull in different directions and, for example, require new and complex relationships to be built between government, service providers, service users and the citizen. However, modernisation, underpinned by a new consensus, is made more difficult when set against the experience of two dominant models of welfare – the 1945 post-war Fabian social democratic settlement and the 1979–97 New Right governments of Thatcher and Major.

Inclusion not equality

The Blair government's approach marks a decisive break with a core social democratic principle of using state welfare as a means of creating a more equal society. Lister (1998, 2001) argues that the current stress on a socially inclusive society, fundamental to Labour's electoral appeal after the divisiveness associated with Conservative policies, amounts to a rejection of redistribution through taxation. 'Social inclusion' is the core concept but this does not involve addressing, either by eradication or by amelioration, the structural inequalities that lie at the heart of a free market system. The goal of equality of outcome has been replaced by equality of opportunity, as reflected in the level at which the minimum wage was set and the pre-election pledge to remain within Conservative spending plans. Social exclusion is equated primarily with non-participation in the labour market (Levitas, 2001).

Individual achievement and security must be secured through personal investment in education, improved qualifications and training, and securing and maintaining a place in the formal economy. A key role for government is to enable and encourage individuals to secure the necessary credentials to achieve a financially rewarding place in the economy. Both positive and negative incentives are employed to this end as in, for example, the basic skills and widening participation agendas and increased regulation of benefit recipients. This process of 'up-skilling' is not to be restricted to the initial point of entry into the labour market (Powell, 2000). Opportunities are first captured by broad objectives such as 'life-long learning' and then translated into specific targets or initiatives, as in the target of 50 per cent of those eligible entering higher education by 2010, the introduction of a 'skills escalator' for continuing professional development, and an expectation that the unskilled amongst the professionally unqualified public services workers achieve NVQ level 2 by 2005 through the Skills for Life initiative (DfES, 2001).

Those at the wrong end of social and economic distribution will no doubt welcome any improvement in their material circumstances. Whether this will be sufficient to alter attitudes and behaviour in more 'socially desirable' ways or to generate a greater sense of national 'belonging' and integration is debatable. While profound inequalities persist, privilege, deference to authority and elitism abound, and prejudice and discrimination are common experiences, it remains more a divided than an inclusive society. It has proved far more challenging and controversial to convert into policy the ideas derived from the concept of social capital, with its emphasis on building trust, or the communitarian stress on a moral order.

Work glorious work

Much weight has been placed by Labour on a productive engagement in the labour market (Levitas, 1996; Jordan, 1998). Human dignity, self-worth, and a sense of societal belonging are assumed to flow from waged labour. Policies such as New Deal, are designed to 'encourage' claimants back into the labour market, making work pay by imposing more restrictions and controls on claimants and offering assistance to move into work. Only through labour market activity can the citizen make a productive contribution to society, ensure financial self-sufficiency and reduce their dependency on the state. This was clearly stated in one of the early Labour initiatives,

> The Government's aim is to rebuild the welfare state around work... Our ambition is nothing less than a change of culture among benefit claimants, employers and public servants, with rights and responsibilities

on all sides. Those making the shift from welfare into work will be provided with positive assistance, not just a benefit payment (DSS, 1998b: 23–4).

Labour has less to say in relation to the nature, distribution, organisation or rewards of paid work, although policies have been introduced to support those on very low incomes such as the minimum wage, the Working Families Tax Credit and a childcare tax credit. It has called for more 'family-friendly' employer policies and by way of an exemplar launched the National Childcare Strategy and National Health Service (NHS) Childcare Strategy. However, the entitlement to unpaid parental leave has not been embraced enthusiastically and the derisory 'right' to ask an employer for flexible hours has suffered the same fate. For the majority of the working population, the nature or experience of work has not altered fundamentally. This appreciation of the need for a better work/life balance appears primarily in order to facilitate access to paid work. Ultimately, the objective is to reinforce the work ethic rather than build a new foundation based on an 'ethic of care' (Williams, 2001). Labour has been much less concerned about the conditions under which the work is performed, the social relations of work, and the meaning or satisfaction that is derived from work. Any work is apparently better than none at all. There has been little acknowledgement of the value of other forms of productive activity, alternative methods of exchange, or more radical measures such as a citizen's income (Gorz, 1999). Rather, all can, and should, be in the workforce with little comfort other than an acceptance of the uncertainties and insecurities associated with the new global economic order.

The belief in the relationship between paid work and social inclusion has been used to justify both the abolition of lone parent benefits and the introduction of policies to afford the disabled 'opportunities' to work. Previously both groups experienced ambiguous and lower expectations in relation to the labour market. By contrast, Labour has remained silent on profit levels, wage differentials or maximum salaries, and has continued and defended both private and public sector bonus payments, golden handshakes, generous executive severance packages, and salary hikes for senior managers in excess of inflation. Labour no longer associates social inclusion with the offer of a secure, guaranteed and adequate income, at a reasonable level, relative to the income of the wealthy

(Townsend, 1979). An adequate income is no longer sufficient in itself to enable individuals to make their own choices about how to lead their lives and decide on what basis to participate in society. This acceptance of work 'as it is', and the assumption that this can act as a unifying force, when many continue to have a negative experience of work and gross income disparities remain, is a fundamental weakness in a strategy for social inclusion.

Active but managed citizens?

Alongside its 'make work pay' strategy, Labour has placed a high priority on devising a variety of complex, consultative and participatory mechanisms along with incentives to encourage participation. Central to its vision is a new relationship between the state and the citizen. This is to be achieved by creating opportunities for engagement in political life, ensuring that the citizen is sufficiently informed, and emphasising the social obligations and responsibilities attached to the concept of citizenship (Blair, 1997). Previous versions of state-led public participation have been heavily criticised as tokenistic attempts designed to co-opt the most vocal, deflect attention away from substantive issues by burying participants in a mountain of procedure and paperwork, and operating to unrealistic timetables while being manipulative in the release of information. Labour now offers a different vision of the active citizen, although the outcome may not be dissimilar.

Mechanisms are required to enable citizens to meet their responsibilities, contribute to community well-being and generate a sense of belonging. As one former minister stated, 'we all owe a responsibility to each other, where every individual... has the opportunity to fulfil the potential that lies uniquely in them; where every family can feel it has a stake in society' (Mandelson, 1997). However, meaningful citizenship is only secured when individuals have an equal ability to pursue their rights and exercise their responsibilities, requiring a commitment to an individuality *de facto* rather than *de jure* (Bauman, 2001). As currently formulated, Labour's concept of the 'active citizen' contains a number of contestable assumptions, namely that:

- It is possible and appropriate for the state to clearly define citizenship, both in terms of the entitlements and duties that flow from belonging to a nation state. Further, to seek evidence of citizenship as a prerequisite of entitlement is not unreasonable.

- Citizens can be expected to act as responsible and autonomous social agents in relation to themselves and their dependents. Consequently they will be, and would seek to be, less dependent upon the state-funded provision.
- Personal independence is to be secured, and the duties of citizenship fulfilled, through an active engagement in the labour market. The state has a concomitant responsibility to remove any disincentives to paid work, including those within the benefit system, and to provide opportunities to maximise citizen engagement.
- If citizenship implies 'belonging' and 'contributing' it also signifies appropriate and inappropriate behaviours, legitimising the role of the state in defining these. In turn, this provides a rationale for the exclusion from benefits and services of those who persist with what has been defined as unacceptable or the imposition of some other penalty.

What is less prominent is the idea that active citizens will want to determine through dialogue the inclusive frameworks within which they will cooperate. Nevertheless, the creation of both informal and formal participatory mechanisms always contains the potential that such fundamental challenges will be raised. State-led participatory initiatives usually release a profound anxiety on the part of their creators and this is no less so within Blair's government.

Socially responsible behaviour

The Blair government has expended much energy distinguishing itself from the traditional image of the Labour Party, and particularly from its left-wing, by insisting that the question of individual social responsibility is a critical but a long neglected area. In pressing its case for socially responsible behaviour as a hallmark of an inclusive society, Labour has adopted an authoritarian response to those who do not conform. It has been quick to pronounce on moral issues and define individual obligations. Often such pronouncements have been made in a manner lacking in sensitivity to the diversity it would otherwise welcome and seemingly without insight into the complex processes required to change behaviour. In doing so it has drawn heavily from the US-based communitarian movement previously influential within the Clinton administrations (Etzioni, 1995; Tam, 1998; Heron and Dwyer, 1999).

At the heart of communitarianism is a concern with restoring the balance between social rights and responsibilities, challenging current understandings of what individual contributions should be made to personal and societal well-being in return for the freedom to exercise rights or receive benefits. Communitarianism goes further by specifying what is believed to be the unacceptable features of social and economic life, such as Etzioni's (1995) comment that 'children should not have children'. Its proponents urge governments to pursue policies that encourage socially responsible behaviour, support traditional family structures, promote active citizenship, and instil a sense of civic duty (Driver and Martell, 1997). This includes policies that make access to provision conditional upon perceived behaviour as judged by welfare professionals acting as gatekeepers. Etzioni promotes an interventionist state urging:

> It is sociologically naïve to sit back and wait for new communities to spring up. It is often necessary, and there is nothing artificial or otherwise improper, in recruiting and training organisers and facilitators of 'we-ness' (Etzioni, 1995: 125).

Communitarianism treads what is a delicate line at the boundary of stating what is 'undesirable' and what is 'wrong' and the particular shading or emphasis that is given to any issue has potentially significant policy implications. Preventative, educative, corrective or positive action measures are adopted to address the 'undesirable' while punitive measures predominate in relation to what is deemed to be 'wrong'. Labour has sought solutions to these dilemmas through the creation of cross-cutting units, such as the Social Exclusion Unit (SEU). Alongside its concern for neighbourhood renewal, it focused on specific social groups including rough sleepers, teenage mothers, truants and school exclusions. Labour's dilemma has been that if it pursues preventative policies it might appear too much like previous social democratic administrations but if it consistently adopts a punitive response it is in danger of alienating its liberal support.

Too often Labour has appeared strident and self-righteous on the need for strong and moral 'communities', and the requirement to re-moralise them where this is absent (Heron and Dwyer, 1999). 'Community', embracing both family and voluntary effort is to be the basis of both a moral and economic revival, where core needs are met and behaviour is policed. Again Labour has faced a dilemma. On the one hand it claims that the classic concept of the welfare state is no longer applicable and new forms are required for a dynamically changing Britain. On the other, it has adopted a very traditional and conservative meaning to the concept of community, ignoring its new and complex formations (Hoggett, 1997). It remains attracted to a vision of the traditional, stable, homogenous, place-based communities that are both individually identifiable, and able to police their members through the employment of new moral gatekeepers, such as super-caretakers and neighbourhood managers. Further, the sum of such place-based communities is somehow combined to generate one national community of common values (Etzioni, 1995; Tam, 1998). The measurable objectives for improving disadvantaged communities have been somewhat limited with the neighbourhood renewal programme offering the prospect that things will improve for 'most of the residents of poor neighbourhoods', alongside the questionable statistical proposition that such neighbourhoods will be brought up to the national average (SEU, 1998).

The origins of Labour's authoritarian tendencies has been a matter of debate. Some have connected it to Blair's personal attachment to Christianity. Others refer to the weakening ties with the party's traditional roots, mounting frustration and impatience with the reluctance or unwillingness of 'traditionalists' – politicians and professionals – to modernise. Rawnsley (2000) argues that the profound fear of electoral defeat and subsequent isolation of a central core leadership anxious to distance itself from 'old' Labour, created an overblown sense of the correctness of the analysis and strategic responses. Policies had to be seen to be working and instant results were required while the leadership could not be seen as a 'soft touch'. Crime and anti-social behaviour are also concerns that require an immediate response, especially for those who live in disadvantaged communities who are often the victims of crime and experience anti-social behaviour on a daily basis. Nevertheless, Labour's authoritarian tendencies on matters of morality, combined with its desire to maintain detailed centralised control of all aspects of policy, suggest a restricted vision of active citizenship.

Capacity building

Another core concept for the Blair government has been 'capacity building' and the role of community development agencies and those within the non-profit sector. Within an enlarged mixed economy of welfare such 'third sector' organisations have been offered an enhanced role as a partner in policy-making, as a service provider, and also in ensuring that communities are more receptive to and participate in the new local strategic planning arrangements (ODPM, 2001). A more cohesive society does indeed require multiple opportunities for citizens to influence and shape the decision-making process, and their collective efforts should be valued and nourished while their individual potential is encouraged and maximised. Allocating a key role to capacity building, as with the concept of the active citizen, highlights the tension between a desire for dispersed and devolved centres of leadership, deliberation, and action and centralised control.

Labour's approach to capacity building has clear objectives both about the kind of general 'climate' it wishes to create and specific expectations about behaviour and attitudes. It has focused on building a community's internal assets rather than on what it needs or should expect from others, especially the state, strengthening its sense of identity, its problem-solving capacity, and its desire to take responsibility to address local concerns. Additional inputs of state resources are closely tied to the capacity or willingness of local communities to pursue these objectives.

Joined-up thinking

'Joined-up thinking' is another element in Labour's programme of modernisation. The potential of a coordinated, collaborative and holistic approach to tackling complex issues is not new. The need for coordinated planning has been recognised since the inception of the post-war welfare state and the difficulty of achieving it acknowledged since the early 1970s in a variety of policy documents on local government management and service configurations, planning or implementation (Clarke and Stewart, 1997). However, what is now suggested is that this comprehensive joined-up strategic approach is to be adopted throughout every stage of policy from planning to front-line service delivery. It is to include all provider

agencies and practitioners at every level of government. Addition-
ally, service users, voluntary and citizen organisations are expected
to contribute and new duties of consultation have been imposed on
local authorities and healthcare providers (Local Government Act,
2000; DoH, 2001a; SEU, 2001).

Labour has adopted a multi-level approach. It has created a
number of Whitehall-based cross-cutting and service specific units,
introduced local initiatives to develop joined-up practice, reformed
certain aspects of service providing agencies, and created new
institutions of local governance. The proliferation of think-tanks
staffed by those recruited from outside the traditional civil service
and drawn from a range of professional backgrounds has been
a particular feature. One of its first actions on regaining office was
the creation of the SEU, and symbolically its initial location within
the Cabinet Office was not insignificant. This has been followed by
other similar bodies including the Neighbourhood Renewal Unit
(NRU), located within the office of the deputy prime minister, the
Regional Co-ordination Unit, the Community Cohesion Unit, and
the Home Office Active Community Unit, recently identified as
the lead agency for civic renewal and community development.

The SEU, the first of such new style bodies, has typified the
approach with its remit to break the 'vicious circle' caused by the
'combination of linked problems such as unemployment, poor
skills, and low income'. Its role is to encourage inter-agency and
inter-professional collaboration, identifying and disseminating
'best practice'. Central to its approach is the concept of 'mainstreaming' or 'shifting the policy and practice of mainline departments' (SEU, 1998). Rather than concentrating as in the past on
special time-limited initiatives focused usually on small geographical localities, operating with a limited budget, and crucially, in
isolation from the policy and practice of the major policy departments, it aims to transfer learning to mainstream practice. To do so,
it first requires the creation of a 'learning culture' within government.
The SEU and NRU attempt to mirror the approach by bringing
together professionals from a wide range of government departments, local authorities and non-profit organisations, and are
supported by a 'ministerial network' from the key government
departments. An early SEU initiative was to create eighteen Priority
Action Teams (PATs) to investigate and advise on key issues. The
PATs have subsequently reported and their recommendations
incorporated into the latest regeneration strategy (SEU, 2001).

Claire Tyler (2002), the Unit's current director, described its work as:

> We do policy development to identify areas that are tricky cross-cutting issues that no particular government department owns, or which have proved particularly intractable (Tyler, 2002).

Other initiatives concerned with service delivery are being reorganised around particular client groups, as in Children's Trusts and Adult Care Trusts, that bring together professionals previously located in the NHS, local authority education and social service departments to commission, finance, and possibly provide direct services for children and older adults respectively.

Other mechanisms for the improved coordination have included the development of central and regional centres of excellence and leadership for different policy areas and the collection and web-based dissemination of 'best practice', as in the proposed NRU's 'knowledge management' system; improved data gathering, and a growing emphasis on programme evaluations. At a local level, a range of initiatives such as the various 'action zones' have been created to experiment with mechanisms to improve coordination and strategic planning. Similarly, in modernising specific services new roles have been created with responsibility for drawing together strategic plans and all those involved in their delivery. For example, in public health a new Director of Public Health located within each Primary Care Trust (PCT) is expected to take the lead, on improving health and reducing local inequalities and is responsible for drawing together the Health Improvement and Modernisation Plans (HIMPs). In 'Shifting the Balance of Power' (DoH, 2001b), the need for greater inter-professional collaboration is spelt out:

> A modern public health function can only be delivered successfully by a workforce which is interdisciplinary in its orientation, training, remit and composition (Annex B, para. 3).

Other strategies focused on provider agencies have included a growing emphasis on the need to develop leadership and internal learning processes, while the Best Value initiative calls for continuous service quality review and improvement. New forms of local governance have also been created. Perhaps the most important of these has been the Local Strategic Partnership, with an oversight of the many service specific partnerships already in existence and responsible for the development of a Community Strategy. Local authorities have been given a new duty to promote local social, economic and environmental well-being. Local government management has itself been reformed with the separation amongst elected members between Cabinet and 'Overview and Scrutiny' committees with extended powers to examine local NHS provision. English Regional Government Offices have been strengthened with a current brief to respond to cross-cutting issues such as crime reduction, drugs and community cohesion.

Leadership development

New Labour claims to have learnt the lessons from the failure of previous, more modest, approaches and to be unwilling to tolerate the threat posed by, for example, professional or organisational rivalry, jealousy, protectionism and narrow self-interest. The determination to pursue this goal only intensifies its desire to remain in control. Such collaborative ventures in respect of both problem analysis and response are assumed to generate the opportunity for 'value added' outputs through the synergy of process. However, while the sum of the parts might be greater than what each can bring separately to any policy situation, the skills and capacities required to make these work are currently not part of either professional or managerial training. In response Labour has stressed, along with its Organisation for Economic Co-operation and Development (OECD) partners, the importance of developing both a stronger public sector leadership and building 'learning organisations' (Cabinet Office, 2001a; OECD, 2001). The OECD document expressed the problem as:

> How to develop more public officials who can draw others into a strong spirit of public service geared to the needs of contemporary society, and thereby make their services to government and to citizens more effective? (p. 12)

Labour's modernisation is an unfinished project and one that is complex and contradictory (Lister, 2001). In its determination to fund public sector growth by extending the mixed economy of welfare and levering in private finance, it has been unable to reassure doubters that this will not inevitably lead to privatisation or a dual market in significant aspects of provision. However, the emphasis given to inter-professional collaboration, partnership, local leadership, evidence-based practice, service quality, service user involvement, capacity building and public participation provides the basis for challenging Labour's limitations and restrictive vision in other areas. Crucially, success in these areas could significantly improve the quality of services for those who depend upon them. The remainder of this book explores in more depth these instruments of contemporary welfare practice, identifying issues that need to be addressed if progress is to be made in ensuring their effective implementation.

3

A Mixed Economy of Welfare: A Plurality of Providers and a Diversity of Service User Relationships

The next two chapters are concerned with the continued expansion of a mixed economy of welfare, an objective supported by all political parties. In this context, a mixed economy is understood as a diversity or plurality of public service providers operating across all sectors of social life, from the informal to non-profit, market and state sectors (Wistow *et al.*, 1994). It also signals a plurality of relationships for the welfare consumer, often in respect of the same provider agency, alternating between a citizen exercising social rights, to that of a purchaser in the market place, or supplicant seeking assistance. If the user is confronted with multiple and diverse providers they are also themselves either required, or choose to act, as purchasers as well as recipients of services. These variable relationships in respect of the provider have, in turn, an impact upon the user's behaviour and provide added legitimation for shifts in the welfare market place.

In practice, there always has been a mixed economy of welfare. Most of our everyday needs have been provided either within the informal sector of immediate and extended family and neighbours or through individual purchases in the market place. The non-profit sector, a key provider prior to the post-war welfare state, continues to offer a range of services, on a charitable, state-funded or self-help basis, and campaigns for the recognition of unmet needs. The market sector offers services to both consumers able to afford them and to employers willing to provide them as a benefit for their employees. Employers also offer their employees, usually after some negotiation, with a range of other occupational benefits, but distributed unevenly and with variable levels of benefit across the workforce. Nevertheless, for some thirty-five years following the creation of the post-war UK welfare services, the state overshadowed all other sectors, both as a provider and responsible agent for all major aspects of welfare.

This perception and experience of the state as the primary provider of collective needs have undergone profound changes since the 1979 election of Margaret Thatcher. For the next eighteen years successive Conservative governments, committed to a diminishing or residual state public sector, vigorously pursued a policy of first privatising and then marketising public services. A mixed economy is now institutionalised in Labour government policy as a vision for the future of welfare as was affirmed both within education (DFEE, 1998a) and in the Health and Social Care Act 2001 (DoH, 2001c). While not a new phenomenon, the relative scale of provision, between the state, market and non-profit sectors, for the collective meeting of need has altered significantly and continues to do so. In contrast to the post-war vision, the state is no longer assumed to be the appropriate service provider. In outlining his vision for local government, Blair argued that:

> The days of the all-purpose authority that planned and delivered everything are gone. They are finished ... Local authorities will deliver some services but their distinctive leadership role will be to weave and knit together the contribution of the various stakeholders (1998: 13).

Policy reform is now premised on the superiority of the mixed economy. Thus irrespective of the depth and breadth of provision, the form it takes will be through a plurality of agencies (Knapp *et al.*, 2001) with different contractual arrangements depending on the provider's commercial or non-profit status (Mackintosh, 2000). The state's primary function is now seen in terms of a commissioner and regulator.

A mixed economy or private market place?

Labour recently reaffirmed its commitment to collective provision (Blair, 2002), but what remains in doubt is both the extent of that provision and the distribution of providers across the sectors. A mixed economy can mean multiple providers, from different economic sectors, who are funded and regulated by the state to provide specific public services. It can also mean a diminished public sector and an opportunity for unregulated private sector organisations to inherit the space vacated by the state to provide market-based services. Under this formulation the state could enable the service user to access such provision by providing vouchers to those who qualify to be exchanged for services. Individuals would be expected to meet any additional costs from their personal income or seek charitable assistance. A mixed economy approach can be embraced both by those who favour diversity of provision and believe that large monopolistic state bureaucracies have proved themselves to be inflexible and unresponsive, and by those who support privatised public services.

For those committed to publicly funded and regulated provision, the concern is that any significant involvement by the market sector will lead to pressure first for a reduction and then abandonment of direct state funding, regulation and thus democratic accountability. It would be a process of privatisation by the back door. The existence of an already profitable sector operating, for example, within the health, housing and social care markets adds to this sense of unease. For this group there is an insurmountable clash of values, principles, and practice between otherwise profit-oriented organisations and those concerned with the delivery of public services. Any suggestion that there should be a financial return on private investment is unacceptable on the grounds that such returns either are always excessive or have been secured on the basis of a universal or personal need and are, therefore, exploitative. Others argue that market sector organisations will only be interested in providing the services that are relatively trouble-free with a compliant service user group whose members retain a measure of autonomy and independence. They will create a two-tier system by literally 'creaming off' the most rewarding services. The 'heavy end' of service delivery, where there are more complex problems to address, challenging or reluctant service users, greater difficulties in measuring success and therefore fewer opportunities to sell the product, would be left to the state or voluntary agencies.

Those who argue for the retention of public services within the state and against any extension to the involvement of market sector organisations, find themselves struggling against a sea of change supported by all political parties. More significantly, mounting a defence based on the resurrection of pre-1979 public provision is unsustainable. Those essentially post-war mechanisms had already been fatally discredited after some fifteen years of mounting criticism by the left and the right, as well as service users and their organisations. Various efforts to reform the bureau–professional model of state provision have proved ineffective in substantially improving public services. Rather, the decline in quality is typically related to a lack of public investment and it is assumed that a substantial increase in resources would revitalise public provision. There is a deep reluctance to address either the need for or the relationship between other aspects of reform, such as organisational structures and processes, improved service standards, professional practice, accountability and management, for fear of further undermining the public sector. Crucially, eighteen years of reforming market-oriented governments have transformed the terrain on which the arguments are conducted over the future of public services.

For the current Labour government, the future role of the state is mapped out to be that of funder, regulator, facilitator, coordinator, and primarily concerned with governance. This does not imply that the state is to play a less significant or involved role since, as Clarke (1996) suggests, 'new relationships and new flows of power are constructed in these processes' (p. 17). The state continues to provide a significant number of direct services, and indeed to be the primary provider, in a wide range of service areas notably health, personal social services, social security, education, as well as neighbourhood regeneration, youth services and employment (Burchardt and Propper, 1999). Even in the rapidly declining area of state housing provision, 18 per cent of householders continue to occupy local authority provided housing, albeit a drop from 30 per cent in 1971 (CIH/JRF/CML, 1999, as quoted in Hawtin and Kettle, 2000). In every aspect of welfare, the state continues to determine, manage and govern public provision. To understand current configurations between the state, market and civil society it is important to locate these within the context of shifting perceptions of the state since the post-war period.

The place of the state

During the post-war period of social democratic reform the state was perceived as the agency with overall responsibility for the identification and meeting of collective needs. It was uniquely capable of ensuring that services were offered on the basis of need, available equally to all those entitled irrespective of an individual's ability to pay or accidents of birth (Clarke, 1996). For many socialists it was both the vehicle of social reform and of greater social and economic equality. The state and the provision of public services were thus seen as one and the same. Consequently, when needs were identified or services provided by non-state bodies, the state faced increasing demands to take responsibility for such provision or ensure that its own services were both protected from and not exploited by other providers. Within the informal sector, the realm of family, kinship and neighbours, the state was expected, although did not always oblige, to extend its responsibilities. A growing number of disadvantaged, abused or discriminated groups, such as victims of domestic violence, began to lobby for state intervention and protection. By the mid-1970s there were few areas of life in which the state was not prominently involved and to that extent the concept of the 'welfare state' had real meaning. The centrality of the state and its perceived role as ringmaster in social welfare often cast a shadow over, but did not obliterate, the efforts of others. This fixation with the state was hardly surprising given the highly centralised nature of the UK provision and the near monopoly held by the state (Glennerster, 1995). Despite an ambivalence and even hostility towards the state, there has been a deeper and widespread belief that it represented the one agency capable of advancing the social democratic cause.

The radical social democratic view of the state as a progressive force contrasted with its function as a capitalist state to secure the conditions necessary to further the interests of capital (Offe, 1984). This involved both protecting and advancing the interests of national capital, including the reproduction of labour power, by ensuring that its citizens were sufficiently educated, healthy, compliant workers, and guaranteeing a level of social cohesion. Those who benefited from its services and those who worked within it often experienced it as a controlling and oppressive body (Cockburn, 1977; London Edinburgh Weekend Return Group, 1980). There had been a continuous tension between demands for a state responsive to perceived or changing needs or unacceptable inequalities, and deep reservations about the nature and objectives of such interventions. Similar tensions existed in relation to state interventions designed to change or manage individual behaviour to protect the vulnerable and 'at risk' citizens or those they may threaten, as well as to efforts to control socially unacceptable or unlawful behaviour. The left critique of state welfare focused on:

- the controlling and oppressive features of any intervention;
- the extent to which state interventions served interests other than those stated;
- the degree to which individuals or social groups were pathologised and held responsible for circumstances or behaviour that could be better understood by an analysis of the social and economic structures and their location within them;
- the inadequacy of any policy response in relation to the scale of the problem.

Paradoxically, its response was often to demand even greater state intervention.

Within such debates, individual agency, relations between citizens and welfare professionals, or the role of non-state agencies in shaping state (in)action were neglected areas. The left saw the possibilities for progressive state action through the recognition that the state was far from being a homogeneous, strategic, single-minded, coordinated and well-organised body. It was a complex web with its own contradictions, conflicts within and between each of its institutions, between different levels of state organisation, and between different social categories or tiers of hierarchy (CSE State Group, 1979; London-Edinburgh Weekend Return Group, 1980). This view was countered by those who believed that over-arching state-wide objectives could never be ignored and that powerful and organised political forces combined with the external economic and political imperatives were always likely to take precedence (Miliband, 1969; Cockburn, 1977). Offe (1984) described these tensions as evidence that, 'while capitalism cannot coexist *with*, neither can it exist *without*, the welfare state' (p. 153).

Globalisation has again challenged such views about state welfare. The power of a deregulated and globally mobile capitalism casts doubt upon the capacity of nation states to protect citizens from the worst consequences of market inequities. Nation states are

caught between the need to restructure in response to the requirements of global markets but also by a more articulate and demanding public. Those who credit the state with a high level of conscious
strategic planning suggest a shift is underway from the Keynesian
welfare national state to a 'Schumpeterian workfare post-national
regime' (Jessop, 1994; 2000). Within this regime the state gives
emphasis to open deregulated markets, promotes labour market
requirements for a flexible workforce in its social policy, and gives
an enhanced role to non-state agencies and their inter-relationships
through networks and partnerships for the delivery of state policies. This is accomplished through a process of 'hollowing-out'
and internationalisation of the state alongside the transformation
of 'identities, interests, capacities, rights and responsibilities...
(producing) more flexible, capable, and reliable agents of the state's
new economic strategies' (Jessop, 2000: 353). Clarke and Newman
(1997) describe what they see as the emergence of the 'managerial
state' and the tendency both towards centralisation of policy and the
'modernisation' of local state and non-state organisations as a pre-
condition for the dispersal or delegation of coordinated state
authority. Such processes, involving a greater role for non-state
agencies, ensure an extension of state power and influence rather
than its diminution. They argue that the mixed economy is better
thought of as,

> a structure of dominance in which one element of the combination (the
> state) both performs its own functions (purchasing and providing
> through the public sector) and allocates the places to the other
> elements...a field of power relations....(p. 27).

The process of constructing such relations of dispersal, however,
involves some structural instabilities as the engagement of a whole
variety of new and often previously critical stakeholders simultaneously creates for the state new points of resistance, creating the
need for welfare professionals to be disciplined to work in new ways.
Clarke and Newman are quick to point out that the identification of
such a strategic initiative by the state does not equate to its successful
implementation.

The Thatcherite New Right defined the post-war interventionist
or regulatory welfare state as the 'nanny state'. Through a process
of ever-expanding its role it became an interfering, intrusive, fussy,
over-protective figure, stifling independence and creating and

maintaining an unhealthy dependency such that those receiving services were unable to cope as independent beings in the 'real' world of market forces (Marsland, 1996). Thirty years of state welfare had created unrealistic expectations about the state's capacity to identify and respond to need and had diverted valuable resources away from more productive areas. To break the spell of the Keynesian–Beveridgen legacy, that kept all eyes fixed on to the state and dulled the UK's competitive edge in the international economy, the New Right was determined to marketise social welfare. This would be achieved by:

- direct privatisation of provision with incentives for those who opted out;
- contracting out services to private sector agencies;
- the introduction of quasi-market competitiveness within remaining state services;
- the managerialisation of welfare organisations;
- undermining the power of welfare professionals and public sector trade unions;
- the encouragement of voluntarism and self-help;
- redefining the service user as a consumer choosing between service providers;
- an intolerance of those who were perceived to be exploiting the welfare system or engaged in anti-social behaviour.

An aggressive individualism or market entrepreneurialism was promoted and any collective responsibility for the well-being of all citizens denied with Thatcher's infamous declaration that 'there is no such thing as society'. Those who succeeded economically were praised while those who fell foul of economic restructuring were labelled weak, feckless, irresponsible or work-shy. Particular social groups, such as social security claimants, the unemployed, teenage and single parents, council tenants, black and ethnic minority communities, trade unionists, were variously scapegoated as 'scroungers', 'fraudsters' or 'irresponsible', and a threat to Britain's economic prosperity, national identity or public order.

The New Right's declaration to 'roll back the state' conjured up a vision of the end of welfare, the abandonment of hard won rights of citizenship and widespread destitution and widening inequality. It marked the end of a political project designed to produce greater social and economic equality through planned state intervention in the market and social provision. Welfare professionals faced an uncertain future as services were cut back and new agencies appeared as competitors. Although the New Right failed in its aspiration to substantially reduce the level of public expenditure, its success in challenging the fundamental assumptions of the post-war welfare state and the introduction of new relations of welfare have had such profound consequences that shaped Labour's post-1997 welfare strategy.

Labour's restructuring of state and market

Greater attention is now given to the question of who should provide and pay for public services and to the appropriate boundaries between state, market, voluntary and community sectors. Labour's (1998) Green Paper on Welfare highlighted the boundary between public and private as central to the future development of welfare. Since its second term election, debate has centred on the concept of public–private partnerships (PPP) and specifically the public finance initiative (PFI) (HM Treasury, 2000). The debate is saturated in emotion as it throws into doubt Labour's commitment to reversing the Conservative market-oriented policies and returning to the principles and practices of post-war social democracy. A report from the influential think-tank, the Institute for Public Policy Research (IPPR, 2001), outlining the findings of its two-year Commission on Public Private Partnerships, argued for the extension of PPPs into core public services, although remaining cautious about their role in healthcare. This received further support from Le Grand (2001), himself a member of the Commission, following the publication of a strong counter argument by Catalyst, a left-of-centre think-tank (Pollock *et al.*, 2001).

The IPPR report argues that while firmly opposed both to a shrunken government and residualised public services, as envisaged by marketeers, it rejects the view that as a matter of principle public services should always be provided by the public sector. Instead, a diverse mixed economy built on partnerships should be seen as an opportunity for future provision, a 'risk-sharing' arrangement in which participants share common policy objectives. Such partnerships would need to guarantee social equity, be responsive to need, offer efficient and high quality provision, and be accountable. The report is also critical of existing PPP and PFI arrangements, highlighting uneven success, and acknowledging that all PFI initiatives are publicly funded and incur future liabilities for taxpayers. A number of suggestions are made for the future improvement of PFIs. These include ensuring that capital projects are contained with capital budgets, inserting explicit provisions for sharing 'super-profits' derived from re-financing arrangements, increasing user involvement including the selection of providers, and the adoption of an evidence-based approach to determine the appropriateness of a PFI and to evaluate subsequent performance. Any PFI arrangement, the report argues, would have to be underpinned by sustainable increases in public funding.

A critical response to the IPPR (Pollock *et al.*, 2001) was published by Catalyst. The Foreword, written by the Labour Chair of the House of Commons Health Select Committee, notes:

> the encroaching presence of an appeased private sector ... (its) abysmal record in quality of provision ... constant draining of publicly-trained staff (p. 5).

The authors argue that PPP would drain public revenues, lower the quality of services, and eventually threaten 'the very principle of universal services free at the point of use' (p. 8). Future generations would bear the cost of current borrowing from the private sector for new capital projects and that, as the IPPR report also notes, all the 1999–2002 PFI funded capital projects could have been funded through traditional public sector borrowing or by drawing upon existing surpluses. Instead, it argues that public agencies are denied access to public funds and given little choice but to pursue PFI arrangements, often in an uncompetitive market with few potential providers. The authors claim there is little evidence to support a value-for-money argument, based on sound private sector management and greater efficiency, and that irrespective of whether a particular initiative offers good value it may nevertheless be unaffordable.

Crucially, Pollock *et al.* question the limited evidence – defended by Le Grand in his later publication – that the private sector can be motivated by values beyond profit-maximisation. They present evidence, including that drawn from Australia and elsewhere, that private sector provision, for example in nursing homes, is of poorer quality or, as in private hospitals, has higher administrative costs or more expensive treatments, some of which are inappropriate, and does not deliver greater efficiency. Further, when private sector companies fail to deliver on their contractual obligations, the state has been reluctant to extract full compensation for fear of jeopardising future relationships. The costs of such failures have been borne by service users or their families with reduced or poorer quality services. Responsibility for service delivery continues to rest with public sector managers and professionals. In respect of healthcare, the report concludes that PFI has failed to deliver improvements to the NHS. It highlights increased inflexibilities, decreased diversity and access, and a failure to respond to health needs. Capital projects have been funded through revenue budgets thereby reducing the level of resources available for clinical services while new hospitals are downsized through fewer beds and the termination of some services. The report questions Labour's commitment to free universal services, pointing to the charges for personal services and the option of redesignating services currently defined as healthcare, and therefore free, into social care which is not free. It claims that the evidence is such as to create serious doubts about the involvement of private sector agencies being anything other than an opportunity to accumulate excessive profits through a transfer of funds raised by public taxation.

There is nothing intrinsically meritorious about state provided services which should be distinguished from state determined, defined, funded and regulated provision (Bryson, 1992; Burchardt and Propper, 1999). Others remain doubtful about any value-added benefits from a substantial private sector role (Ball *et al.*, 2001; Propper and Green, 2001). What is required is a clarity about the objectives and ethics of public provision and appropriate regulation in respect of *who* can provide, *how* services are provided, and the *quality* of those services. A plurality of state and private agencies delivering such services should not prevent the achievement of those objectives. Difficulties arise when such dispersed services are either inappropriately or over-regulated, or when services are offered to agencies operating to conflicting values and objectives and without any requirement to change.

The market sector already invests resources without the incentive of an immediate profitable return. Philanthropic support through the funding of research and policy development, direct grants or donations in kind, staff volunteer time, and managerial expertise offered in the UK through Business in the Community, has long been a tradition amongst market-based companies, especially in

North America. The 2002 *Guardian* 'Giving List' based on the
Financial Times Stock Exchange (FTSE) 100 Index suggests that
the UK corporate giving stands at 0.95 per cent of pre-tax profits,
up from 0.4 per cent the previous year, although the bottom 41 gave
a mere 0.12 per cent. The overall rise is partly accounted for by
falling profitability, improved measurement and the listing of world-
wide, rather the UK-only, contributions (*The Guardian*, 2002). In
its latest report, the Directory of Social Change indicates that
'community contributions', including donations, from the top 400
corporations was no higher in 2000–01 than it was in 1990–2001 at
0.42 per cent of pre-tax profits, although it has risen from a 1995–96
low of 0.29 per cent. There is increasing pressure for companies to
publish reports on their economic, environmental and social impacts.
Two private member's bills have now gone before Parliament while
public opinion polls suggest nearly 75 per cent believe that companies do not pay enough attention to the communities in which they
operate, while the proportion of consumers including an ethical
dimension to their purchasing stands at 44 per cent (Mori, 2002).

Corporate social responsibility or 'ethical' capitalism does not
diminish the importance given to profitability but acknowledges
the importance of trading relations, investment decisions and
community relations. Conditions of employment for employees, the
proportion of profits used to inflate corporate director income,
and the reciprocal norms of competition agreed between producers
operating within 'industrial districts' are also relevant (Ekins, 1992;
Lorenz, 1992). Companies are increasingly marketing products
under a 'fair trade' label that their policies on purchasing raw
materials contribute to local economic and environmental sustainability, support disadvantaged groups and are less exploitative.
Conversely, voluntary non-profit organisations have increased
their involvement in profit-making enterprises by selling existing
knowledge-based services, such as consultancy or publications, or
establishing new trading outlets. The expansion of the 'social economy' has sheltered a plethora of small, profit or surplus generating,
organisations, for example, worker and community co-operatives,
partnerships, and companies limited by guarantee (Pearce, 2003).
These are owned and managed by their members, seek to trade on a
more equitable basis and, working to social objectives, invest a per-
centage of any surplus in local social development (Quarter, 1992;
Shragge, 1997). Such trends, while slow, uneven and inconsistent,
blur sectoral boundaries.

The strength of public provision

Public provision continues to be significant. In 1995–96 public provision accounted for just under half of the total expenditure on welfare, having shown only a slight drop, from 52 per cent to 49 per cent since 1979 (Burchardt and Propper, 1999). The amount spent on privately financed services grew in the same period, from 27 per cent to 31 per cent of total expenditure, as did expenditure on privately provided services, up from 41 per cent to 49 per cent. Certain welfare services have for a long time been provided on the basis of quite different and competing value systems, for example, housing or residential care. Such provision, offered in the for-profit market place, through voluntary not-for-profit agencies, as well as by the state, has mirrored wider economic inequalities and different lifestyles. The key issue is not whether all housing is offered on the same basis but whether non-stigmatised, high quality and well managed social housing is provided as to promote social inclusion rather than reinforcing or contributing to exclusion (Hawtin and Kettle, 2000).

Strong objections were raised during the early 1980s against the Conservative's sale or privatisation of council housing (Whitfield, 1983). While individual tenants benefited from substantially reduced valuations, sales creamed-off the best quality houses from the collective stock, denying access for future tenants, and a reduction in the social diversity of council tenants (Malpass and Murie, 1990). There is now much greater acceptance of mixed housing provision although continuing the concern about the 'residualisation' of the remaining council housing stock. Part of the explanation lies in the absence of a strong sense of tenant 'ownership', and has lead Scottish authorities to propose the wholesale transfer of ownership to community-based co-operatives. In other areas of provision, such as healthcare or education, there has again been strong opposition to mixed provision, especially in relation to market-led services. In these settings, the private sector's presence is felt to undermine state services, because it recruits scarce human resources that would otherwise be employed within the public sector and takes advantage of any available public provision. Market-based services, for example in education, attract those who are ambitious for their children, see the competitive advantages of private provision and are sufficiently wealthy to afford it and who, it is assumed, would demand better quality state provision, had they been using it.

Any significant exodus from public services by the aspiring middle classes reduces the pressure to deliver high quality services. While private education remained the province of a minority from highly privileged backgrounds, it appeared not as a threat to state education but as a bastion of class privilege. Now that more middle-class parents choose to send their children to private schools, state education is consequentially more vulnerable. In a context that promotes active consumerism and values individual choice, while under-investing in public provision, this middle-class drift away from state schooling appears as the rational choice of parents 'wanting the best' for their children. State schools then compete for these 'desirable' pupils in an attempt to prevent the drift to private provision or entice middle-class families back to the benefits of state provided post-sixteen education. This reinforces the mentality of individual rational choice and inevitably distorts the distribution of resources within and between public schools with disproportionate resources being allocated to schools located in middle-class areas. As Burchardt and Propper (1999) argue, the choice of service is determined by pragmatic decisions based on what can be afforded against what most meets their needs.

The blurring of boundaries

Current debates about the politics of a mixed economy in public services need to acknowledge the existing combinations of state, market-based and non-profit sector services. The traditional four sector distinctions between the state, market, voluntary, and informal sectors no longer adequately describe what is a much more complex and graded set of arrangements. A substantial number of market transactions already take place within what might be perceived of as universal state services. There is no longer a sharp distinction across an expanding number of services between the state and the market. As boundaries become blurred, service users find themselves engaged in several different types of exchange within the same service. What used to be thought of as anomalies within an otherwise comprehensive state system are increasingly defining the service. Some of the complexities within state provision are illustrated below:

- *Universal state provision*, free at the point of need, funded through taxation, delivered by state employees. This pure welfare state model, with no immediate cost to the user (e.g. child benefit, primary and secondary healthcare services and most treatments) is in decline.

- *Partial universality*, in which the state provides the 'core' element, that remains free and universally available, whilst other aspects are only available to those who can afford to pay, perhaps at a subsidised level, or when costs can be met through voluntary fund-raising. For example, in education what has often to be purchased by parents might be thought of as essential (such as, textbooks, equipment, curriculum-related visits), or inessential to core curricula but relevant and enriching (cultural, leisure, social activities or exchange visits). Some services will be offered on a concessionary or 'no charge' basis to poorer families. What is made available to all, and what is fee-paying and concessionary is continuously shifting and is determined locally, against which there is unlikely to be any form of appeal. Typically, the systems by which concessions are offered are arbitrary and badly managed. A personal request for help has to be made on each occasion while the availability of concessions is not always made known. The process by which these concessions can be secured can be potentially humiliating and exclusionary.

- *Restrictive state provision*, is another common variant of the purist model. Services are available to those qualifying on some 'objective' criteria, such as competitive examinations, length of residence, and/or a capacity to pay an entry fee (e.g. higher education tuition fees). More informal systems also operate by which needs are prioritised.

- *State pay-as-you-go provision*, are those services that may be subsidised but increasingly offered at a rate comparable to the market sector. They are available by payment of a user charge or to those excused from some or all the amount, by virtue of their membership of a designated concessionary category (for example, public transport, social housing, leisure and cultural facilities, adult education and careers advice).

- *Selective or targeted state provision*, a traditional and growing form of provision. These are either means-tested or accessible only to those who fall below a certain income level (usually equivalent to the level of state non-contributory benefits), or qualify because of previous paid contributions (unemployment benefit), or are perceived to be socially excluded (residents in disadvantaged neighbourhoods).

In addition to acting as provider, albeit one where the provision is heavily conditional, the state has entered into a number of relationships with private bodies. Such agreements have, for example, generated:

- *Joint state and private provision*, where the service is provided privately but some are offered free at the point of need to particular, often age-related groups, or to those who qualify via a means test. Services offered in these ways are funded by the state, while all other users pay a market-based fee (e.g. dentistry or ophthalmic services).
- *State/private contractual relationships*, in which the state contracts a private organisation to provide a certain level of service, who is then free to determine those who qualify (social day care). State support may come in other forms such as grants to the organisation, service user vouchers or payments, direct fee payment to the provider (residential care) or subsidies (social housing).
- *State regulated and managed provision*, in which services are ostensibly provided by the state but are dependent upon a large number of individual volunteers (adult literacy tutors) or paraprofessionals to whom a fee is paid to cover costs (foster parents).

Market-based provision also provides some variation in the criteria on which services are offered.

- *Market-based provision competing with or complementing state provision*, with a significant proportion of the cost paid directly by the user or indirectly by a sponsor, such as employer or insurance company. The provider and/or user might also benefit from a state subsidy (private healthcare, private education). The user pays for what is believed to be a superior service or privileged access to long-term benefits, as in education.
- *Market-based provision but with concessions*, for particular categories, typically based on age or family structure (cultural or leisure services).
- *Market-based provision, accessible only to those that can afford it*, but offering different income-related 'levels' of access.
- *Pure market-based provision*, with no concessions or variable access (private rented housing, residential accommodation).

Even within the purest form of universal state provision the market sector has not been absent, particularly in respect of capital projects such as building or maintaining hospitals, schools, residential homes, day care provision, youth centres, social housing, museums, libraries and so on. In revenue costs too, it has been the major supplier of materials for state provision, as in healthcare drugs, school text-books or furniture and equipment. Tax-generated revenue has been used to fund other market-based enterprises, for example the arms industry, whilst the state has offered subsidies by providing tax-free incentives and concessions to business or tying overseas development aid to the purchase of UK products. Current debate over the role and limitations of the private sector is fuelled by the profit levels that are predicted to flow to it from public funds (Monbiot, 2000). Labour has argued that an expansion of welfare can be secured only through private sector funding with decreasing dependence on public investment. This has lent support to the view that PPP, and PFI in particular, signals the continued break-up of the classical welfare state. Labour has fuelled concerns by its reluctance to accept that while there may be some justification in offering private investors a financial return on any investment, this should be both proportionate and limited, especially given the low level of risk involved.

The April 2002 budget announcement of a 1 per cent increase in National Insurance contributions (a regressive tax) to fund growth within the NHS and Treasury statements on the limits of private involvement suggest that the government is not united in its position. The announcement in January 2002 to create not-for-profit public interest company 'foundation hospitals' from those trusts applying with a 3* performance rating, appears to be an attempt to balance the attraction of using private finance with the need to ensure public accountability and local control. Foundation hospitals, fully oper-ational from April 2004, will be given greater autonomy from direct Whitehall control, will be able to fix their own staff salaries, raise funds through borrowing or the sale of land, retain surpluses and make investment decisions. The assets will continue to be publicly owned and legislation will protect them against private sector take-overs. Crucially, they are to be managed by a 'stakeholder council' that will include representatives from the local communities and hospital staff.

While the best hospitals can entertain the prospect of greater autonomy, those that are judged by the Commission for Health

Improvement as persistent failures could face 'special measures' including the management franchise to an external organisation. Former Health Secretary Alan Milburn, summed up the proposals that contain the core features of Labour's modernisation programme – provider diversity, centralised strategic direction plus local autonomy, inspection, user choice and greater local control,

> Our reforms are about redefining what we mean by the NHS. Changing it from a monolithic, centrally run, monopoly provider of services to a values-based system where different health care providers...provide comprehensive services to NHS patients within a common ethos; care free at the point of delivery, based on patient need and their informed choice and not on ability to pay. Within a framework of clear national standards, subject to common independent inspection, power will be devolved to locally run services so they can have the freedom to innovate and improve care for NHS patients (DoH News Release, January, 2002).

The satisfaction of welfare needs

If we consider how individuals and families attempt to satisfy their welfare needs further complexities arise (May and Brunsdon, 1996). Current welfare discourse stresses our personal responsibility for the satisfaction of need. Any social benefits that are derived from individual well-being are minimised, as are our mutual interdependencies. As part of the Thatcherite legacy, the ideal is that of the market-oriented consumer with rewards flowing in proportion to personal investment and achievement. The private sector has always provided need satisfying services for the wealthy or those unwilling to participate in any service designed for the masses. Increasing numbers now find themselves the beneficiaries of an employer benefit giving free access to private welfare services. Those dependent upon state provided income, typically experience one of three relationships when seeking to satisfy needs. First, they can secure these through self-help or the support of any informal networks. Second, they have access to the full range of state-funded services, as benefit dependency acts as a passport to other services, regardless of who is the provider. They may be dissuaded, however, from pursuing this option by what they experience as a humiliating and complex application process. Third, they can look to the market where a lack of disposable income will exclude them from all but the cheapest goods and services. For those above this de facto poverty line, multiple and more complex relationships are now the norm.

The non-poor continue to benefit from a diminishing range of universal state provision, but have little choice but to engage in market exchange relations for other related services felt to be essential but not otherwise available. These include, dental treatment, spectacles, medical prescriptions, miscellaneous educational services, including diagnostic services for those with special educational needs such as dyslexia, pre-school nursing provision, and social care for elderly, sick or disabled dependents. A growing proportion of the non-poor, however, are now active consumers in the welfare market place, seeking to take advantage of whatever service best meets their needs and is within their available resources. In some markets, such as housing, those able to purchase, usually with the benefit of a mortgage, can expect to generate a surplus from their initial investment. Home ownership is a highly desirable commodity and has become a major source of personal wealth generation. To rent, either privately or within the social housing market, is not a good investment, and is increasingly reserved for economically marginal social groups or those faced with a temporary or short-term housing need, such as students or young single workers.

In other markets, such as education or health, private provision increasingly acts as an alternative for more reluctant consumers, with either personal capital or insurance. A belief that public services have declined to such an extent that to be solely dependent upon them would cause unacceptable suffering or disadvantage for themselves or their dependents drives them to private provision. Pragmatic decisions are made to purchase selective services, while a commitment to one sector for a particular period does not preclude subsequently switching or returning to another sector. Other desirable services may only be available from the private sector, for example, the 'talking therapies' for a mental-health or inter-personal problem. The willingness of the non-poor to become evermore active and discerning consumers in the market place of well-being and self-improvement is reinforced by the markets' inherent desire to expand by increasing the range of 'essential' commodities and colonising services previously dominated by other sectors. The market in non-prescribed drugs and remedies, or 'personal growth', are examples of how the private sector both capitalises on genuine but insatiable health concerns and redefines 'health' to mean not simply treatment or preventative medicine but a state of perfect health irrespective of age or other factors. It creates a new market in health, beauty and inner well-being.

The state acts similarly, constantly redefining what is considered as a core or universal service, a collective good funded by taxation. Where it expands its provision in response to rising user expectation, as in public library held collections of videos and CDs, it offers these on a market-related basis, extending the cash nexus into most areas of social provision (Baldwin, 1997; Jordan, 1998). Once public provision is redefined either as non-essential or only available on a selective basis, such as adult or higher education, it becomes susceptible to consumerism and commodification. Private membership-based leisure facilities have grown as users have withdrawn from the cheaper, more limited and overused state provision. Private residential care is similarly perceived as offering a better quality service with more choice, matched to personal preferences and tastes. Unless there are significant differences in the quality of provision, opportunities for private sector expansion will be limited as long as the state provides services free to all those who qualify.

The introduction of fees or charges into state provision both expands the opportunities for private sector competitors and increases the likelihood that state provision will be privatised. The proliferation of service charges converts welfare into a market place that demands consumer-like behaviour. In response to the imposition of charges, those able to afford them are free to 'shop around' for the best price. In doing so they may discover that choices are limited or inaccessible, that they do not have sufficient or relevant information or expertise to make 'good' decisions, and that they will have to be skilled in the techniques of the aggressive competitive shopper to get what they need. They may also come to regret the consequences of having made the 'wrong' decision. There is more at stake in choosing the right school, hospital, consultant or residential care home than in other consumer goods. Despite these risks and disincentives, the lure of 'consumer sovereignty' and the exercise of free choice act as a powerful force and are exercised by those who can when they can. Ultimately, it enables consumers to use their purchasing power to become providers. Thus one can become an employer by recruiting a nanny or au pair, or a landlord by subletting part of a home, or by buying a second house for rent, perhaps to support children through their higher education.

It is increasingly common for the non-poor to have multiple relationships to the state, market and non-profit sector. Some are embraced positively while others are entered into only with considerable reluctance. Even those that create the greatest discomfort can be rationalised or tolerated. When one is in need of a service it is often not the time to argue about how it is funded. There are other priorities, and decisions can be taken from the comfort of having a range of choices although the use of private welfare in relation to the two major areas of health and education remains a relatively small albeit growing feature (Burchardt and Propper, 1999). However, such estimates do not take account of the individual market transactions that take place within the context of public provision, and ignore childcare costs and personal pension additions. The housing sector has already been transformed and private ownership is now the desired objective.

In a society in which personal identities and the satisfaction of personal preferences are increasingly linked to well-being, the question of what should be guaranteed and provided by the state and what left to individuals to secure by other means is increasingly uncertain. There are few services, beyond immediate life-and-death situations, in which questions about access, cost, and payment do not regularly arise. Even in core areas of provision, such as education, what can be expected of a school in meeting ever-expanding educational needs or desires is a matter of debate. What was previously a luxury, such as computer literacy, is now seen as an essential feature of basic education. Schools must decide whether and how much to invest, at what technical level, and with what access to facilities or policies.

Democratic debate

A significant minority continues to live in poverty, struggles against high levels of risk, and is denied access to opportunities necessary for personal development. In such circumstances, the logic of allocating public funds to targeted services for the economically and socially disadvantaged while creating a mixed economy with greater choice to the majority carries considerable political weight. For the non-poor a mixed economy is already a reality. Questions about how specific services are to be provided and by whom will be determined not by appeals to the principle of universalism but according to how the non-poor respond to and organise around the satisfaction of need. Conflict will continue because the category of the non-poor conceals wide variations in economic and personal resources, two essential requirements for success in a mixed economy. The resultant competitive culture will ensure that large numbers of the non-poor will lose out in the search for secure markets in welfare services. Only a renewed democratic debate can prevent the complete abandonment of public goods and services, except for residual provision for those unable to provide for themselves. The critical test for the future will be whether democratic control can be established over all those that provide social welfare services.

4

The Changing Role of the Non-Profit Sector

The changing shape of the mixed economy of welfare is having a profound impact upon the UK non-profit sector. From a position of being relatively marginal to service provision, following the post-war reforms, it is now positioned at the heart of government strategy (HM Treasury, 2002). From having to struggle for any voice or recognition in strategic policy planning or evaluation, the sector is now welcomed as a partner in the process of policy-making. From learning to survive on few resources in a cold, uncertain and frustrating climate, non-profit agencies are promised additional resources, long-term security and the opportunity to shape events. Such offerings, however, come with a price and this chapter explores some of the potential dilemmas facing the sector as it comes to terms with its enhanced role. Attitudes to the role of non-profits in relation to the production of welfare have long been ambiguous. Concerned about mounting criticism from ministers, such as Bevan, in the post-war Labour Government, who railed against the perceived parochialism, amateurism, particularism and paternalism of the sector, Beveridge (1948) felt it necessary to mount a stout defence suggesting that:

> the vigour and abundance of voluntary action outside the home, individually and in association with other citizens for bettering one's own life and that of one's fellows are the distinguishing marks of a free society (p. 10).

Defining the sector

A variety of terms – third sector, voluntary sector, non-profit sector, independent sector, non-governmental organisations, the social economy – are used to describe the third arm of the mixed economy (Paton, 1991; Burns *et al.*, 1994; Pearce, 2003). While there are conceptual difficulties with all descriptors, the preferred North American term the 'non-profit sector' will be used. Within this broad category, the concern here is with those welfare-related organisations operating within the sphere of civil society that are private in nature, formal and organised, operate to a non-profit distributing principle, are self-organising, and involve an element of voluntarism (Salamon and Anheier, 1997). The concept of a 'non-profit' organisation highlights both a motivational factor and a specific relationship to the provision of goods and services.

In the UK, the tradition has been to use the terminology of the 'voluntary sector' to describe such organisations. In the latter part of the nineteenth century, it was the primary provider of welfare services, hostile to state intervention although deeply involved in the moral policing of the poor on its behalf. Thus, 'voluntary' simply meant being independent of the state. However, the emphasis on a sector constructed on voluntarism no longer reflects either the common understanding of what is meant by that or the reality of those involved in service provision. The discourse of a voluntary sector may serve a useful ideological function but fails to reflect its professionalisation or dependence on state funding (Kendall and Knapp, 1996; Leat, 1996; Lewis, 1996).

Another useful distinction is that between these more formal bodies and those in the 'community sector'. The latter tend to be informal, small-scale, locality or interest based, concerned with mutual-aid, localised campaigns, service provision or local coordination (Chanan, 1993). Thus we need to distinguish between not one but at least two distinct segments or sectors in civil society – private non-profit agencies providing either a membership or public benefit in the form of services, and those civic organisations concerned with individual and collective self and political expression (Marshall, 1996). In addition, there is the informal sector of nuclear and extended family. The non-profit sector's sphere of activity has grown, as kinship and neighbourhood support has declined (Marshall, 1996). Pearce (2003) makes a further important distinction between those elements in what he calls the third economic system, rather than civil society, that engage in trading and those that do not. The former is defined as the 'social economy'.

Non-profit organisations can typically adopt a number of roles in relation to the state such as offering parallel services, supplementing or complementing state services, or as a substitute or an alternative to state provision (Kramer, 1989; Lewis, 1996). They can be state critics or service innovators, as well as agents of the state. Services can be offered either on a membership basis or as a public benefit. When broadly defined, the sector makes a significant contribution to the national economy both in relation to paid and voluntary workers, as well as operating income (Taylor, 1997). Government sources calculate that it has a paid workforce of 563,000, a total income of £15.6bn (£4.53bn of which derives from government sources) and some 3m volunteers (HM Treasury, 2002).

The importance of a vibrant associational life is shared by many contemporary writers (NCVO, 1996). The free association of individuals in their autonomous organisations can, as de Tocqueville's early nineteenth study in the US argued, be a significant benchmark of a healthy vibrant democracy. It can be, as the Deakin Commission (NCVO, 1996) noted:

> portrayed as the backbone of civil society... their presence as the essential precondition for the health of democracy (p. 15).

The Wolfenden Committee (1978) praised its diversity, its innovative nature, flexibility, capacity for a rapid response to social need, cost effectiveness, and its ability to mobilise quickly a number of 'publics' in response to unpredictable or critical events.

There is, however, tremendous diversity amongst the organisations of civil society in respect of goals, values, methods, structures and processes. It should not be assumed that the sector is progressive in nature (Taylor and Hoggett, 1994). It lacks collective coherence and contains a plethora of agencies rooted in a variety of competing historical traditions, from paternalistic charities, self-help groups, social rights and justice organisations, to community-based radical politics. If the vibrancy of civil society is equated to citizens joining together through organisation to achieve shared goals then a substantial number of non-profits would not qualify. The recent focus on service provision has led to a tendency for the organisations of civil society to be increasingly dominated by those who can satisfy this function, thereby depoliticising and restricting the sector's role and potential significance. To ascribe a grand political role to agencies led by largely unaccountable professionals, concerned with urban management and the public service needs of particular social groups, is to obscure their purpose and limitations. There are dangers for participative democracy when associational life is co-opted by the state to act as its agent while maintaining the perception that it continues to have the same political function. The incorporation by the state of a large element of the non-profit sector, through financial dependency and regulation, represents a weakening of civil society and not the strengthening of local democracy.

Key trends

There have been five discernible trends within this broad sector. First, the sector has been encouraged to move to expand direct service provision. This has been reinforced through changes in funding arrangements so that contracted funding is rapidly becoming the norm for individual organisations. Since the 1990, NHS and Community Care Act state bodies have been encouraged to ensure that an increasing proportion of services are delivered by non-profit organisations (Lewis, 1996). Prior to that, a substantial number of non-profits had already taken the initiative to provide services. Often these were not otherwise available, sometimes because the 'need' had yet to be acknowledged by the state or accepted as a sufficient priority. Alternatively, existing services were defined as inadequate, deficient, or so reduced in scope that a self-help or 'voluntary' approach seemed more effective as a supplementary or complementary service. Other services were created to challenge the perceived injustices, discriminatory treatment, or overall neglect by the state and some to enable the beneficiaries to remain independent of the state. Non-profit service providers frequently joined in the chorus of those critics of statutory provision and called for additional funding on the grounds that they could provide a more efficient and effective service, and one that was more closely in tune especially with difficult-to-reach service users. The New Right governments of Thatcher and Major responded positively to such claims as these fitted closely the twin public service goals of privatisation and voluntarism.

Second, the sector has become professionalised. In part, this is a direct consequence of its enhanced service function. It also stems from the early urban regeneration efforts of the late 1960s to the mid-1970s. During this time the response to declining community networks and support systems and a concern over public participation was to offer small- and medium-sized, often informal, organisations access to state funds. Additional funding opportunities were made available under the Urban Programme and European Social Fund, as well as local authority grant-aid. Such funds were used to build, sustain or staff the organisation to provide a specialist service, such as advice work or counselling, but perhaps most commonly were employed in a developmental capacity working to enable the organisation to achieve its stated objectives. Such 'single employee' organisations generated a high level of dependency on that person, blurring the roles of 'employee' and organisational 'representative'.

As its potential was recognised, the non-profit sector expanded, partly as a consequence of the formalisation of community sector agencies transformed by the new funding. Such agencies demonstrated their worth and were judged by their capacity to identify and plug service gaps, relieve pressure on statutory agencies, and build local capacity, or establish contact between the authority and difficult social groups or challenging neighbourhoods. Where appropriate community or non-profit organisations did not already exist, the local state recruited development professionals to help initiate and support them. Within disadvantaged neighbourhoods and under the umbrella of urban regeneration, the state established quasi-independent bodies, such as the Community Development Projects (1968–76), with a license to act, until such time as they were withdrawn, as though they were outwith the state (Loney, 1983). As numbers increased and employment opportunities expanded, development professionals moved between statutory, quasi-statutory and non-profit employers.

Third, the creation of a diverse and fragmented mixed economy of welfare along with the complexity of the social issues confronting service providers and urban managers highlighted the need for improved collaboration between those involved and the local communities. The non-profit sector has been accorded a privileged place within such collaborative arrangements and it has been able to argue with some justification that such cross-boundary working had always been a feature of its practice. Increasingly, inter-sectoral collaboration became increasingly a condition of both government and private sector funding and was otherwise considered good practice.

Fourth, in response to a perceived democratic deficit, non-profit organisations have been promoted as a vehicle to revive democratic engagement. Here, the terrain becomes complicated. The relationship between an extension of democracy and professionally led non-profit bodies is at best tenuous. An investment in membership-based community sector organisations is more likely to have a direct impact on direct democracy. Between these two stand, perhaps, the majority of non-profit agencies. These are theoretically rooted in civil society and may indeed contain elements, such as a voluntary Board, to support the claim. However, the employee effectively runs the organisation and also acts as its representative in formal inter-agency structures or other public arenas, and with little effective account-ability. Consequently, the democratic engagement is often reduced to a meeting of professional employees (see Chapter 10).

Fifth, the Labour government has extended this democratic role by giving non-profit organisations a key role in the strategy to combat social inclusion, both as an outlet for an increase in volun-tarism and as a means of facilitating development, enhancing social capital and rebuilding community (Boateng and Stowe, 1998). The sector's potential in this regard is also annunciated within its own national commission on its future (NCVO, 1996) and by other national agencies that claim to speak for the sector's interests, including the Community Development Foundation, a long-standing government quango. As Blair (1998) noted in relation to the new 'compact' between the government and the sector,

> The work of voluntary and community organisations is central to the Government's mission to make this the Giving Age. They enable indi-viduals to contribute to the development of their communities ... they promote citizenship, help to re-establish a sense of community and make a crucial contribution to our shared aim of a just and inclusive society (p. 1).

The impact on the sector

The changes in role outlined above have rarely been acknowledged for their differential impact on or meaning for the various subdiv-isions within the non-profit sector. The state has successfully manoeuvred the sector in its preferred direction with the promise of improved resources and greater access to decision-makers. Overall, the sector has acquiesced because it too has made demands on the state for recognition, claiming that it could deliver better services. In accepting an ever-greater role as a service provider, non-profit agencies can expect the state to insist upon greater regulation and accountability. As Stewart states:

> Those who exercise public power should be answerable to those on whose behalf they exercise it (Stewart, 1995: 289).

As the primary funder and regulator of welfare services, the state legitimises those needs that are to be met, prescribes the ways they should be met, and controls the resource envelope with which to do so. Moreover, the public and especially service users will urge government to ensure greater and more transparent account-ability. Those non-profit agencies that espouse different goals need to question whether they want to be confined, or confine them-selves, to being private, professional bodies, surviving only through this para-state agency function. A minority has always defined itself in this way, and for them there is no conflict between aspira-tions and practice, but for the majority this is both a relatively new and restricted experience. It is not yet a role that has been fully embraced nor does it sit comfortably with the espoused mission or history of many individual agencies. Such a close and dependent relationship with the state threatens the sector's historic claim that they are value-driven organisations, independent organic products emerging from and rooted within local neighbourhoods or social issues.

Service delivery

The sector's dynamic, risk-taking and entrepreneurial features, that sometimes enabled small and under-resourced organisations to have a disproportionate impact, can appear to relate closely to the modernising energy of the Labour government. It has defined the sector's strengths as,

> to challenge, complement and reinforce public services ... (it) brings a distinctive approach... This comes from its close relationship with service users. This distinctive approach ... (HM Treasury, 2002: 30.2).

The government sees the value in harnessing the sector. As expressed by the minister responsible for the Review,

Independent of Government, the voluntary sector is free to side with
the user against the perceived threat of authority. For marginalized
groups who are hard to help, this identification with the user perspective
is crucially important (Boateng, 2002).

What is ignored is the extent to which any such 'identification
with the user perspective' is transformed once the agency becomes
the service provider. The increase in service provision by non-profit
organisations has been accompanied by a move from a system of
general non-specific grants to a contract financial regime. Whilst
these have varied in their detail and requirements they are regulatory
in nature and designed to ensure that the state, usually at the local
level, is confident that services are delivered in a manner it considers
appropriate. Such contract–service relationships focus attention
on the sector's independence and its capacity to maintain a campaigning or policy development function. Some commentators
predict a drift towards self-censorship, a reluctance to bite the hand
that feeds, and restrictions derived from a growth in competition
with the market sector (Lipsky and Smith, 1989; Wolch, 1990;
Lewis, 1996). Others fear the sector may become characterised by a
market-led philosophy, managerialism and self-interested competitive practices in place of sectoral collaboration (Taylor, 1996).

Other commentators argue that organisational independence
can be retained through a combination of multiple funding sources
so that none dominate, the relative absence of other competitors,
and the state's inability to effectively monitor the activities of such
diverse organisations (Kramer, 1989; Gutch, 1992). Nevertheless,
as they become embedded in the detail of service provision, which
becomes defined as core business, and dependent upon state
finances, so they will become more vulnerable to state control.
Moreover, the state has extended and become more proficient in its
regulatory expertise, a process that is likely to continue. The output
driven nature of these requirements, aimed at achieving specific
policy objectives within limited time frames, undermines the sector's
orientation towards process and capacity building in which the
benefits are more diffuse and difficult to measure. Indeed, if non-
profit agencies as service providers working to government targets
find themselves in conflict with their service users, they may feel they
have more in common with the state. Those remaining non-profit
organisations, reluctant to sacrifice their autonomy and methods,
may find they have little choice if they are not to be excluded from

local state funding as the latter prioritises and directs its resources to those willing to provide services (Miller, 1998).

By extending their service delivery role, non-profit organisations encounter a number of difficulties including continuing financial insecurity through reduced allocations for core funding and short-term contracts. The services they do provide have not been fully funded although, following the Cross Cutting Review, agencies can now factor in an overhead cost (Treasury, 2002). To meet the required service standards, non-profits will have to cope with increased regulation and monitoring, a stronger managerial presence, and pay more attention to user throughput in place of longer-term developmental activity. Currently there are still an insufficient number of non-profits with the capacity or willingness to meet the service delivery and strategic planning requirements. If the sector meets the enlarged service delivery role, as annunciated within the Review (Treasury, 2002), it will face the prospect of state incorporation and a dramatic loss of independence.

The sector will also be forced to grapple with the challenges arising from their responsibilities to service users and the requirement to involve them in service planning, delivery and evaluation (Bradshaw *et al.*, 1998). Unless non-profit agencies invest in their governance structures, the influence of sector professionals will increase with a corresponding weakening of lay management. As services expand, many non-profit agencies will experience a capacity problem that is likely to result in organisational mergers and the disappearance of smaller agencies. There is also likely to be a decline in campaigning and pressure group activities and the emergence of new powerful 'broker' organisations mediating between the sector and the other partners in which the appropriateness of individual agency behaviour will be a central concern.

Working in partnership

While Chapter 7 considers partnership working more broadly, this section explores it from the perspective of the non-profit sector. Under both the Major and Blair governments, the non-profit sector's role in the maintenance of the social and political formation has been actively promoted. As confirmation, it has been offered 'reserved' places and a key role in policy formation and strategic planning, as well as policy implementation. This change in policy direction presents the sector with a considerable challenge. To engage positively in partnership working, it must be seen to contribute to an improvement in policy formulation and implementation. Successful partnerships are those in which partners retain an independence that permits the freedom to be critical and to engage in conflict, not just over the details but also the strategic direction, principles, priorities and available resources. Success is also related both to the earlier experience of the other partners and to the differential sources of power and how these are mobilised in practice. To be such a partner requires considerable skill, reflexivity, a capacity to work within uncertainty and a confidence in the relationship's long-term stability. To take up this role, and have it confirmed by others, requires dedicated time and effort with no immediate or automatic benefits for such investment. On the surface, the non-profit sector enters into partnership work from a position of distinct disadvantage.

A commitment to partnership working has been endorsed, following the report of the national 'Deakin' commission (NCVO, 1996) and an earlier Labour Party policy report (Labour Party, 1991), in the signing of a 'compact' between government and the sector (Home Office, 1998). This, in turn, has led to the creation of a number of local compacts, supported by central government guidelines, on how to proceed (Craig *et al.*, 1999 and 2002; DETR, 2000b). The position was confirmed in the conclusion to the Cross Cutting Review of the sector's role of service delivery (Treasury, 2002) in which it stated:

> The Government needs a Voluntary and Community sector that is strong, independent and has the capacity and skills, where it wishes, to be a partner in delivering world-class public services. It wants a new partnership with the sector, drawing on the sector's strengths to challenge, complement and reinforce public services (HM Treasury, 2002: 30.2).

Labour's language of 'joined-up thinking', and a 'Third Way', is symbolically powerful for those in the non-profit sector with its implicit assumption, 'as practised by people like us'. The sector's own discourse and public perceptions of it – as diverse, autonomous, voluntary, self-governing, for public-benefit, flexible, responsive, rooted in community – makes it ideally suited to achieve these objectives. However, securing new institutional arrangements is a complex process. There are long-standing tensions specific to each of the partners. Persuading all of them to join together, including those who are more used to being on the outside of policy-making, is a challenging process. Indeed, non-profit organisations might be wise not to invest too heavily in such relationships or to neglect the lines of accountability to their members or constituencies. The state retains the capacity to shape the conditions and nature of such arrangement and these may threaten the sector's autonomy. Further, there can be no guarantee of a long-term commitment by the state to partnerships in the face of other economic and political pressures.

Labour's embrace of collaboration in a socially inclusive project holds a particular appeal. The non-profit sector has chosen to put aside its more reflective, cautionary and critical tradition in favour of a journey of hope and the promise of resource investment, and has embraced the model of partnership with the state and market sectors. Despite the associated uncertainties, partnership working is thought to represent the best opportunity for achieving justifiable, and long overdue, recognition. Instead of displaying caution about the sector's elevated status, the primary concern has been with the continuing weakness of such partnerships. The market and state are accused of being unwilling to listen to non-profit sector contributions, take seriously what is said, or implement properly what it promises. The sector remains hopeful that the promised benefits will materialise and enjoys the experience of being included. Yet, it appears enraptured by the mysterious 'invisible hand' of the market and the concept of entrepreneurialism which has been rapidly adapted as 'social entrepreneurs' to reflect the sector self-image (Miller, 1998).

Anxieties remain over whether partnership can be achieved, the sector's capacity to deliver its part of the bargain, and more especially whether the offer is more rhetorical than real, a symbolic relationship rather than one of substance. Thus, non-profit sector personnel tend to highlight the lack of sincerity, the shortcomings, inequalities or exploitation within such relationships. Other partners are accused of offering insufficient resources for the sector, of not ensuring it has the capacity to participate, or of creating inequalities in the decision-making processes. The government has responded to the need for additional resources to assist with the sector's capacity building. In 1999 it introduced Community Empowerment Fund, alongside the Neighbourhood Renewal Fund, to support the creation of local non-profit networks and infrastructure. As part of the Cross Cutting Review (2002), it has increased its funding of the Active Community Unit, from £35m in 2002–03 to £65m by 2005–06 (Treasury, 2002) to contribute to the Review's implementation and allocated a one-off £125m three-year 'futurebuilders' fund to support the sector's service delivery work.

If the sector continues to insist on working to an ideal template of partnership working it is in danger of becoming fixated by internal working arrangements (Taylor, 1995; Craig and Manthorpe, 1999). It has paid less attention to the appropriateness of the relationship and the consequences for its role, values and independence. Thus the loudest cry has been a cynical 'what partnership?' or pragmatic 'could do much better!' rather than a challenging 'why are we doing this?'. The sector has been reluctant to pursue the question of why partnerships so often fail to get beyond the rhetoric. It prefers to act on the assumption that current shortcomings are the combined result of inefficiencies, a failure to understand the sector's particular requirements, or another example of policy by 'muddling through'. There is little sectoral theorisation of the state in practice and rarely does it appear willing to consider the viability of other independent options beyond such arrangements.

Crucially, it has neglected those relationships with members and constituents that are central to its capacity to act as an expression of democratic voice. Even the umbrella coordinating bodies, created to support the partnership process and often dominated by paid employees of the sector, can suffer from poor attendance, poor decision-making and a lack of accountability. Such weak representational and accountability links can be used to the sector's disadvantage should it fail to deliver its part of the partnership bargain. There are huge risks involved for the sector. So much depends on establishing relationships of trust based on how partnerships are conducted in practice, on their capacity to secure outcomes that make a positive difference, and the avoidance of 'drama', in which partnerships are theatrical events in which all have defined roles and well-rehearsed lines.

For the state and market partners, the price of involving non-profit sector colleagues is relatively negligible. Although it is sometimes troublesome, this is a price worth paying to achieve greater legitimation and a muted or managed source of opposition. Formal partnerships require the non-profit sector to act responsibly, focus on problem-solving, engage in less conflict, abide by, take responsibility for and publicly defend, collective agreements (Miller, 1998). The state can delegate this function to the non-profit sector precisely because of the latter's nature as a disparate, diverse, often divided arena, in which agencies compete with each other in pursuit of a variety of agendas, not least of which is their own organisational survival and competitive advantage.

Survival may be directly related to the establishment and success of a partnership. If workable partnership arrangements can be achieved between what are essentially safe, reliable and responsible agencies (and there are mechanisms and pressures to filter out or manage those who are not), subsequent newcomers can be expected to work within established structures and processes. New members will seek to meet the requirements of existing partners. Labour appears less concerned to secure maximum citizen engagement, which has all the dangers of being uncontrollable and unpredictable. Rather, it is for a managed approach to public engagement, the creation of particular forms of relationship between the state and the citizen (see Chapter 10). In practice, this poses a challenge for the state, as any perceived over-interference is unlikely to produce the desired outcomes. Those civil society organisations sympathetic to the goals of partnership, maintaining a paternalistic relationship with their users, or holding a strong sense of entrepreneurialism and low level of sectoral identity, can perform a useful function in this respect. For others, the new regime is more problematic.

Professionalisation

The changes within the sector have been facilitated and are reinforced by its own internal process of professionalisation. Its professional staff has enjoyed increased levels of responsibility and influence. As non-profit organisations adapt to a contract-driven regime, albeit sometimes with reluctance and misgivings, they are required to deliver services to a specified standard, to account for the efficient and effective discharge of public funds, and to operate professionally. These requirements encourage a cross-sector dialogue of professionals rather than one between the state and representatives from civic organisations. Often it is the professionalised non-profit agencies that dominate the sector's representation within any partnership and sector employees, rather than lay members, act as its representatives, dominate sector umbrella bodies, network with each other and relate with professional colleagues employed beyond the sector. Both groups share an interest in working together to generate work and to offer themselves as the solution to a series of complex social problems that they have helped define.

There now exists a shared labour market and a growing proportion of professionals have been employed in both the state and non-profit sectors, and increasingly, within market agencies (Bruce and Raynor, 1992, quoted in Taylor, 1996). Although often lower-paid and with poorer working conditions (Popple and Redmond, 2001) non-profit professionals, relative to their state employed colleagues, enjoy privileged access to decision-making structures but are less accountable to democratic processes. However, not all non-profit employees are equally privy to such relationships or choose to invest their time in cultivating them. Consequently, a potentially damaging division of knowledge and access to local decision-makers could emerge within the sector. When paid staff do have delegated authority to represent the agency, clarity is required about the boundaries and legitimacy of such authority. To this end it is critical that non-profits have effective Board management. Similarly, inter-sectoral professional dialogues should not be confused with dialogues between state, market, non-profits and civic society. To counter this tendency, non-profit organisations need to strengthen their relationships of accountability with the membership and wider constituencies and invest in sustainable community capacity building (Miller, 2002).

Partnership arrangements also create some immediate dilemmas for the state, including managing the overall relationship with the non-profit sector given its diversity and lack of coherence. There often exists a more basic lack of understanding and appreciation of how non-profit organisations work both individually and as a sector. Many areas have been required to create intermediary non-profit forums in order to have a single body with whom to engage. Given the previous encounters and common perceptions of each other, the state will need to invest in relationship and trust building. While it has been convenient for government to extol the sector's capacity to 'challenge authority', it now expects those who delivered and received such challenges to embrace each other in a partnership. Finding a creative way to close the cultural and value gap between the sectors will not be easy.

Unresolved issues

A mixed economy of welfare in which organisations from different sectors provide a rich and diverse range of services to service users is likely to remain a characteristic of contemporary welfare provision (ODPM, 2001). The post-war state near monopoly seems unlikely to return. A genuinely mixed economy, offering a range of service providers equally accessible to service users and offering services of comparable quality, could make a qualitative difference to provision. However, within each of the three sectors of the state, market and non-profit, there continue to be a number of difficult issues that have yet to be addressed. Any partnerships between the state and either the existing market or non-profit sector, especially those involving public funds administered by the state, are likely to come with a number of concerns and issues. Unless these are addressed, the efforts that have gone into partnership building and increasing the mix of service providers may do little to enhance the quality of provision for service users.

The last two chapters have examined some of the dilemmas arising from the expanded role of both the private and non-profit sectors. For quite different reasons there are those who would argue that neither should be deeply involved in service provision. What is clear is that none of the three sectors can be presented as a 'natural' provider of public services. Each faces substantial challenges. Considerable energy has been devoted previously to demystifying the role and function of state provision and challenging the detail of specific practices. This looks set to continue in relation to both the private and non-profit sectors. This should not, however, deny the potential benefits of having more and different voices and perspectives in service delivery and strategic planning. Having established three-way partnerships, the next step must be to introduce a fourth arm of citizen-based associational organisations.

5

Managing, Leading or Learning?

This chapter explores the growing interest in the leadership of public services. It examines the introduction of public service managerialism during the 1980s with its abrasive assertion of the 'right to manage' in the face of professional, bureaucratic and political resistance. Within this discourse, managers not only oversaw the implementation of policy but also led the organisation. The current Labour government, in line with others, shows signs of a shift towards a greater emphasis on the need for more 'leadership' capacity rather than 'management'.

> Leadership is a critical component of good public governance.... When we say we want more leadership in the public sector, what we are really looking for is people who will promote institutional adaptations in the public interest. Leadership is . . . a positive espousal of the need to promote certain fundamental values that can be called public spiritedness (OECD, 2001: 7).

Whether this current focus implies adherence to a traditional view on leadership or embraces a post-modern dispersed leadership remains unclear (Cabinet Office, 2001a). The alleged crisis of leadership and desire for strong leaders at the top of public service organisations reflect familiar heroic models. The opposing position is that what is required are organisations characterised by a culture of learning (Iles and Sutherland, 2001) in which leading is equated with learning (Vaill, 1999). This challenge transforms our understanding of leadership by detaching it from its association with hierarchy and formal role. Leadership becomes something that is available to all and can be held by more than one person at any point of time. Within the model of organisational learning, leaders are expected to model the processes of learning, exposing themselves as 'not knowing', implying that they too are involved in what is a collaborative journey, and that the knowledge of others can authorise their leadership. The concept of organisational learning offers both a richer perspective on leadership with far reaching ramifications for the existing hierarchical structures that dominate organisational life.

From public administration to management

The post-war welfare state model provided a rather uncomplicated organisational framework for the delivery of public services. The impact of organisational processes on policy implementation and outcomes was a largely neglected area. Efficient or 'sound' administration rather than management was what was felt necessary and 'leadership' would be provided through the political process. Elected representatives framed the legislation that entitled citizens, either on a universal or selective basis, to receive specific state provided services. The state provided the overall financial, human, and organisational resources required to deliver what had been so agreed. It was assumed that the state could solve the most challenging of social issues through carefully designed policies, providing appropriate levels of resource, and ensuring that a sufficient number of qualified professionals were in place to respond. Local government had some limited capacity to interpret the intention and meaning of legislation, especially in relation to discretionary Acts that gave powers but not duties, and to shape the way local services might be offered. Local politics mattered to the extent to which authorities both interpreted permissive legislation and determined the level and organisation of resources necessary to meet their responsibilities. The excitement lay in local battles over the relationship between local proposals and central government policy. Typically these were concerned with the sufficiency, fairness and appropriateness of local plans; resource levels and organisational capacity; the relationship between the policy goals and the core principles; and the level of discretion available to front-line staff in the interpretation of policy. The level of autonomy available to different professions varied but all were subject to agency regulation.

Within those local authority departments, and the NHS, responsible for the service delivery, detailed rules and procedures
governed the process. Occupational groups were organised around
job descriptions, linked to qualifications, within areas of expertise
and departmental location. Occupational expertise was often
restricted as many lacked any professionally specific qualification.
Each was expected to have an understanding of their contribution
to any provision, although that did not prevent service users being
passed from one agency to another, with sometimes tragic outcomes,
as disagreements broke out over who was responsible for what. Few
held a strong professional identity. They were local government
officers employed to administer policy, charged with dispensing
services to those who were eligible. Applicants for quite junior
positions in local authority departments were frequently interviewed
and directly appointed by elected members rather than managers or
professional colleagues.

When supervision was provided, both in respect of whether
interventions were appropriate and followed agency procedure, it
was done by a more experienced professional from within the same
occupational group. Management, as such, was largely invisible and
concerned more with administrative coordination. The key managerial task was to ensure that both an appropriate policy response
and bureaucratic regulations were in place. The prevailing view
was that a sufficiently detailed web of procedures would guarantee
that occupations worked in predictable ways but could be identified
if they failed to do so. Industrial relations focused mainly on career
development, salary levels, access to training, working conditions,
and from the mid-1970s public sector financial cuts. Until the
late 1970s, National Association of Local Government Officers
(NALGO) (now UNISON), the trade union of local government
officers, was renowned for its moderation (Sharron 1980; Price,
1983; Joyce *et al.*, 1988; Laffin, 1989).

The reorganisation of personal social services, outlined in the
1968 Seebohm Report, was the first major change in the configuration of post-war services. This was part of a wider package of
liberal reform measures, described by Hall as the 'legislation of
consent' (1980: 2), that characterised the late 1960s, alongside an
upsurge in public sector industrial action. The resultant 1971 Local
Government Act abolished the roles of childcare, mental health,
and welfare officer and created the generic social worker, responsible for the social care and community mental health needs of

children, adults, families and communities. Seebohm outlined a vision of a qualified professional service in social care that was responsive and needs driven. The number of appointments increased significantly and the projected public service growth patterns attracted younger, more educated recruits. A number of authors believe this only increased management and bureaucratic control at the expense of professional autonomy, although there had been little evidence of an independent practice pre-Seebohm (Satyamurti, 1981; Howe, 1986).

New ideas for the 'rational management' of local government appeared in the Bains Report (1972) that called for the strengthening of strategic corporate management and modelling private sector management practices. Corporate managerial structures proved short-lived but the emphasis on better integration, improved efficiencies, planning and control from the top continued as a response to a growing fiscal crisis (Bennington, 1976; Cockburn, 1977) as well as a more effective way of addressing social problems (Clapham, 1985). While many individuals worked diligently and creatively in response to complex problems presented by those seeking a service, organisational proceduralism remained dominant. The professionalisation of social welfare occupations faltered and lost direction by the mid-1970s. Although a growing number of practitioners continued to pursue a 'radical' agenda, this remained a minority position and one that rarely explored the nature of radical practice, confining itself to converting workers to an activist trade union identity (Miller, 1996).

It was not until the mid-1970s that the post-war service delivery system faced its first real crisis. Instead of the continuous growth that had taken public spending up to 28 per cent of the gross domestic product (Gough, 1983), welfare services were faced with social spending reductions triggered by the 1973 rise in oil prices and the conditions attached to the International Monetary Fund loan. Coupled with growing dissatisfaction amongst service users, the politicisation of public service workers and prolonged industrial conflict, the reaction was one of retrenchment rather than creative invention (Bolger *et al.*, 1981; Jones, 1983). During the early 1980s, a significant number of local authorities experimented with decentralised services and what was termed 'local socialism' (Boddy and Fudge, 1984; Goss *et al.*, 1988) that questioned traditional departmental and professional boundaries, as well as extending participative and direct democracy (Hambleton and Hoggett, 1984).

Although often popular with service users such initiatives faced strong trade union opposition (Miller, 1996). Overall local government was too preoccupied with central government criticisms and threats of privatisation or service cuts. By the end of the 1980s, it was adjusting to the imposition of market principles and the emergence of the generic public sector manager (Audit Commission, 1985).

As we saw in Chapter 1, under the Conservative governments of Margaret Thatcher there was a decisive shift away from the social administration model that was by now rather battered by service user assertiveness, social action, disaffected public service trade unions and a declining resource base. Generic management, oriented to the espoused practices of the private sector, was the Thatcherite solution to the organisation of public services, after direct privatisation and stringent financial controls (Cutler and Waine, 1994; Pollitt, 1995). Based on a belief in the superiority of the market, public sector organisations would have to learn about private sector management practices, the ideology and social relations that underpinned managerial power and the capacity to authoritatively demand the 'right to manage'. Managerialism marked a dramatic break with the past but had the New Right not emerged as a political force, the inability of public services to respond to the turmoil of the 1970s suggests that an alternative to the model of public administration would still have been required.

Managerialism

Managerialism was central to the New Right restructuring of public services and it continued to be a core element during the first term of the Labour Government. There is some evidence that during Labour's second term, enthusiasm for the skills of management is receding to be replaced by the concept of 'leadership' (Cabinet Office, 2001a). Nevertheless, managerialism has been and remains significant. It is important to distinguish between management as an activity and managerialism as a discourse. Within a stable organisational environment, management as an activity is concerned with two essential tasks: the integration and coordination of people and enhancing the quality of subordinates' work (Salaman, 1995). It is by working through others that management seeks to improve the quality of that work. Coordination is related to the achievement of complex tasks, within a particular resource and environmental context, to secure agreed objectives that may often be in tension.

Management can only be understood in its context. Within advanced capitalism it is located between the demands of complexity and the maximisation of profit or increased productivity. Moreover, profit maximisation is itself subject to political constraints. Thus, what can be achieved through others is deeply contestable and is likely to be prefixed by such concepts as 'reasonable' or 'legitimate', and determined by what is feasible politically. Although the enhancement of a subordinate's work can bring both material and psychological benefits to that person, the real object can be to enhance organisational goals at a minimum cost, although it is feasible to secure both simultaneously. Yet, too often it can mean getting more for less. The workplace is an arena in which individuals and social groups struggle to advance their particularistic interests, usually expressed as a general interest, and management must negotiate a path between such claims, making judgements on their relative strengths and relationship to organisational goals. All such claims are also to be judged against those interests as represented by management itself.

Within public service organisations there is the added dimension that objectives are determined within the political arena and workers are charged with carrying out the political will. As citizens, workers will themselves have played a part in creating those political objectives and will identify with them to varying degrees, which will influence work-related behaviour. For example, a recent report found that the desire to make a social difference through the production of a public good remains a powerful value across the whole of the public sector and at all levels (Steele, 2000). However, in any organisation in which subordinates have limited autonomy or influence in relation to work tasks, feel undervalued or unfairly treated, then the likelihood of experiencing the workplace as providing intrinsic rewards is diminished. In this context, attempts by management to 'get things done' are likely to be met either by compliance or resistance as subordinates attempt to inject some personal distance or self-determinacy over the demands of an imposing and unresponsive environment.

The managerialisation of public services involved much more than looking at the tasks of management within a complex environment. For the New Right, managerialism referred to the transfer of market sector concepts and practices into the public sector

(Hood, 1991; Dixon *et al.*, 1998), and a decisive shift from an administrative orientation to a managerial consciousness and profit-oriented culture (Lawton and Rose, 1991; Thomson, 1999). Management was identified as superior to administration, and private sector management as more dynamic and rigorous than its public sector counterpart (Metcalfe and Richards, 1990; Farnham and Horton, 1993). By claiming to possess a discrete body of knowledge that had universal applicability, management could be transferred across sectoral boundaries (Pollitt, 1993).

The introduction of sound management within the public sector was to solve a variety of problems by improving performance and service quality, while curtailing spiralling costs (Pollitt, 1993; Horton and Farnham, 2000). The new management would bring an end to the illegitimate power and domination of both professionals and trade unions, and secure the interests of the consumer. Public support would be regained through cost containment, improved performance and increased service quality. As Clarke and Newman (1997) argue, in contrast to the rule-bound, inward looking, ossified and compliant centred bureaucracy, management was portrayed as dynamic, innovative, performance centred and externally oriented. The private sector focus on customer satisfaction, with an emphasis on results, transparency, and market product testing was contrasted with the tendency for professionalism to be paternalistic, opaque, inflexible on standards and insistent upon self-regulation. Whereas local politicians were cast as dogmatic or ideological, an interfering and essentially unstable force, managers were projected as strategic, enabling, pragmatic and decisive. However, bureaucrats, professionals and politicians did not disappear but continued to claim a legitimate place in public service debates. Managerialism demanded the freedom to act, but managers had to learn to work alongside other stakeholders even if the image of the manager as in control was central to the reforms (Flynn, 1993).

A new set of practices emerged from the new generic managers recruited into the public sector. Typically, these included:

- output focused target setting;
- individual performance management and appraisal;
- close and detailed supervision of what had been seen previously as a professional domain;
- the decentralisation of managerial responsibility with increased middle manager accountability for subordinate performance;

- the dual imposition of resource restrictions and increased productivity;
- a competitive culture between individuals and units in relation to resources and performance achievements and the rejection of past working practices;
- management by instruction, an unwillingness to consult or negotiate and greater use of disciplinary structures.

The portrayal of the manager as standing above the narrow sectionalism of the bureaucrat, professional, and politician, able to work proactively and strategically with the best interests of the 'customer' in mind provided managerial legitimacy and the freedom to operate to make unpopular decisions. However, such declarations of a 'right to manage' (Pollitt, 1993) do not in themselves secure a legitimacy that cannot be guaranteed or offered unconditionally. With its more restricted vision of the implementation and management of policy (Dixon *et al.*, 1998), managerialism clashed with the more discursive cultures within the public sector where front-line staff expect to debate both the specific policy measures and how they could be further developed (Cabinet Office, 2001a). When externally recruited general managers were introduced in the NHS, during the mid-1980s and the early 1990s, in parallel with the creation of internal markets, they encountered strong resistance from both still powerful clinical professional bodies and from trade unions (Horton and Farnham, 2000). As one government report notes,

> Most of the leaders brought in were experienced managers...yet many failed to reconcile the demands of the role and left the service within a fairly short period of time (Cabinet Office, 2001a: para. 5.5).

In other management areas, existing personnel remained in place albeit with redesignated titles. The conversion of professionals into managers required convincing them that what was required was both desirable and realistic. The failure to provide managerial training and socialisation into the managerial role left them vulnerable, with divided loyalties between a professional and managerial orientation. Professional principles and practices were not easily or entirely abandoned while cynicism about the managerial project remained. Those who wished to embrace the vision of themselves as part of the solution often had limited managerial

skills. Although hailed as the new saviours, public service managers could not in fact be entrusted to carry out the task without
strong incentives. Instead of a freedom to manoeuvre, they were
driven by the demands of centrally determined external audits,
performance targets and reduced budgets. Working within this
framework, anxious, untrained and often unskilled managers
sought to exercise their 'right to manage' through a command and
control culture with a stress on competence and performance.

Contemporary attempts at close and detailed managerial control are referred to as 'neo-Taylorism', following the largely failed
efforts by Frederick Taylor in the 1920s America, to design a
system of 'scientific management' to maximise productive output
within the emergent large scale industrial production plants
(Pollitt, 1993). The blanket utilisation of such strategies in the
1980s public sector, requiring considerable front-line autonomy
and flexibility in response to complex problems, was not only inappropriate but ignored changes that had occurred amongst private
sector management. Management strategies that offered a combination of command and control alongside monetary rewards and
job (in)security had been challenged since the 1930s by the 'human
relations' school of management (Morgan, 1997). This approach
focused on more complex motivational factors, inter-personal
dynamics, personal validation and autonomy that influence work
performance and attitude. Systems theories, highlighting the importance of the relationship between an organisation and its environment,
suggested that openness and flexibility were keys to success when
operating within turbulent environments (Burns and Stalker, 1961).
Such well-respected advances in managerial insights were simply
ignored by the New Right in their efforts to overhaul public sector
management.

In sharp contrast to the restrictive prescriptions of the New
Right, private and public sector managers were being exposed to
the so-called 'excellence approach' to management (Peters and
Waterman, 1982). This offered a 'new managerialism' to succeed
in a constantly changing and deeply uncertain environment.
Managers had to become more accessible and visible, act as inspirational role models and transformational visionaries, take risks,
innovate and communicate face-to-face with their employees. The
most successful companies would be those that adopted an asset-
based approach to the workforce. This emphasised that workers
were 'people with ideas', and that in order to exploit this creative

potential, organisations should seek low levels of hierarchical functionalism and strive for high levels of worker participation, team work, open information systems, and devolved operational control. The central task for management was to build organisational cultures that encouraged employee commitment and an identification with corporate goals.

Managers, at all levels, were to be participative leaders operating within flatter hierarchies, and decentralised and flexible structures. Successful organisations would be customer driven, focused on quality, networked with others operating within the same environment, dynamic and innovative. Rigid, inflexible and stifling organisations would simply fail to succeed. What was required were organisations that enabled employees to exercise discretion, to be autonomous, self-regulating and empowered to take initiatives (du Gay, 1994).

Handy (1995) notes that this requirement to be both controlling and delegating is but one of a number of paradoxes of our times and has to be held simultaneously. Any New Right sympathy for the dynamic entrepreneurialism of the new managerialism was offset by a deep antagonism towards the public sector. Any capacity for local organisational change and innovation remained severely constrained by central government directives and monitoring. Public service staff experienced a stark mismatch between the force and boldness of the 'excellence' rhetoric and the more old-fashioned Taylorist realities (Clarke *et al.*, 2000). If the dynamism and entrepreneurialism of the excellence model appealed to individual managers, neo-Taylorist practices offered a safety zone whenever the new management rhetoric was taken too seriously or their judgements questioned too forcefully.

New Labour and managerialism

Labour has not ended the competitive environment but it does have different priorities and requirements for public service managers. The emphasis is now on the development of collaborative practices and partnership relationships (DoH, 1997; NHS Executive, 1999; ODPM, 2001). The combined effects of an extended mixed economy, the separation of purchaser and provider, competitive funding regimes operating to an annual cycle, and greater internal decentralisation has resulted in too much fragmentation, creating inefficiencies and ineffectiveness (Cutler and Waine, 2000). The uncritical transfer of private sector practices ignored crucial differences between the sectors, particularly the political dimension to decision-making and accountability (Dixon *et al.*, 1998). Instead, Labour proposes strategic partnerships and insists, if contemporary challenges are to be met, all stakeholders must be fully involved (White, 2000).

The Labour strategy fuses together, in what can be an uneasy alliance, the concept of working collaboratively with the competitive urge to be the best and it requires managers with high levels of confidence who are secure in what they do. It implies a common commitment to the sector as a whole and to its continuous improvement. It also assumes that individual organisations not only strive to deliver high quality services but also seek to stay ahead of sectoral expectations. Managers are expected to be aware of the environment in which they are located, to work with it as a system, to be well networked, proactive, and able to work across boundaries with a range of professionals, users, and elected members (Lupton *et al.*, 1998). The key to this reformulated management role is accountability and transparency in service delivery (Lowndes and Skelcher, 1998). Behind this lies two contradictory notions, the deeply pragmatic 'what counts is what works' but also that learning is iterative, offering the potential for innovation, and diversity of practice (Schein, 1993). It marks a change of emphasis away from one that privileged managerial solutions against other perspectives to one of thinking more broadly about how best to achieve policy goals. In making this shift, the concept of leadership assumes a particular significance.

The emergent focus on leadership

Working from within a 'whole system' or a user-focused, collaborative stakeholder model, the concept of leadership – utilising informal processes to mobilise people through values and vision – offers greater utility than that of management with its focus on formal systems, processes and incentives. Recent government thinking (Cabinet Office, 2001a) highlights the scarcity of high quality and widespread leadership across the public sector and points to the constraints in its development. These are cited as:

- a public service aversion to risk;
- a prevailing blame culture;
- limited rewards and personal recognition following success;
- the uncertainty around the leadership boundary between elected members and appointed officials with ultimate authority resting with democratically elected members;
- the restrictive nature on innovation of central government control;
- the absence of consistent leadership challenge; and
- the historic undervaluing of leaders (Cabinet Office, 2001a: para. 2.13).

The popularity of 'leadership' is also reflected in the creation of a number of government 'leadership centres', including those for education and health. There has also been a growth in postgraduate educational provision that explicitly challenges the traditional private sector-oriented Masters in Business Administration, and senior staff emphasise the need for leadership development within in-house service-related continuing professional development training.

If the public sector is to address the challenges presented by more complex and less hierarchical organisations, sound leadership is essential at all levels. Success will depend on recognising and working with organisational inter-dependency, and responding to a more assertive and self-confident user. At a generic level, leadership encompasses a combination of personal qualities and the ability to mobilise and extend organisational capacities including its relationships to others. The OECD document suggests that,

> the core of leadership is how individuals influence others, particularly in respect to accessing their inner motivation. Leaders appeal because those who follow them believe that their values and deeper interests are served by doing so... leadership differs from management in so far as the latter tends to be about more tangible incentives on behaviour (OECD, 2001: 11).

Leadership is identified with:

- an ability to maintain a following in a particular situation through the building of trust founded on success, consistency, role modelling and a favourable interpretation of a leader's behaviour;

- being strategic by having an awareness of the whole system in which one is operating;
- offering and communicating explanatory narratives;
- constructing, with others, possible futures through a common vision, values, and overall sense of purpose along with a capacity to adjust or modify this in anticipation of changes in the environment;
- the ability to motivate, inspire initiative, and get the best out of followers;
- enabling diverse voices to speak and be heard equally and drawing upon the full range of interests and experience within the organisation;
- flexibility and creativity in the construction of effective implementation processes to secure objectives and the capacity for risk-taking;
- the capacity to be decisive when appropriate.

Within a public service context additional features are crucial, such as:

- the ability to lead and work collaboratively across boundaries to define and achieve common objectives through building trust via networking, alliance and coalition building;
- the capacity to balance multiple stakeholder demands and accountabilities;
- maintaining a focus on and remaining connected to the quality of services delivered working within an ethical framework.

As the Cabinet Office report puts it,

> Leaders today...need to collaborate more, manage change through others and focus on customers whose problems may not be susceptible to solution by a single agency (Cabinet Office, 2001a: 2.10)

and

> good leaders are people who can see the importance of making wider connections, are sensitive to the needs within the locality, and find effective ways of participating in partnerships and build coalitions, joint ventures and inter-organisational networks (op. cit., para. 3.8).

Leadership and followership

Leadership theory is riven with competing interpretations over the identification and significance of the essential characteristics of leadership and the difference between leadership and management (Stogdill, 1974; Palmer and Hardy, 2000).

Even apparently successful leaders are unable to pinpoint the basis of their success (Yukl, 1989). Ultimately, any understanding of 'leadership' must be located within the relationship between the leader and the followers and the achievement of consent (Prince, 1998; Joyce, 1999). However, the literature continues to be dominated by a view that equates the capacity for leadership with an individual leader, operating within a command and control relationship and based on the leader's authority and the subservience of the followers (OECD, 2001). Prince (1998) describes this as a 'structurist' model, due to the over-association between leader and occupancy of a hierarchical position. Implicitly, the assumption is that such leadership capacities are to be found in only those few who succeed to such positions.

Such models of heroic leadership have been challenged by the concept of 'dispersed leadership'. This relational model suggests that the qualities of leadership are to be found in all organisational members, can be held simultaneously by a number of people, can move between people, and that teams and individuals can be self-managing. However, the concept of dispersed leadership has had little impact on traditional hierarchical structures and their associated reward systems. Rather, its active promotion may reflect its utility as a device to extract more effort and responsibility from subordinates without any change in differential rewards or hierarchical structures, while concealing the operation of more informal relations of power.

Capacity

Another rather different concept closely related to that of dispersed leadership within a complex uncertain organisational environment is that of 'capacity'. Leaders must be able to act, to make reflexive judgements, to take decisions, whilst retaining a sense of the more immediate contradictory demands and long-term visions within which they operate (Palmer and Hardy, 2000). It is that ability to stand still, as it were, to remain reflexively grounded when all around seems chaotic, uncertain and anxiety-making. In acting, leaders must be reflexive in relation to both self and context, constantly expanding their learning and acknowledging what they do not know, yet being decisive when appropriate. A failing of 1980s managerialism was the inability of many managers to be reflexive about themselves in role and the expectations or purpose of that role, to subject themselves to the discourse of managerialism. A critical understanding of one's social or organisational location provides the freedom to explore the possibility of acting differently.

In relation to others, capacity means to be able to hold or contain for others the uncertainties, complexities, ethical dilemmas for which there might be no 'solution', and for not knowing the answer to the problems confronting service providers (Broussine, 2000). It is to provide a space that contains the conditions, material and emotional, structural and processual, within which others can learn and be productive. To be able to work in what is an empowering way requires a belief that others have the capacity to be as critically reflexive as oneself, to work with unresolvable dilemmas, and remain ethical. Leadership capacity is more than a capacity *for* leadership. It suggests that effective leadership involves being able to contain what often appears as opposites. For example, having an eye for the detail and being able to engage effectively in strategic visioning, or being responsive to both the needs of people within the organisation and to the performance of the task (Hart and Quinn, 1993). Within a framework of organisational learning, it also implies that leaders and followers must learn together.

Leadership as relational

Senge (1990, 1999), focusing on organisational 'systemic forces and collective learning' (1999: 340), speaks of the leader as the designer and steward of the organisational vision, displaying 'responsibility without possessiveness', and the teacher of how to learn about current realities and the tension between these and organisational vision. Senge (1999) locates 'leadership' within the 'collective community' and its capacity to address contemporary challenges. Leadership in this sense is understood as the ability to mobilise the full capacity of members both within and between

organisations. Grint (1995) speaks in terms of the leader as someone who can,

> embody, articulate, channel and construct the values and direction that
> the followers think they ought to be going in ... the embodiment of the
> collective (p. 148).

This relational approach (Prince, 1998) stresses the interdependencies between leaders and followers as a dynamic and complex
process. Prince argues that,

> Contexts, critically, are set and developed by sets of actors in interaction
> with one another, in a cycle of mutual creation and influence .... (p. 125).

In other words, there is a process of negotiation about the
nature of leadership required at any moment and who is most
suited to take it up. Leadership can only take place in the context
of what Prince describes as 'bounded trust' (p. 110), when there is
consent from followers, who authorise the leadership of others,
and equally are able to withdraw consent and authority (Merton,
1969; Bass, 1981). The meanings and interpretations that followers
apply to situations and behaviour define leadership. Grint (1995)
argues the critical role of the leader is to ensure that key actors in
the determination or maintenance of leadership are made familiar
with the interpretation of events most supportive of their cause.

The concept of relational leadership offers a better opportunity
for loosening the deeply assumed connection between leadership
and hierarchical positions and relationships, either within or between
organisations. It allows for the possibility that any of the multi-
sectoral organisations involved in public services can take or be given
the responsibility for leadership, and that within any single agency
all can similarly feel able to go beyond their designated role and
indeed can be expected to do so. It is possible to underestimate the
difficulties of ensuring the circulation of leadership. Those who
have experienced leadership develop the skills and capacities to
perform the role effectively thus making them both more confident and more attractive to followers as future leaders. Indeed
trust between leaders and followers is built over time, the result of
proven success in the role. Similarly, those followers who regularly
find themselves so can internalise that the perception of themselves
and can be seen by others in this way. Breaking such cycles

requires a conscious effort on the part of any group as old patterns tend to be highly resistant to change (Freeman, 1973). Although there is a growing recognition of the need to strengthen leadership in the public sector in the face of 'unprecedented challenges' and a scarcity of good leadership, there is little clarity of what leadership behaviour works in practice or what qualities are required (Cabinet Office, 2001a). The solution lies in creating organisational environments that promote good leadership, providing both a creative space in which to lead and one in which leadership can be challenged in a manner that facilitates further understanding and development.

Traits and circumstances

Traditional and still dominant approaches to the question of leadership focus on the assumed inherent characteristics or traits of the successful leader. The problem is to both establish what these might be and identify those individuals who possess them. Research into leadership traits, however, has failed to identify a common set of dispositions or a strong link between those with the most favoured traits and those who secure leadership roles (Grint, 1995). Whilst charisma (Bryman, 1992; Grint, 1995), elusive and imprecise, is considered to be a core trait and the one most sought after, others include the more widespread ones of ambition, curiosity, initiative, self-confidence, self-control and cognitive skills (Bass, 1981). Not all writers recognise the existence of charisma and of those that do a number highlight what are felt to be associated problems for subordinates, such as over-dependency, the blocking out of other effective leaders, and the potential for unethical behaviour by the leader. Moreover, as the recent government paper acknowledges (Cabinet Office, 2001a), charisma is in the mind of the beholder or has, as Grint puts it, 'a hard job emerging when there is no one to be impressed' (Grint, 1995: 135). Charisma is, therefore, a relational quality rather than a trait possessed by an individual. More recently the focus has shifted away from inherent traits to learned skills stressing the importance of self-awareness, self-management, social awareness and social skill (Goleman, 2000).

If leaders cannot succeed in all situations, they need to be matched to situations or be suitably adaptive to the demands of the moment (Fiedler, 1978). Leadership becomes contingent. Contingency arguments suggest that the style of leadership, ranging from the coercive through affiliative, to coaching, and participative, must vary according to the particular context. The leader's orientation, the need to either emphasise the task at hand or the people/relationships, along with the capacities or maturity of the followers are key considerations (Hersey and Blanchard, 1982). Thus, leaders need a repertoire of skills, the ability to be highly adaptable, the capacity to judge and the skill to implement the most appropriate style for the circumstances (Blake and Mouton, 1964). Some contingency theorists are more cautious. Context is crucial, both in relation to the capacities and dispensations of the followers and the nature of the task, but it is unlikely that any one individual can be so adaptable. Either the leadership must change or the situation must be changed to one in which the leaders are more able to function effectively by being able to maximise their skills and dispositions (Fiedler, 1967; Chemers, 1993).

Transactional and transformational leadership

A number of archetypes have been offered to describe different approaches to gain influence over others, such as, authoritarian, transactional transformational and empowering. A key distinction is that between transactional and transformational leadership (Burns, 1978). The former relies on winning people over through negotiation and bargaining by appealing to and satisfying their interests in an instrumental but mutually satisfying exchange (Hollander, 1993). The emphasis is on demonstrating concern and interest in the individual, supporting teamwork, listening, delegation and trust, and offering recognition and reward. Thus, in return for 'following', or not taking leadership, personal or collective rewards, either material or status, would be forthcoming. Transactional leaders are not only considerate but also organised. Their focus is on roles and objectives, service quality and productivity, performance, resources and infrastructure as sites for negotiation. Trust in a leadership is accumulated over time as a consequence of consistently attending to and meeting stakeholder interests and ensuring that appropriate structures are in place. In contrast, by being inspirational, purposeful or stimulating, transformational leadership focuses more on emotions, values and higher collective goals to persuade followers to subordinate personal or sectional interests (Bryman, 1992; Bass and Avolio, 1994). Such leaders are said to be future-oriented, innovative, outward-looking, problem-solving and able to take decisive action.

In reality, it is difficult to envisage organisations that do not require both a vision and purpose, and hence an inspirational element to create a sense of identity, but also ones that attend to the real interests of organisational members (Palmer and Hardy, 2000). To be without purpose or inspiration can lead to organisations that are aimless or stultifying, whilst to be overly dependent on emotional appeal would generate dysfunctional instability and unpredictability. Similarly, an over-reliance on transactional features can create mechanistic organisations, whilst a failure to attend to the needs of its members will have a negative impact on morale, recruitment, retention and service delivery. Again we are left with the question of whether anybody can in all circumstances effectively provide both transactional and transformational leadership and, if not, how to ensure that each is possible.

Building 'follower' capacity

Contemporary ideas on leadership have given greater acknowledgement to the importance of 'followers' and their willingness to accept that the solution rests as much in their own hands rather than those of a leader (Bass, 1981; Grint, 1995). Prince (1998) describes it as:

> a negotiated social order in which influence is achieved through trust, reduction of uncertainty, and the achievement of frameworks for action which are largely acceptable to followers (pp. 95–6).

Within this conception of the self-organising and self-disciplining unit, the leader's essential task is to facilitate the process through which followers can both adopt this position and begin to act upon it. This requires that more attention be given to capacity building amongst the followers. As an organisational safety net, committed, engaged, and active followers can compensate for the shortcomings of the formal leadership although how long they might be prepared to do so unconditionally is another matter. To avoid 'group-think' (Janis, 1982), organisational cultures should both express a unified value system and encourage discourse, facilitating and supporting emergent, divergent or dissenting voices. The constructive dissenting voice, prepared to question, seek clarification, challenge, or posit alternative interpretations and solutions, whilst sometimes uncomfortable to have around, should nevertheless be acknowledged as crucial to organisational development. Some officially sanctioned dissenting voices, offering an alternative source of leadership, can be found within formal roles, such as the trade union representative. Such perspectives should be incorporated into the formal decision-making process even though they create additional pressure on that leadership which, in order to sustain credibility and legitimacy, has to retain its independent relationship with its following and avoid co-option into formal structures.

Organisational learning

Organisational learning is increasingly seen as a critical prerequisite for organisational survival and a primary task of leadership (Dixon, 1992; Gilmore and Shea, 1997). Building a learning culture within public service organisations is now seen as essential (SEU, 2001), and leadership is essential to this task. Senge (1990) argues:

> the organisations that will truly excel in the future will be the organisations that discover how to tap people's commitment and capacity to learn at *all* levels in the organisation (p. 4).

There is a growing list of prescriptions concerned with the development of organisational learning, although the evidence for it occurring in practice is less apparent. Within the model, leaders are not only expected to act as role models for organisational change, as they would within almost all leadership models, but the very concept of organisational learning has fundamental implications for our perception of leadership. Leaders cannot be separated from the need to be learners. They can no longer hide behind the pretence of 'knowing' but must expose themselves to the more risky business of uncertainty and 'not knowing'. Followers cannot absolve themselves of their responsibility for learning through their dependency upon the leader and their projections of omnipotence. Learning occurs unevenly between people, over time, and according to the subject of concern. Leadership through 'knowing' cannot be claimed by single individuals but must rather flow between and be shared by people.

Learning is a demanding and challenging process as well as being rewarding and, under the right conditions, enjoyable. If all organisational members are to be engaged attention must be paid to the labour processes that either inhibit or facilitate learning. Vaill (1996) suggests that leadership in the context of learning should be self-directed and continual, with action following as a consequence of learning. It should be 'on-line' in that new ideas and possibilities are explored in real time rather than in simulations or role-plays. It should be creative, expressive and concerned with feelings, exploring and stretching boundaries and processes, developing new abilities, and learning through dialogue and intuition. Above all, it should be reflexive with attention paid to process while in the midst of action.

Harvey and Denton (1999) identify six factors, equally applicable to public and private sector organisations, to explain the rise in popularity of organisational learning, a concept that, they suggest, provides a 'binding, integrative force' within an organisation (p. 898). The six motivating drivers are:

1. The growing importance of factors of production and of intellectual labour, as identified by writers such as Drucker (1992), Handy (1989) and Peters (1992).
2. The accelerating pace of change as an accepted part of organisational reality (Kanter, 1984; Morgan, 1988).
3. Knowledge as a source of competitive advantage (Drucker, 1992).
4. More demanding consumers (Croft and Beresford, 1996).
5. A dissatisfaction with the existing management paradigm as an effective way of dealing with the increasingly complex and paradoxical environment in which risk-taking and employee trust are essential (Senge, 1990; Handy, 1994).
6. And the increasing intensity of competition (Kanter, 1989).

Change and turbulence create a crisis for the stability of organisations. Organisational learning offers an opportunity for maximising the capacity of individuals and groups to work effectively within such an environment. It is concerned with identifying and encouraging the processes, structures, behaviours and understandings that enable organisations to learn and unlearn continuously. Yet, while offering the prospect of change and development, learning especially when institutionalised can also lead to a reinforcement or preservation of existing practices. Further, as a number of writers argue

(Easterby-Smith, 1997; Palmer and Hardy, 2000), there is no consensus as to the meaning of organisational learning or whether it is possible to speak of a 'learning organisation'. Whilst some speak of it in aspirational tones (Senge, 1990), others are more cautions, even dismissive. Krantz (1998) describes the idea as:

> a leading fad...a cult-like movement with its own cliches and rituals, (it) amounts to a defensive neutralization of these potentially disruptive and anxiety producing ideas (p. 94).

Opinion is divided as to whether learning is primarily an individual activity (Argyris, 1993) – and if so whether to include emotional as well as cognitive and tacit learning – or a collective one (Schein, 1993). Similarly, opinion is divided as to whether the focus should be on learning as a process or on the outcomes of learning. Is the aim to bring about new ways of understanding and thinking or to alter behaviour? Cook and Yanow (1993) suggest that the crucial issue is the relationships between individuals in the social construction of meaning, identity, and sense making within organisations, a process best achieved through the establishment of 'communities-in-practice' and the use of participatory action research (Hendry, 1996).

Isaacs (1993) argues that organisational learning can most effectively be achieved through the development of a 'container' to enable the practice of 'dialogue' to emerge, whilst Schein (1993) describes dialogue as:

> a central element of any model of organisational transformation (p. 40).

Isaacs defines dialogue as a conscious process of learning how to think together

> A sustained collective inquiry into processes, assumptions, and certainties that compose everyday experience (1993: 25).

Dialogue is contrasted with other ways of talking such as discussion, dialectic, and debate – all that involve large elements of securing a 'victory' for one's point of view. Dialogue involves the initial suspension of personal defences, putting on hold at least temporarily personal perceptions, judgements, feelings and impulses, while attempting to listen carefully to and reflect upon what others are saying, accepting differences, and allowing trust to develop. Those involved in dialogue search for hidden assumptions or how, as Schein states:

> our perceptions and cognitions are preformed by our past experiences...
> how our thought processes work (1993: 43).

Common ground is to be created through the mutual exploration of assumptions and feelings and the sharing of tacit knowledge (Polanyi, 1970). As a consequence, a new 'metalogue' can emerge that reflects the thinking and shared assumptions of the whole group. This form of learning extends Argyris and Schon's (1987) concept of 'double-loop' learning, which requires the capacity to consider alternative perceptions and understandings of what is before us by exploring the context of learning. They also identify a third level of learning, or 'deutero-learning', where learning is directed at the learning process itself. Isaacs argues that this collective thinking and communicating can occur,

> If people can be brought into a setting where they...can become con-
> scious of the very processes by which they form tacit assumptions and
> solidify beliefs, and be rewarded by each other for doing so, then they
> can develop a common strength and capability for working and creating
> things together (Issacs, 1993: 25).

As Schein (1993) acknowledges, the real test for such practices is whether they facilitate problem-solving in areas of sharp conflict. For those seeking above all else to secure a victory, there is nothing in the concept of dialogue to prevent them doing so, and for it to succeed participants must be committed to working together. Within the public sector where collaborative partnerships between agencies, professionals and sectors is a requirement, dialogue offers the possibility for exploring underlying assumptions. Collective learning and unlearning could serve us much better than either the traditional managerialist strategies or the growing regulatory regimes to be discussed in the next chapter. However, before dialogue or any other learning process can be developed, the container for learning must be in place to the extent that organisational members feel sufficiently safe to engage. The development of a distributed leadership would go some way to securing this, along with the expansion of intra- and inter-organisational collaborative work teams, and ensuring that organisational members felt secure in their respective roles and their relationship to other roles (Krantz, 1998).

The managerial paradigm that dominated the 1980s has begun to reveal its limitations in the management of complexity and difference. While this is slowly being replaced by a focus on leadership, this too is still often confined to the traditional and somewhat redundant accounts of the heroic leader blessed with special qualities. However, within the current discourse there are opportunities to develop further our understanding and practice of dispersed leadership, within the context of cultures that promote organisational learning, but with significant implications for hierarchy and current reward patterns. Such possibilities hold out the promise for a different kind of relationship within and between welfare organisations and with their users.

6

Producing Quality Services

Improving the quality of provision is a key objective within Labour's programme of public service modernisation (Kirkpatrick and Lucio, 1995). The Cabinet Secretary recently highlighted both the changing context in which public services are to be judged – alongside goods and services purchased from the private sector – and the impact this has on the performance of public sector professionals.

> Public services in the past tended to be something which people got, not as a right but as a favour…Along with that went a tacit understanding that the service might be a bit shabby, slow and bureaucratic…(not) as good as something which you paid for. That is not how most people see it now. People expect from public services the standards which they themselves are expected to provide in their own jobs. They expect service of the kind which they would get from the private sector (Sir Richard Wilson, Cabinet Secretary, 2000).

Judging public service quality on the basis of what is offered by the private sector is another legacy of the 1979–97 New Right governments. What is less acknowledged but is what everyone knows is that the private sector offers goods and services of variable standards, everything from junk to the latest 'perfection'. Public services must provide consistently high quality services, which must by definition include a choice of service, as one service irrespective of its technical quality and appropriateness for some will not be experienced and evaluated in the same way by other users. The incentive to aspire to quality is a commitment to the values of collective provision for the enhancement of individual and social well-being, and a sense that these are superior to the competitive self-centred individualism of the market. Welfare professionals have

110

been entrusted with stewardship of the principle that we are all, 'our brother's keeper'. There is a duty to provide the highest possible quality services, for as Bauman (2000) argues:

> The future of...the welfare state...depends...on the ethical standards of the society we all inhabit...better to be moral, even if this does not make people wealthier and the companies more profitable (p. 11).

That there is 'something special about public services' (Blair, 2002) is emerging as part of Labour's second term re-evaluation of public provision.

> At its best the notion of public service embodies vital qualities – loyalty, altruism, dedication, long-term relationships with users, a sense of pride. It is an ethos that is the motivating force... (Blair, 2002).

This chapter explores the concept of quality in public services, the current efforts to measure and enhance quality, and the implications for professional practice.

What is this thing called 'quality'?

Quality has come to be defined as 'fitness for purpose' – that is, does it do what it is meant to do? As outlined in the White Paper, The New NHS,

> doing the right things, at the right time, for the right people, and doing them right – first time. And it must be the quality of the patient's experience as well as the clinical result.... (DoH, 1997: para. 3.2).

Lewis and Hartley (2001) argue that defining quality in the public services is complicated by the three characteristics of 'intangibility', 'heterogeneity' and 'inseparability' in service provision. This makes it difficult to test for quality in advance, to define one specific service transaction as applicable to all users, and to separate the relationship between provider and user from the product (p. 479). User obligation or the lack of choice within many public service relationships further complicates the picture so that quality cannot be judged simply on the basis of user preferences. To understand the implications of using a patient or user's judgement about service quality, account needs to be taken of the circumstances or environmental quality, in which the service is delivered, the manner of that delivery, and its relational aspects (Stewart and Walsh, 1989).

For many services, such as counselling or residential care, it is impossible to separate these elements from a notion of 'fitness'. An important distinction between a market product and a public service is that the quality of the latter is altered by the engagement of the service user in the process. Service users not only judge whether a service is of sufficient quality, they also contribute to that level of quality. Since much of the encounter is focused on the relationship between the service user and an individual professional providing the service, the quality of the provision can be experienced as quite different from an overall judgement of the service. The extent to which a service is primarily a relationship determines whether and how far the quality of the service declines with the overall level of resources. A drop in the number of encounters, a reduction in the time allocated to each encounter, or if the provider has less energy, commitment, or attention due to the impact of service reductions elsewhere, then the quality of that service for that user is reduced. Other users may be denied access to the same service as a consequence of an overall reduction in resources.

Our understanding of quality, and the way it is measured, depends on our interests and circumstances. Consequently, the meaning given to it at any moment is the result of a negotiated process between different interests (Gaster and Deakin, 1998). As in any other negotiated process, there are trade-offs to be made between different aspects within the complexity that is quality. Service users' views on the quality of provision are variable and are closely related to both their expectations of and their relationships to the service at the precise moment of evaluation (Gaster, 1995). Any engagement with service users on quality takes time, requiring numerous discussions, before the meaning of quality and the richness of the experience can be fully explored and understood. The need for such ongoing dialogue is something that the popular survey methods within the consumerist model of user involvement (see Chapter 8) cannot adequately capture.

Quality must also be measured against what are considered to be minimum standards, what is achievable within current constraints, and what is desirable, and all these are contestable.

Quality targets are too often established without clear links between what can be realistically expected now and how one might move closer to the desired target. The concept of 'good enough' services acknowledges both the weighing up of provision against contextual considerations and the gap between what is offered and what might be desirable. While some slippage can be expected between what can be reasonably expected and what is achieved, the line between reasonable expectations and minimum standards is critical, since 'minimal' is also inextricably connected to context. The distinction is significant when for whatever reason an agency is unable to deliver what others judge to be attainable. In such instances, minimum standards provide an ultimately poor safeguard for those dependent upon the service. To distinguish between current expectations and minimum standards, we effectively apply the latter to standards of delivery previously thought reasonable but applicable in different conditions. In this sense, minimum standards can act as a trigger to signal the imminent replacement or upgrading of a service if there is evidence of further decline, as a consequence of rising standards or through wear and tear, such that they are no longer acceptable. To equate minimum standards with 'quality' seems something of a contradiction in terms.

Pfeffer and Coote (1991) identify five different perspectives on quality:

1. an expert model, with standards set by specialists;
2. a managerial or 'excellence' approach, concerned with maintaining or extending a market position;
3. a consumerist or user model, focused on individual experiences
4. a democratic model, with standards or expectations specified through political debate and contestation, and;
5. an elite model, in which emphasis is given to different goods held by groups of people as a mark of privilege and status.

In reality these five perspectives overlap and are inter-dependent, so that all are evident at any given moment (Davies, 2000). Thus, managerialist and consumerist perspectives share many of the same concerns in respect of what factors are considered in judging service quality and can have similar outcomes in relation to user satisfaction. To apply the democratic model requires a mature political process with provider organisations embedded in local communities, working to a negotiated local mandate, holding a service philosophy determined through a stakeholder dialogue, receptive and responsive to front-line professionals. Standards determined in the polity rely on professional experts for translation into measurable and/or practical processes, outputs and outcomes.

A choice has to be made as to where to draw the boundaries around any quality model. Comparisons could be restricted to within a nation state or evaluated against what occurs elsewhere, breaking away from what Deacon *et al.* (1997) describe as the Fabian reformist 'national ghetto' (p. 8). Yet, international comparisons are complicated, slow to develop, and a reminder of the importance of history and context in grappling with meanings and interpretations of quality. Another evaluative technique measures all models against generic public sector core values such as, equity, fairness, inclusiveness, solidarity, identity, accountability, justice, and community or some broader commitment to health and autonomy in relation to basic human needs (Doyal and Gough, 1991).

Although all five perspectives, as identified by Pfeffer and Coote, have been evident in respect of public provision, no single one has dominated, and indeed expectations about standards have largely been characterised by a lack of clarity. For it to be a meaningful measure, an approach must identify the benchmarks against which quality is to be judged, and any preconditions for its achievement. For example, within the consumerist approach the central concern is with the service users' evaluation of their personal experience. This 'experience' is itself complex, involving both a separate and overall 'satisfaction' judgement against a number of different criteria, including:

- service outcomes, and whether needs are met to the desired and/ or expected extent;
- the processes by which providers consider needs, priorities and resource allocations;
- transparency of and ease of access to such processes, including both physical and psychological proximity;
- the amount and nature of information provided about the range of available services;
- relationships with service professionals;
- a sense of fairness and equity in treatment and in outcomes;
- a willingness to use the service again and recommend it to others.

An individual may feel more or less satisfied with each of these bench-marks but may not consider any one to be especially significant in relation to an overall judgement of the service. They may be highly satisfied with their level of involvement in the decision-making processes but if they were disinterested in this then the satisfaction value would count for little. A high satisfaction rating against service outcomes might be explained by low expectations, and gratitude for what is received. To imagine or expect anything more may be beyond their experience, and unhelpful if it is unlikely to be forthcoming. Conversely, there can be deep dissatisfaction with the provision that is subsequently modified, having acquired a better understanding of the circumstances in which that service was offered. Thus, the consumer approach cannot be applied unless it is done within a participatory democratic process, in which expectations can be raised and debated, alongside other considerations, and judgements are explained and re-evaluated.

Quality, choice and market influences

Pfeffer and Coote (1991) argue that the 'elite model' is not applicable to the public sector since a better quality service is understood to mean a better overall service than previously experienced. It does not reflect qualitative differences within a service, or those experienced by different groups of users. The association between the elite model and market-based transactions lies not far beneath the surface in public service quality debates, especially in relation to user choice. Criticism over the absence of choice, the explicit prohibition against users expressing any sense of personal ownership of a service received, and the limitations of homogeneous products was first aired by the left in the late 1960s and early 1970s.

The New Right rejected the post-war standardisation of essential services and made 'choice' a legitimate expectation. As monopoly providers with guaranteed markets, state provision faced none of the incentives for improvement found in the more competitive market place, resulting in low quality public services. Professionals were accused of exploiting the protected environment of the public services to set minimum or self-protective standards (Harris and Seldon, 1987). It was assumed that the incentivised private sector produced the best quality services, that everyone naturally seeks the best they can afford, and therefore should be free to opt out of public provision and purchase private sector produced services.

Conversely, since providers should be able to compete for customers, private sector organisations should be allowed to expand into markets previously restricted to public provision.

The market offers goods and services for every size of consumer wallet or credit card where quality and price are equated, although all goods regardless of price are said to meet minimum quality standards. Earlier post-war generations saved for the new consumer goods, occasionally taking advantage of 'loan schemes' offered by major retailers. Today purchasing goods on credit is the primary form of purchase. It is the payment, not the purchase that is deferred. This demand for easy access to credit is driven by the prospect of the immediate purchase of better quality products than could otherwise be afforded. The extent to which the product conveys status, as in the popularity of designer clothing or brand name products, is an added incentive (Klein, 2000). Personal identities are endlessly made and remade without reference to the wallet. The expansion of product diversity, away from mass standardised goods towards niche marketing, creates the impression of immense product variation based not only on the richness of consumer tastes but infinite price-related marginal qualitative differences. Empirical evidence to the contrary does not necessarily undermine the logic of the argument.

The market makes a number of unsustainable and contradictory claims about the relationship between price and quality. These are closely related to the seller's perception of the buyer from that segment of the market they wish to attract. A dissatisfied purchaser may be told that, 'you get what you pay for'. In other words, that there is a correlation between price and quality. Conversely, the seller will attempt to persuade buyers that there is unlimited choice for all tastes and pockets and that, irrespective of what you pay, you will receive in return a product of quality. 'Quality' implies that more has been invested into the production whether this is in the form of craftsmanship, creative design, advanced technology or durable components. A quality product, and therefore one that is more expensive, offers the prospect of enhanced profits, although profits can be generated just as easily by selling goods that quickly fail in their purpose or have built-in short-life obsolescence.

Extensive product diversification and differentiation, along with misleading claims about product quality and performance, have generated a parallel and influential consumer movement of product testing, comparisons, and rankings to create a more discerning consumer by information, education and protection. The 'green' movement highlights the environmental impact, and the risks to individuals and to particular social groups of specific products or their production process. It also exposes the myth of 'continuous growth'. The market's response has been to invest more in product marketing by equating the kind of person who buys the product with a limited range of fantasy role models. More limited attempts have been made towards increasing their credibility on environmental 'friendliness'. This is, no doubt, to avoid exposure to public criticism and litigation, and gain a better market advantage, but also because consumers have become more discriminating and markets can collapse. Pressure to do so can lead to real improvements to the quality of products.

The contemporary obsession with product quality and market consumer expectations of continuous improvement has inevitably influenced our approach to public services. The idea that a product is 'good enough' appears acceptable, albeit reluctantly or grudgingly, only when we do not have the time or energy to investigate the product range, or alternatively become exhausted by, the search for the 'best buy'. The discerning consumer is a powerful image and used to promote the adoption of a mixed economy of welfare for the non-poor. The failure of the political left within the policy community to address this desire for choice and quality has further exposed public provision as something that is preserved for those unable to afford choice, or somehow not deserving of it.

The left has concentrated on the important task of highlighting the limitations of choice, the difficulties of providing it in relation to particular groups of service users, or the way in which it can work to further disadvantage groups (Gewirtz *et al.*, 1995). This highlighted the complexities in the category of service user and warned that to engage as consumers requires some difficult adjustments in previous behaviours and expectations. Drawing upon their research of consumer ideal types operating in the social care market, Baldock and Ungerson (1996) construct a useful typology, based on expectations of who should provide care and how much energy or participation, would be required to secure what was needed. They describe four categories or 'types of disposition', of social care: 'consumerism', 'privatism', 'welfarism' and 'clientalism', although acknowledging that in most instances consumers demonstrate aspects from all. Each is based on the 'norms' or 'intermediate values' that influence an individual's daily decision-making.

For the consumerist, the expectation is that care would be provided either by the market or informal networks, and that they would largely determine what they received. Privatism refers to those who adopt a passive consumerism, rarely engaging in the social world other than to take what is offered. Welfarism reflects the welfare citizens who are active in the pursuit of their rights, expecting these to be met through collective provision. Finally, clientalism refers to those who are grateful for what they receive, uncomplaining and passive, with few expectations in relation to services, and who therefore do rather badly.

These are important insights but they do not represent a sufficiently strong argument against 'choice' per se, irrespective of whether such choices are made on the basis of real or perceptional differences. To have choice, and to use quality and appropriateness as critical dimensions in the decision-making process, is important. Different agencies, for example, in residential care could target specific service user groups through the re-creation of different lifestyles. Given a sufficient supply of users, each agency could strive to provide the highest quality service and could do so without being in a competitive relationship with those who target a different group. However, as soon as multiple provider agencies target the same user group, an element of competition is present. All can strive for excellence but each may want to be better than the other, or to highlight some distinguishing feature, which if effective in attracting users will produce a counter response from other agencies. The prospect of failure is never completely removed and those who fail to compete effectively face closure. However, for those providers who remain, the competitiveness within their relationships does not exclude the possibility of collaboration in pursuit of their mutual interest in the health of the market place. Competition and collaboration can live alongside each other, provided that the boundary area that contains the tension between them is carefully managed.

The determination of what is meant by 'quality' involves the negotiation of the criteria to be applied, such as the views of experts or the experience of consumers. It also requires clarity in the relationship between the particular service (outputs), the impact of the service (outcomes), and the resources required to produce the service (inputs). Much of the quality debate has hinged around whether it is possible to improve the processes involved in the production of services within the present resource envelope through greater efficiency, or whether additional resources are a prerequisite for quality improvement. Key resources include technological developments and improvements to plant and equipment, but above all the people performing the work. Doing things differently to increase efficiency or effectiveness always raises anxieties amongst those affected. The potential impact of change in relation to employment security, reward and status differentials, re-training, and changes in role are always sources of concern. The implied criticism that previous systems and performance were inefficient and the prospect of not being at ease or competent within the new requirements creates further anxiety. Defensiveness is a common response to anxiety with workers predisposed to challenge proposals designed to generate quality improvements through new working practices.

Public services are heavily dependent upon the capacity of human capital available to it. Staff recruitment and retention are important concerns, as is the level and nature of the initial training and continuing professional development. It is unlikely that front-line staff will be willing to make the personal investment required to deliver an enhanced service if their perception is that they are undervalued and unsupported in their work. The restricted vision of the 1980s neo-Taylorist management failed to comprehend these realities. Instead, the government preferred a confrontational strategy with professional and trade union organisations. The legacy of that approach has not entirely evaporated although there is greater acknowledgement of the need for human resource investment through improved training and professional development, more family-friendly measures, and a better work/life balance (Bryson *et al.*, 2000; DTI, 2000). Some measures have been introduced, such as improved maternity provision, paternity leave and unpaid time off for dependents. However, it has been European rather than UK legislation that has been the driving force behind improved working conditions and entitlements. Beyond addressing the minimum wages of the working poor, Labour has avoided tackling pay differentials and workplace inequalities or creating ways to enable front-line staff to participate in policy and organisational development. Managers remain reluctant to abandon the traditional approach to exercising their 'right to manage' while UK employees work some of the longest hours in Europe and are experiencing increased work related stress (Good Housekeeping, 2000).

Labour and quality provision

Labour has staked its future on improving the quality of public services and this is reflected across the policy spectrum (ODPM, 2001). As stated in the 1997 White Paper, The New NHS,

> Every part of the NHS and everyone who works in it should take responsibility for working to improve quality (DoH, 1997: para. 3.2).

The 'Best Value' regime, first outlined in Modern Local Government – In touch with the People (DETR, 1998a), was formally introduced under the Local Government Act (1999). This placed a duty on local authorities to provide continuous service improvements balancing costs and quality in consultation with partners and local people, and identifying the most appropriate method of delivery, securing,

> Not just with the best that other authorities provide but the best that is on offer from both the public and the private sectors (DETR, 1998a: para. 7.1).

Best Value has been further extended by the introduction of a system of Comprehensive Performance Assessment (ODPM, 2001). The desire for improved service quality first gained prominence at the end of the 1980s, and has since flourished both in the UK and elsewhere (Gaster, 1995; Bovaird and Halachmi, 2001). The social democratic model of the pre-Thatcherite era had relied on four factors to ensure the delivery of quality services:

1. A bureaucratic organisation bounded by impartiality and equal treatment, standardised rules and procedures, clear role differentiation, internal accountability, and job security.
2. Professionalism, both a self-regulating mechanism and a process for setting standards based upon training, education, and a commitment to professional practice and development, linked to vocational self-sacrifice, status and reward.
3. Hierarchical relations based on qualifications, expertise and experience in respect of both the service organisation and between professional groups, to ensure decision-making based on appropriate relations of authority.
4. Above average and continuous level of national economic growth.

This implementation process was underpinned by a political system in which politicians working through and accountable to democratic processes determined policy goals and objectives. The detailed implementation was left to the discretion of those professionals responsible for service delivery. Financial probity was a further safeguard on the use of public funds but not one that was necessarily linked to the quality of provision.

The reforming zeal of Margaret Thatcher's first government was devoted more to a real and substantial reduction of public provision than with a concern for issues of quality. Services that were to remain were targeted for improvements in efficiency and economy, effectively a reduction in quality, alongside greater accountability. The New Right's aversion to public provision ensured that even after the 1987 election, government ministers continued to insist that quality could best be guaranteed within the private sector. Alternatively, public sector services would need to become like private sector organisations. Thus, for the New Right, public service quality would be achieved through a variety of methods that have since been strengthened by Labour:

- The separation of service providers from 'purchasers', now referred to as 'commissioners' to reflect Labour's move away from a market-orientation.
- A more competitive 'market place' between a greater number of provider agencies to ensure service users greater choice. Commissioners are able to use the selection process to achieve threshold service standards as specified by central government, and include an opportunity for local creativity, while matching the lowest cost with what is judged as the appropriate combination of economy, efficiency and effectiveness.
- The devolution of responsibility for individual contracts to managers giving them incentives to lower costs, deliver more and innovate.
- Greater emphasis on the individual consumer in service evaluation and in the determination of their own service package.
- Increased use of performance indicators and targets, linked to individual and organisational benefits, most recently captured in the concept of 'earned autonomy' offering fewer external audits and extended devolved decision-making.
- The use of inspection bodies with powers to take over from failing providers.

The production of high quality public services is central to the Labour agenda. However, there is much that is continuous with the previous Conservative regimes in the way it has interpreted and applied the concept. Labour continues to rely on external audits and performance management as core tools in the monitoring process, combined with sanctions should agencies fall below requirements. The ethos of performance measurement dominates local concerns and threatens any potential gains that could be achieved by benchmarking (Ball *et al.*, 2000). Maile and Hoggett (2001) describe what they see as the managerialism of politics, by which performance indicators become, 'the new currency of accountability, not votes gained and seats lost' (p. 512).

The 'New NHS' White Paper (DoH, 1997) calls for continuous improvement in clinical practice, and a Commission for Health Improvement has been established to examine the work of NHS Trusts in relation to advancing quality provision (DoH, 1998c). Within local government, following the White Papers Modern Local Government – In touch with the People (DETR, 1998a) and Modernising Government (Cabinet Office, 1999a), the Local Government Act 1999 placed a duty of Best Value on authorities to provide quality services. Under Best Value, local authorities are required to review their functions, publish annual plans with past and projected performance and secure continuous improvements in both quality and service cost across all their provision while giving due regard to questions of economy, efficiency and effectiveness. An exploration of alternative ways of procuring and delivering services is also expected. Best Value requires authorities to pay greater attention to service effectiveness and therefore encourages a dialogue with other partners, as well as users and citizens, to address what is another dynamic, negotiated and contested arena (Ball *et al.*, 2000).

When first introduced, Best Value linked improvements in policy effectiveness to local circumstances and requirements, as well as national comparators or benchmarks. Working to national frameworks, each authority must engage in local consultation to establish performance targets. In setting targets, authorities are expected to address four areas: the challenge of why and how a service is provided, a comparison with the performance of others, consultation with local stakeholders, and competition for delivering the most efficient services. Authorities are judged against agreed targets but also in comparison with others. Bovaird and Halachmi (2001)

locate Best Value at the intersection between the managerialism
of New Public Management and community involvement in policy
planning within a community and local governance model (p. 458).
Based on a review of Best Value pilots they conclude, 'Best Value
has liberated a spirit of enquiry and energy to pursue continuous
improvement to an unusual degree' (p. 460). Local Public Service
Agreements (LPSAs) were also introduced alongside a new 'Best
Value Inspectorate' charged with driving through the government
agenda (Martin and Davis, 2001: 89). These are voluntary in
nature but enable local authorities to be more ambitious in push-
ing forward government priorities with additional resources and
greater autonomy as the reward.

Audit and performance management

External audits and inspections as a mechanism for quality assurance are now a well-established, although often unwelcomed, feature
of daily life across the public services. A joint Audit Commission
and DETR consultation document (DETR, 1999) identified some
192 performance indicators for metropolitan and 101 for district
authorities against which local authority performance can be
compared with others and against itself over time. The most recent
(2002–03) performance indicators identify some 95, a reduction
from the previous 123, for Best Value. These are sometimes
expressed in relation to the overall service, as in the NHS National
Service Frameworks identified by the National Institute for
Clinical Excellence (NICE) created in 1999, or embedded within
specific policies, as in the children's Quality Protects agenda (DoH,
1998b). Many of these performance measures and frameworks are
overlapping and have become the source of confusion that the
introduction of comprehensive performance assessment aims to
address (ODPM, 2001).

The number of inspection bodies has grown and covers both
specific services and an agency's overall provision. Some focus on
professional practice whilst others address broader themes of efficiency and effectiveness. Key agencies include the Audit Commission, Best Value and Social Services Inspectorates, OFSTED,
Quality Assurance and Audit in Higher Education. Regional
Commissioners for Care Standards, recruited under the Modernising Social Services White Paper, have been appointed uniting

health and social care inspections (DoH, 1998a). Such bodies represent the architecture of a highly regulated state. The stakes are high for any agency in the throes of an inspection. The cost of failing can be enormous in terms of agency reputation, staff morale, loss of business, and therefore income or funding, the additional burden of inspections and ultimately the prospect of local management replaced by government appointed personnel. National inspection 'league tables' dominate both the popular and professional press. The more exacting the inspection and the greater the consequences of failing, the more likely organisations will re-position activities and priorities to match those of the inspection regime.

The preparations for each inspection absorb substantial amounts of agency resources, in terms of finance, staff time, focus and emotion. A successful outcome can produce little beyond a confirmation that quality standards are being met. However, the concept of 'earned autonomy' promises both additional funding and greater freedom. Ironically, success in securing a badge of approval against performance targets can marginalise other valuable activity and create organisations that are resistant to further learning. As audits and inspection increase in number and complexity, they also become an exercise to be negotiated. Successful completion becomes an end in itself, quite removed from service delivery priorities or whether service users receive a better service as a result. Instead of more closely binding front-line staff with the goals of inspection, they generate a deep cynicism as staff witness, and participate in the bending of data to satisfy the prescribed requirements and the energy devoted to impression management. Once a system of auditing leaves participants questioning the relationship between a successful audit and real performance, it risks losing its credibility, although it might continue to be something that has to be endured.

National public service standards accompanied by mechanisms of accountability are neither new nor unreasonable, and were at the heart of the post-war welfare regime. What is evident is that neither the various professional bodies directly concerned with service provision nor local politics can be solely relied upon to produce services that demonstrate continuous quality improvements. However, a number of concerns have emerged in relation to the current inspection regime. These relate to the tools and mechanisms of inspection, the inspection process, and the consequences of a target driven regime. Common examples include:

- The 'tick-box' shallowness of the approach to measuring the complexity that is quality, for example, quality judged by the number of times something occurs rather than a judgement about the content, context, and impact of that occurrence.
- The proxy nature of some benchmarks that can conceal rather than illuminate the real objective and do not demonstrate that the particular measurement in use can assess whether the underlying objective has been achieved.
- The focus on output targets neglects service-related processes, such as participation, choice, advocacy, and equity, that have a significant bearing on longer-term outcomes.
- The amount of preparatory work involved deflects agencies away from service delivery, and encourages the use of presentational skills to create a closer fit with inspection requirements. Compliance costs appeared to outweigh any potential benefits.
- The sheer volume of inspections and the extent to which these are inflexible, overly prescriptive, intrusive, focusing on weaknesses and failings rather than rewarding good practice, with a detrimental impact on those individuals whose work is given close attention, and act as a deterrent to learning.
- The overly prescriptive nature of standards at the expense of legitimate local considerations.

The introduction of the concept of 'earned autonomy' is an attempt to address these dilemmas by offering more concrete incentives than in earlier initiatives, such as the achievement of 'Beacon Council' status. Critical to the success of any quality inspection regime is whether the standards and targets are appropriate and realistic along with how and why they have been determined. Those who are to be inspected should have an opportunity to shape how standards can best be measured. The rationale behind any target needs to be transparent and opportunities provided to raise other alternatives. There is a greater likelihood of a collaborative and developmental approach to inspection if targets are shared by those involved. The contribution of each agency to the achievement of a target needs to be clear, as do the consequences of not meeting them.

The government has insisted that service providers work in partnership across service and agency boundaries but the inspection regime displays a lack of trust in the motivation and practices of public service providers. Some of the current audit systems, such as Office for Standards in Education OFSTED, pay little attention to partnership or cross-boundary work, but prioritise what is happening within the institutional boundaries. Local agencies are capable of generating sound systems for audit and inspection. Attention needs to be given to the construction of standards and targets from the bottom-up, an essential process if they are to be owned by those who will be the subjects of inspection. National standards must be sufficiently flexible to take account of local conditions and variations. However, it is unwise to leave quality control entirely in the hands of the agency responsible for its provision. External inspection and verification is important in accrediting quality standards and ensuring accountability. Government has begun to show greater awareness of the stifling effect of external inspections on local initiative and innovation, reconciling the need for 'intervention protocols' and finding the balance between,

the need for strategic direction and performance improvement targets with the need to allow local leaders enough discretion to innovate and take risks to deliver better service (Cabinet Office, 2001a: para. 4.24).

The Prime Minister has also acknowledged this:

I readily accept that there may be a tension between guaranteed standards, the machinery to underpin and enforce them, and the freedom necessary for local autonomy and diversity to flourish.... Hence our intention to extend 'earned autonomy': a right for the successful who are achieving good standards to manage their affairs and innovate with greater freedom from central oversight and red tape.... (Blair, 2002: 24).

The White Paper, Strong Local Leadership Quality Public Services (ODPM, 2001) proposed to further build upon Best Value and Local Service Partnerships. This introduced comprehensive performance assessments within a national standards and accountability framework and defined priorities, set out in a Central Local Partnership, while removing some control over local inputs, processes and decisions. Local authorities will be expected to reflect government priorities within their approach to Best Value and local PSAs. Authorities will be subject to regular comprehensive assessments, undertaken by the Audit Commission, focused on their performance against such defined standards and priorities.

Using a 'balanced scorecard', that draws together data from a number of performance reviews, councils will be ranked as 'high-performing', 'striving' 'coasting' or 'poor-performing'. Separate inspections on specific services are to continue.

For those that successfully meet the requirements, new freedoms, such as fewer ring-fenced budgets and planning requirements, additional resources, and a more 'lighter touch' inspection regime, are offered. For those who fail, new penalties are promised. These include the appointment of an administrator to ensure sound financial management, the franchising of management from other high-performing councils, or the transfer of functions to other bodies through enforced contracting-out that may be accompanied by a loss of any statutory responsibility for that function. Overall, a streamlined, proportionate and integrated inspection approach is to be adopted. The outcomes of the CPA will in turn influence future Best Value reviews. Local PSAs will be used to deliver improvements in specific priority areas more quickly through the provision of greater flexibilities and additional targeted funds. As Local Strategic Partnerships (LSP) develop they will be expected to play a key role in shaping the PSA.

Further devolution to regional and local level is still required. Local agencies could be required to construct and implement, in partnership with regional and central government, a local/regional inspection regime for both individual agencies and others as part of a consortium. Making local organisations responsible for the process and practice of inspection would increase the likelihood of organisational learning based on that experience. Moreover, it could also increase the possibility that all stakeholders, including service users, front-line staff and trade unions, are part of the process.

A new professionalism

An important implication that flows from the earlier discussion on consumer choice, quality enhancement, and relationships at the point of service is the need for a new approach to public service professionalism. Professionalism, as traditionally conceived (see Chapter 1), has never been attained by the vast majority of welfare service occupations, not even as 'semi-professions' (Etzioni, 1969), despite the many proclamations emanating from 'professional' bodies across the sector. Only the medical profession has experienced the power, status, and control associated with what has always been a fundamentally elitist occupational strategy and even their omnipotence has recently been challenged. Other welfare or public service occupations have always encountered too many obstacles to secure the privileges accorded to those who have successfully claimed a hold over scarce and complex knowledge.

The legitimacy and survival of public service occupations have been too dependent upon the state and its adoption of policies that guarantee them a clientele. Many public service occupational groups remain over-dependent upon the professional judgement of others. In healthcare this is reflected in the deference shown to the medical profession, the control exercised over other subordinates and in the uncertain relationships with service users. This mix of professional arrogance and occupational anxiety has done little to facilitate a sense of measured autonomy and self-regulation.

Although educational standards and occupational qualifications, an essential ingredient for professionalism, are an increasing requirement across the public services, standards have remained low. It is only since the 1970s, for example, that social work progressed from being a poorly educated and untrained workforce. Attempts to introduce prescribed competency-based approaches to education and training programmes (Hodkinson and Issitt, 1995; Banks, 1998) reflects it. It is only in 2003 that the first degree-level programme of initial qualification for social work will be introduced. Post-qualifying programmes have been required to compensate for the relatively poor prior-entry general educational qualifications of many of the recruits. This has been justified in terms of a wholly defensible strategy of widening participation and ensuring equity with a particular emphasis on the recruitment of working class, mature, and black and ethnic minority students. However, as an appropriate response to the public service workforce composition and the needs of service users, the strategy diminished the likelihood of professional recognition, an occupational strategy highly correlated with the social background of occupational members and their personal and social networks.

Not only was the professionalisation project, mirrored on the established and deeply conservative professions, unattainable for most public sector occupations, it was also misplaced and misguided. There is no honour in public services attempting to emulate the elitism of a privileged minority. The pressure for greater transparency and accountability, for an increased role for service users and citizens, for improved standards and quality of service, for greater flexibility of role and function, and for inter-professional collaborative working, undermine traditional professional practices and outlook. While public service occupations continue to enjoy public sympathy, it is at best a fragile relationship, and what is required of them is demanding and complex, in which ethical conduct are far from obvious (Bauman, 1993).

To successfully intervene in socially and culturally heterogeneous communities has become a central challenge. Different interests, experiences and value systems compete for attention. To work effectively requires considerable ethical and emotional capacities. 'Capacity' cannot be learnt in the same way as skills or competencies but is rather a developmental category. It is the ability as a reflective practitioner, 'to hold something for another as well as for oneself' (French, 1999: 1223). Thus practitioners need to hold and work with the uncertainties of a situation, with 'not knowing'. They must allow for difference in others, act on the basis of judgements that refrain from simplifying complexity, avoid locating ethical correctness in themselves in an unreflective fashion, and yet retain their capacity to act decisively.

They also have to manage complex individual and group emotions. In distressed neighbourhoods, professionals may have to work with those suffering from various forms of mental distress (Jarman *et al.*, 1992). A key element of the engagement process is what Hochschild describes as 'emotion work' (Hochschild, 1983), whether it be arousing enthusiasm and building capacity, or responding to hurt and frustration. Practitioners need to be skilled at recognising and attending to their own emotions, dealing with their own sense of anxiety or depression, or the projected anger, cynicism, depression and even despair of those they work with. They need the capacity to employ paradoxical skills – to tolerate uncertainty and be decisive – in order to work through a series of dilemmas for which there are no easy resolutions. The literature on coping styles and resources used to understand human resilience and change (Lazarus and Flokman, 1984; Williams *et al.*, 1999) suggests that practitioners must draw upon internal (biographical) and external (social networks) resources, creating routines as a 'social defense system' against anxiety, stress and burnout (Menzies, 1988).

Public service occupations face considerable challenges in their work and it is doubtful whether they are able to respond effectively. The requirement to work across professional boundaries adds new skills, knowledge and disposition to training and practice. To reduce or contain their autonomy, limit their role in policy-making, while increasing the voice of others such as service users, can have undesirable consequences including a further loss of commitment and decline in self-respect (Foster and Wilding, 2000). For the future, what is required are public service occupations that are:

- educated, well-trained, committed to continuous learning, confident in their role, willing problem solvers and collaborators in multi-professional teams;
- working with a passionate sense of the public good and within an ethical code of practice;
- proactive in their efforts to be democratically accountable;
- grounded in the communities to which they relate;
- engaged in an ongoing dialogue with service users and other stakeholders;
- dedicated to the highest quality services and sensitive to the diversity of user needs.

In return, public service professionals can expect to operate within a relationship of trust in which there are fewer mechanisms of control. Ultimately, high quality public services cannot be produced by order but depend on the trust there is between provider and recipient, and between provider and the society in which they function. The growth of audits, targets and performance management is indicative of a low trust relationship. It can only further undermine rather than enhance the quality of provision as greater effort is invested in navigating the managerial hurdles, avoiding sanctions, and internalising the perception of self as someone not to be trusted.

Labour remains centralist in its desire to force change, displaying a fear of local democracy and a low level of trust in those professionals on whom its policies depend. Labour has demanded that public service organisations provide the highest quality services. They must achieve this objective in an ever changing and increasingly complex and diverse environment. Conscious of the real difficulties in resolving long-standing social issues, and regularly reminded by discerning and demanding publics, public service bodies must act in ways that combine effectiveness with resource constraints. To be effective, they must proactively collaborate with a wide range of other agencies. They must be open to scrutiny by others to ensure that standards are met and services are delivered effectively. Skilled leadership is required, with a capacity to hold these complexities and uncertainties while meeting their objectives.

7

Working Collaboratively, Working in Partnership

The previous two chapters explored the growing emphasis on service quality, leadership, organisational learning and a redefinition of professionalism. This chapter examines the equally extensive and profound shifts required in the ways provider organisations and social welfare professionals work collaboratively across boundaries (Leathard, 1997). The continuing presence of complex and seemingly insuperable social problems has brought universal acknowledgement that no agency or profession can be expected to address these single-handedly. Organisational and professional partiality and territoriality, with their inherent tendencies towards restrictive practices, alongside organisational, philosophical and cultural differences, have long been a detriment to the service user and have contributed to policy failure (Huntingdon, 1986; Jones *et al.*, 1994; Vanclay, 1996).

Professional 'failure' has been especially evident in each enquiry into the death or abuse of a child since the now infamous Maria Cowell enquiry (1973) continuing through to the most recent cases of Ainlee Labonte (2002) and Lord Laming's inquiry (2003) into the death of Victoria Climbie. The Labonte report notes, 'The agencies were compartmentalised in their knowledge and responses'. Elsewhere Murray (2000) noted that:

> The absence of integrated working is long-standing, culturally embedded, historically impervious, obvious to all concerned and deeply entrenched in central and local government (Appendix C, p. 105).

Such concerns have generated increasingly loud calls for the development of a culture of collaboration and partnerships between agencies, professions and across sectors. The expanding mixed economy of service providers, involving a greater number of marketised and fragmented agencies, stretching across three distinct sectors, coordinated and regulated by the state, has increased the need for collaboration. Government commitment to greater social inclusion, through 'joined-up' thinking and the dovetailing of policy objectives and practice expectations reflects and reinforces the message (PAT 17, 2000). Consequently, collaborative practice is expected and assumed to be good practice or is required by legislation.

There has been a marked growth in the number of formal and informal collaborative relationships across the policy spectrum between state agencies and the market, voluntary and community sectors, as well as within and between state agencies themselves. These have emerged in parallel with efforts to build 'partnerships' between service users and providers (see Chapter 8). To work in collaboration with other providers appears self-evident, irrefutable and long overdue. However, the extent to which the expectations surrounding collaborative working can be realised is much influenced by the surrounding context. These are ambiguous and contested concepts and their application can lead to the replication of the previous hierarchical professional and organisational relationships, as well as to the dilution of professional expertise.

The context

Public service marketisation included the creation of an organisational distinction between service provider and those purchaser agencies concerned with identifying need and strategic planning. Relationships between provider and purchaser organisations were to be conducted via a contract. Services became fragmented as competition was encouraged between the restructured state services and those from the market and non-profit sectors (Maddock and Morgan, 1998). This intensification of market relations generated mistrust and inter-sectoral hostility, deepening the low morale felt amongst those responsible for service delivery and reducing the capacity for strategic planning (Coote and Hunter, 1996). By the end of the 1980s such service fragmentation and the absence of sufficient coordination led to the statutory imposition, as in the 1990 NHS and Community Care Act, of inter-agency joint strategic and operational working.

On gaining office in 1997, the Labour government gave a clear signal that it would 'end competition and replace it with a new statutory duty of partnership' (DoH, 1997) so that services would 'pull together rather than pull apart'. Health authorities were required to produce a strategic health improvement programme (Himps) in which local authorities were involved and consulted. Managerial costs associated with running the internal markets were to be substantially reduced, the system of annual contracts between purchasers and providers was replaced by three to five year contracts to encourage more longer-term planning, and compulsory competitive tendering for local authorities was replaced by the 'Best Value' regime. The 1999 Health Act introduced 'flexibilities' to enable collaborative working by enabling local authorities and health care agencies to delegate functions to each other, pool funding, act as the lead commissioner on behalf of the other, and deliver integrated provision through the same organisational structures.

The twenty-six Health Action Zones, located in areas of high deprivation, were tasked with developing a range of creative partnerships to achieve health improvements. The Health and Social Care Act 2001 placed a duty of partnership on both local authorities and the NHS that requires Strategic Health Authorities and Primary Care Trusts to have local authority representatives on their Boards. It also permits the Secretary of State to designate as 'Care Trusts' those NHS Trusts and PCTs with partnership arrangements with local authorities. Partnership permeates the 2001 White Paper, 'Valuing People', on people with learning disabilities in which local Learning Disabilities Partnership Boards are fundamental for the realisation of the goals of 'person centred planning' and the transition from childhood to adulthood.

The Local Government Act (2000) requires local authorities to create a new inclusive non-statutory and non-executive body, a Local Strategic Partnership (LSP), and urges the development of smaller neighbourhood-based partnerships (DETR, 2001a). Eventually, these are to be established in all local authorities and accredited by regional Government Offices but initially have been a requirement only in the eighty-eight priority areas eligible for support under the Neighbourhood Renewal Fund. LSPs are identified as the key mechanism to bring together under one umbrella, local authorities, residents, private, voluntary and community sector organisations. They will be expected to act as the partnership overseeing all other partnerships, exercising a powerful influence over their constituent elements and beyond. Partnership strategies focused on specific policy areas, such as public health or children's services, will thus be subjected to scrutiny by the LSP.

The extent to which an LSP will be able to require detailed changes to service-specific strategies, however, remains unclear, as the expertise will ultimately lie within the more specialised partnerships. Rather, it is more likely that service-specific strategies will be constructed with reference to the broader strategy as devised by the LSP. As LSPs grow in confidence and build a knowledge base they will be able to identify connections and gaps between the more service-specific strategies. There are now few serious challenges to the principles of collaboration and practice, and few argue for a return to the professional and organisational silo mentality characteristic of the post-war period.

Collaborative concepts in use

A number of concepts, some well-established, attempt to capture current or proposed relationships between stakeholders in the delivery of public services. Collaboration is central to all. Nevertheless, there are significant differences between the different concepts although there is a tendency to view them as interchangeable. There are conceptual overlaps but in the orientation, focus, values and potential offered by each concept there are important distinctions. Three dominant concepts, those of inter-agency, interprofessional and partnership working are considered here. Although each has a specific meaning, they continue to evolve and retain flexibility in their usage which requires clarity in their application.

Inter-agency work

The concept of inter-agency work is not new to UK public provision. It was, for example, central to the Seebohm Report (1968) on personal social services. In proposing the creation of a 'generic social worker' within a single agency to replace the three previously distinct Child Care, Mental Health and Welfare Officers, Seebohm took the first step towards a beyond-disciplines position.

However, the importance given to inter-agency work diminished during the competitive climate of the 1980s only to be revived again at the beginning of the 1990s. A 1991 inter-departmental document, 'Working Together Under the Children Act' (DoH, 1991a), provided a framework for joint and multi-agency work, with emphasis on joint commissioning between agencies as a means to provide a 'seamless service' (DoH, 1995a).

Inter-agency working belongs to an era of professional certainty and rational planning in which providers were encouraged to find ways to improve strategic planning and delivery mechanisms. Incremental rather than planned change, together with professional and departmental rivalries, has ensured that the erosion of service boundaries has been very gradual and that individual agencies have rarely contained the full complement of professionals necessary to fully meet their responsibilities. Policies and practices designed to meet the needs of those working from one agency have often been at odds with those of another. At the agency boundary, precise duties and responsibilities are frequently an area of ambiguity and duplication.

Inter-agency work is closely associated with a geographic place, with those agencies that work in the same 'patch'. There are a number of levels on which this can take place. Collaboration might require some boundary adjustments, both physical and organisational, to ensure greater coterminosity. Failure to secure such adjustments has repeatedly proven to be a stumbling block in achieving successful inter-agency work. In a complex world of multiple providers, spatial coterminosity for two agencies can create spatial disunity for others. Boundary sharing might be restricted to those agencies with a special or significant relationship, but with multiple providers it is unlikely that 'significance' can only be applied in relation to one other agency. Agencies located in different structures of accountability, sometimes reinforced by political boundaries, face the additional challenge of balancing the potential advantage of coterminosity across all agencies within the structure or between themselves as a single agency and another located elsewhere. Political differences between areas of government may prevent any redrawing of boundaries irrespective of the potential benefits to service users.

Most commonly, inter-agency work involves the sharing of information, tasks and/or resources, agreeing procedures or protocols to address particular problems, reaching shared decisions, or planning and reviewing policies and procedures. Agencies frequently approach collaboration committed to their own agendas, priorities, perceptions, habits and customs, and with little intention of fundamentally changing these as a consequence of inter-agency activity. Too often, inter-agency working involves negotiating with others, while remaining firmly within one's own organisational framework. When participants work to their own agency agenda, the question of who owns inter-agency work becomes critical. When adopted as an 'afterthought' to organisational life, inter-agency activity will remain marginal and will not encourage investment and risk-taking. The more inter-agency work is perceived to be peripheral, the more difficult it becomes to ensure that beneficial outcomes permeate throughout each individual organisation (Hague *et al.*, 1995). This has been evident in the gap between joint strategic planning and joint working and is often the product of two distinct sets of players involved in each process and the inability of one to communicate effectively or convincingly to the other (PAT 17, 2000). If the outcome is that joint working becomes costly and prohibitive, it is likely that the collaborative work would cease, rather than risking organisational restructuring. Where change is anticipated, it is often perceived as having a marginal impact upon its core activity.

One of the strengths of inter-agency collaboration is that it is not restricted by sectoral boundaries but permits organisations to engage with any state, market or non-profit body. However, it is the agency that is the focus and determinant of membership in such a relationship. To that extent the concept and the practice has excluded the involvement of service users unless through a formal, usually proxy, organisation that can represent such interests. The direct involvement of service users or other community-based stakeholders has been circumscribed and limited by the emphasis on the organisation within the concept, despite often being the centre of such collaboration. Only recently, with the emergence of user organisations, have those interests been able to claim a voice at an inter-agency meeting and then only if they make an adjustment in their self-identity from user organisation to agency. Their entry is unlikely to be trouble free, as the approach is often top-down and managerial, focused on service providers, organised around professional knowledge, marshalling their collective resources and reaching agreements on how best to deliver services.

Inter-agency work is equivocal on the direct involvement of the various professions found within any single organisation and on how different perspectives can best be represented. The principle of inter-agency collaboration implies that in representing the interests of the organisation, it is management, standing above the interests of any one intra-agency subgroup, that is best able to lead such initiatives. In practice, it is not only agency managers who directly engage in the process and government guidelines explicitly state that the concept implies a commitment to joint work at all levels of the organisation (DoH, 1995b). Nevertheless, agency perspectives, policies, approaches and priorities are central to it and such organisational identity and ownership can only emerge via agreement at the level of senior management.

Where inter-agency work involves non-managerial professionals, the issue of agency accountability is one that needs clarification and is often the source of conflict. Hambleton *et al.* (1995), amongst others, highlight this tension between effectiveness in the achievement of the stated purposes underpinning the inter-agency collaboration and internal agency accountability that can result in a drift towards a relationship characterised by 'talk' rather than 'action'. When participants do not bring the authority to make decisions that in some way commit the agency, the exercise can quickly become ineffective and futile. Where there are differential levels of authority between participants, those with least authority can become marginal to or spoilers of decisions.

The need for collaboration can be so apparent that those involved can no longer justify continued separation and decide to merge (Audit Commission, 1993). Data to emerge from recent efforts at greater integration between local government departments involving, for example, former education departments and children services within social services departments, highlight a number of difficulties. There is some evidence that where energy has been directed at building integrated organisational and managerial structures the development of seamless service delivery are neglected, creating resistance amongst front-line staff and placing such initiatives at risk (DoH, 2001d).

Change strategies of this nature tend to be managerially driven with declining ownership of the change process and outcomes, the further one moves from the 'centre' of change. There is professional resistance too when integrated management structures result in professionals being managed by a professional from another discipline. Such restructuring highlights the differences between agencies in the respective understandings of what appears to be a common language. Concepts such as 'management', 'supervision', or 'responding to need' can have quite different meanings depending on the professional context in which they are applied. Such different meanings are then embedded in professional practices and understandings of professional role. The more extensive are such differences and the more they appear to have been neglected by management in the change process the greater the resistance amongst professionals.

The emergence of new organisational structures creates tensions at the boundary between the new structure and other agencies. For example, in mergers between education and social services relationships with primary healthcare and schools become critical. Mergers involving more than two organisations are likely to create conflict around differential power and influence, reflecting the variable relationships to whatever is defined as the 'core' business of the newly merged body.

Agency mergers built on integrated professional practices can leave organisational structures intact with staff continuing to operate separate line management, budgets, decision-making and accountability structures. However, working from within such 'intact' organisations can allow for greater creativity in designing integrated approaches to user-focused service delivery. A capacity to hold the vision of integrated provision that is seen to deliver better service outcomes could prove to be sufficiently resilient to overcome organisational differences, provided integrated structures are the next step. Without them it is likely that the organisational differences will prevail and undermine joint practice. The new voluntary 'Care Trusts' that bring together adult health and social care provision face the challenge of finding the right balance between a focus on professional practice and organisational structures.

Inter-professional collaboration

Professional loyalties, knowledge and insights offer the possibility of reaching out beyond organisational boundaries to colleagues located elsewhere. Inter-professionalism focuses not on organisational boundaries and procedures but on encouraging collaboration between those with different professional roles in any common situation. Inter-professional working is considered essential given the complexity of the issues to be addressed and the partial knowledge and skill base of any single professional group. By combining distinct contributions each is valued and all benefit from what others bring.

At a pragmatic level, inter-professionalism is oriented around a problem-solving approach that concentrates on the range of skills, knowledge and experience contained within the multi-professional team. Such teams can be contained within single or multiple agencies. Policy and practice guidelines encourage the development of a jointly owned strategy, agreed procedures, shared resources, the exchange of information, and regular reviews based on common criteria for the evaluation of effectiveness. Inter-professionalism needs to be distinguished from multi-professionalism that is more a by-product of inter-agency collaboration. This does not require participants to abandon or re-examine their professional cultures, practices or knowledge base. It is not an integrative approach requiring the development of new professional practices but is concerned with the harmonisation of different and sometimes competing disciplines.

Inter-professionalism challenges the bureaucratic tendencies within public service organisations. Professional expertise can be restricted and autonomy curtailed by the boundaries, rules and procedures imposed by organisational requirements. Professionals can look beyond the confines of any single agency and, holding the service user as the central focus, identify the contribution of other professional colleagues in the satisfaction of user needs. Unlike inter-agency work, inter-professionalism acknowledges the range and diversity of professions within a single agency. It thus encourages the development of horizontal linkages within and across organisational boundaries (Audit Commission, 1992).

As in inter-agency work, while the objective is an improved service, inter-professionalism does not directly engage either the service user or other non-professional workers, such as volunteers or carers. However, as new user organisations emerge there is a tendency towards the creation of the 'professionalised user'. Thus individual users who become involved in consultative processes, and have not been too critical or disruptive, are regularly invited to participate in subsequent consultations and are offered training and support to enable them to be more effective. The pressure to involve service users combined with the difficulties of engaging them in formal structures ensures that those recruited are a scarce resource. Their presence, as semi-permanent user 'representatives', acts as a legitimating mechanism reducing the pressure to develop more appropriate structures with a larger constituency (see Chapter 8).

Inter-professionalism remains neutral as to whether some professional perspectives, however partial, are valued or count for more than others. To admit to a differential weighting in values, status, and power undermines the concept's potency as the discourse and outcomes would be seen to reflect those more powerful professions. Such historical and entrenched hierarchical relationships highlight the need for behavioural and attitudinal changes before the potential of inter-professionalism can be realised (Maglacas, 1988). While inter-professionalism provides an opportunity to identify, explore, and overcome rivalries and restricted perceptions, there is no requirement to do so and in practice there is a tendency to neglect them (Walsh *et al.*, 1981).

Inter-professionalism is equally silent on whether all public service occupational groups are entitled to be designated as a profession. The denial of professional recognition to any key occupation undermines the development of productive relationships founded on a single unifying concept. Conversely, internal occupational anxieties associated with status or identity weakens the collaborative relationship, producing deferential and defensive behaviour. While some professions such as medicine, planning or architecture remain secure, others such as social work, nursing or regeneration works do not, and remain ambivalent about embracing professional status. Inter-professionalism implies some agreement and shared understanding on both the nature and desirability of professionalism. Differential power and influence, relative success in the achievement of professional recognition, disagreements over the desired meaning of professionalism, and a commitment to what have been the consequences of professionalism all continue to be sources of contestation within and between occupational groups and between them and the state.

A professional identity is only one of a number of identities available in the workplace. Other powerful and competing identities such as trade unionist or employee as well as those constructed around social identities such as race/ethnicity or gender are also present. Individuals hold multiple identities and the significance of a professional identity will fluctuate over time and between occupational groups and agencies. Unless professions take greater account of other significant identities, efforts to encourage inter-professionalism will flounder as a basis for collective identity amongst public service workers. Historically, professionalism has worked against the interests of particular social groups. As these have grown in strength and found a voice and identity, professionalism continues to be trapped by its past. On the one hand it provides role confidence and offers the promise of status and labour market security whilst on the other it is a symbol of privilege, elitism and the pursuit of self-interest.

Working in partnership

Current policy, in response to increased complexity, both in relation to the issues to be tackled and the range of stakeholders involved, requires not only improved coordination but partnerships involving all stakeholders (DETR, 2001a). This inclusive approach is to include the recipients of any service or programme (McArthur, 1996) and for some writers is 'premised on the bottom-up notion of community consultation, involvement and ultimately ownership...' (Hughes and Carmichael, 1998: 1).

By involving all stakeholders, partnerships are expected to produce a deeper understanding of the problem and its context and consequently more creative, and mutually owned responses (Wilkinson and Applebee, 1999). They are a means to generate information sharing, improve communication, enable a better understanding of stakeholder contributions to emerge, avoid duplication, reduce inefficiencies and identify opportunities for the effective sharing of resources. They are also meant to act as effective vehicles to lever in external resources inaccessible to any one party, facilitate mutual learning and, through dialogue and risk-taking, discover new approaches (Maddock and Morgan, 1997). More significantly, partnership implies an openness in decision-making, responsibility and accountability (Pugh, 1997). In an ideal form, they are characterised by trust, respect, reciprocity and mutuality. Such coalitions seek agreement on strategic priorities, committing their wider constituencies to a set of objectives, values, and action plans that impinge not only on others but also on themselves. Recent government publications suggest that partnership is, 'a mechanism for change...the maximising of influence...being able to build a way of working for the future, something that will last longer than the life of the project...' (DfEE, 1998b: 9).

Partnerships are active relationships, built up over time and not abandoned when difficulties arise. To achieve this they require, 'regular maintenance and support on a continuing basis, if they are to survive and flourish' (Mayo, 1997). They rely on an active commitment to networking, searching for and maximising 'win-win' situations, an open and reflexive dialogue, and a willingness to invest without the expectation of short-term dividends. Participants require a proficiency in inter-personal relationships and sensitivity to group dynamics as well as a capacity to deal with the formal business. Successful partnerships cannot be imposed but require participants who genuinely want to work in partnership (DoH, 2001).

Guidelines for effective partnership working are increasingly available (Taylor, 1995; Audit Commission, 1998; LGA, 1999, 2001, 2002). Stewart *et al.* (1999) identify nine drivers in a positive cycle of collaboration:

1. Consultation or engagement at all stages with all stakeholders
2. Open and facilitative organisational structures to ensure dialogue
3. Flexible and responsive systems
4. Clarity on task definition and accountability
5. An implementation culture of 'can-do'
6. A capacity to act strategically
7. Rewards for innovation
8. Impact evaluation
9. Continuous learning.

The Department of Health paper, 'Keys to Partnership' (2001d) identifies nine building blocks in what it describes as a 'partnership readiness framework':

1. Shared vision, values and principles
2. Specific goals in relation to policy and service changes
3. A willingness to explore new service options
4. Clarity about the boundaries to the partnership
5. Clarity about organisational roles in relation to commissioning, purchasing and service provision

6. Agreement on shared resources
7. Effective leadership
8. Dedicated partnership development capacity
9. The development and sustaining of good personal relationships.

A further ten components for partnership working are then added:

1. Strategic partnerships concerned with governance and the overarching framework and objectives
2. Engagement with users and other local people
3. Promoting ownership via effective communication and sharing the benefits of partnership
4. Planning and delivery of strategic decisions to ensure the achievement of planned changes in service delivery
5. Shared assessment and care management systems
6. Integrated information and support systems
7. Shared training
8. Joint workforce planning
9. An integrated monitoring and review system
10. Shared approach to performance and audit.

Partnerships can operate either within a formal structure or as a set of informal relationships. They range from the very pragmatic, in which the parties collaborate on a single short-term task, to longer-term relationships such that it becomes hard to imagine working in any other way. Mackintosh (1992) identifies three partnership models. In the 'synergy model', the sum is greater than the parts with the outcome better than that produced by all those concerned when working separately. The 'budget enlargement model' is designed pragmatically to lever in additional funds. The 'transformative model' is innovative and change oriented. Snape and Stewart (1996) identify three similar types described as, 'facilitating', 'coordinating' and 'implementing' partnerships. Facilitating partnerships manage entrenched, highly problematic, contentious and/or politically sensitive issues in which issues of power are at stake, and trust and solidarity are essential for success. Coordinating partnerships focus on less contentious issues and where partners agree on priorities but are equally concerned with other pressing demands specific to themselves. Implementing partnerships are more pragmatic, and time limited, concerned with specific and mutually beneficial projects.

Partnership work is the most inclusive of the collaborative concepts. They can transcend organisational, professional and sectoral boundaries, and can operate at different levels of government, local, regional, national and supranational. It is the only collaborative concept currently in use that explicitly embraces the service user and other community stakeholders. According to the PAT 17 Performance and Innovation Unit (2000) report (DETR, 2000a), a holistic approach can be achieved only by creating, '...a new relationship between the public sector and the individuals and communities they serve' (p. 21), based on dialogue. Yet, its flexibility creates problems in establishing whether or not an appropriate partnership is in place, in relation to both its inclusion of all the legitimate stakeholders and nature of its work.

Unlike other collaborations, partnership includes the democratically elected representative, as well as those government officials who might have no service provision responsibility, but who can add a new dimension to the more established relationship between service provider and service user. However, inclusive and powerful partnerships could be seen to threaten the traditional role of the elected representative (Lowndes *et al.*, 1997). Partnerships, such as those envisaged for LSPs, offer the prospect of a powerful coalition of unelected and unrepresentative, professionals and corporate interests working in ways in which decision-making, responsibility and accountability are opaque. While the need to include those participants who feel marginal to the process has been recognised, less attention has been given to the difficulties non-participants will have in influencing what will be powerful decision-making bodies.

The seductiveness of collaboration

It is difficult to find a contemporary policy document or set of good practice guidelines that does not have collaboration as the central strategy for the delivery of welfare, whilst the professional literature extol its virtues (Huxham, 1996; Gillies, 1998). The pressure to collaborate and join together in partnership is overwhelming (Mayo, 1997).

The dominant perception is that collaborative partnerships are an essential prerequisite for the organisation of contemporary welfare practice. Such was the fragmentation between and within public service organisations and professionals that working together around the same objectives had much merit. Similarly, the issues to be tackled are often complex, multi-faceted, and obdurate (Wilkinson, 1997) and the multitude of previously uncoordinated efforts have failed to address them. For those managers, professionals and other stakeholders with an insight into the limitations and shortcomings, as well as the strengths, of fragmented services and partial contributions, the prospect of addressing the 'wicked issues' (Stewart, 1996) with a systemic or comprehensive approach has a strong appeal. The diversity and complexity of contemporary life is such that any one organisation or professional is unlikely to have a sufficient grasp or understanding of the range and significance of emergent needs amongst the population. Pooled knowledge and experience is therefore crucial to any credible and sustainable problem analysis. Critics might suggest that this pooling of knowledge could lead to a dispersal of responsibility such that all can contribute, but no one can be held responsible for any shortcomings.

In working together, opportunities are maximised for identifying and pursuing innovative approaches that go beyond the boundaries and experience of any one of the partners. Such innovations can be effective vehicles to challenge well-established perceptions of professional narrow-mindedness and provide opportunities for organisational change. The inclusion of those who have traditionally been marginal to any service planning or implementation process, especially in the voluntary or community sectors, creates the possibility of levering in new and additional resources. These include voluntary labour, access to local networks and knowledge. It also increases the likelihood that any emergent strategy will have local ownership and legitimation. Such additions are important and their absence has been identified as a contributory factor in earlier failures. The recognition of the non-profit and community sectors as legitimate stakeholders and their inclusion in the service delivery process does more than adding local legitimacy. Their sense of ownership and engagement contributes directly to the likely success and sustainability of any initiative (Gillies, 1998). Energy that was previously directed at criticising the work of mainstream providers is now devoted to the pursuit of common goals and the resolution of more immediate and practical problems of delivering services. The inclusion of the market sector offers the prospect of levering in additional financial resources, although such resources are often perceived of not as 'additions' but rather 'substitutes' for public finance. In practice, too, it has more frequently generated resources in kind such as private sector secondments to local agencies, or training opportunities, as well as a public perception of approval.

Collaborative partnerships offer a number of secondary benefits to participating stakeholders. Indeed, these by-products of the process can be the primary reason for becoming involved or continuing to be so. Thus, for those in the non-profit and community sectors, partnerships with colleagues in the state and market sectors bring with them increased prominence, recognition and status. They are no longer to be on the margins, offering supplementary or complementary services, or occasionally recognised as path breaking and innovative in response to a previously unidentified need that henceforth will be adopted by mainstream providers. They are now central to the process. To be at the heart of decision-making, a player of importance who is able to make a difference or claim that one's presence was influential, has its own intrinsic rewards. With this, too, comes status and recognition, along with opportunities for advancement, not only for specific agencies or the sector as a whole but also for those individuals acting as its representatives.

The non-profit sector's espoused values and attributes have been identified as precisely those now required throughout the organisation of social welfare. Flexibility, responsiveness, innovation, voluntarism, organisational diversity, networking, closeness to both the service user and local community, and a capacity to provide services on limited budgets are all key attributes of a modern service. The values and methods of the poor cousin of welfare are now to be the benchmark for all. The very concept of partnership or collaboration can be claimed by the voluntary and community sectors as the traditional way of working, the importance of which has finally been understood by government and policy makers. The espousal of such values and methods does not mean that these will always be found in practice. Nevertheless, the promotion of collaborative work and establishment of formal partnerships is perceived within the sector as an endorsement of its way of working and a vindication of its constant urging of a holistic approach.

Formal partnerships can also be a mechanism by which professionals can be held to account and dominant modes of professional thinking challenged. However, the inclusion of service users and the non-profit sector, with the explicit message that they are part of the solution, suggests that they too must take greater responsibility for the meeting of individual and collective needs. There is also the expectation that this will generate a flow of resources to the sector commensurate with its new significance. While there may be some inverted sectoral pride in its capacity to do much for little, in reality most agencies would like to see more funds.

The prospect of additional funds, greater influence and the apparent endorsement of a way of working can have its drawbacks. The sector has at least temporarily forgotten why it previously prided itself in its autonomy and independence from the state and the market. Partnership work might bring advantages to all but at a price, and for non-profit organisations that may well be the price of silence, the end of criticism. However, successful and more consistent experiences of working collaboratively may enable participants to feel secure and adept in managing, if not always resolving, conflict.

For the market sector, participation in inter-sectoral collaboration offers few immediate benefits. The market place remains the primary orientation and source of reward, be it material, public recognition or personal enhancement. Partnership working may place new demands on the sector as it comes to terms with different values and approaches that need to be understood even if the perceived task is to then change them. Partnerships do provide the market with an opportunity to demonstrate the relevance of its own long established approaches and persuade others to adopt these. It is an opportunity to promote its priorities and secure their inclusion on the policy agenda, and to control what the market sees as the excesses of others in respect of expenditure, bureaucracy and policy responses. The requirement that all partners endorse proposals to central government for funding is a guarantee that market priorities are taken into account.

The general endorsement of partnerships has already had an impact on corporate giving to the non-profit sector (Mullen, 1997, see Chapter 3). There is some evidence of a more strategic approach and an expectation of a more interventionist and hands-on role, as a condition for what is still often only limited funding (Marx, 1999). This includes both a greater say in which projects are to benefit from funding and a requirement to open agency structures, processes, and programmes to direct influence by the funders.

These are presented in the form of executives making a personal contribution to a good cause, fulfilling their civic obligations, or as an example of the sector offering expertise to individual agencies within a more ethical approach. Yet, irrespective of their genuineness, such initiatives offer the market greater influence over service provision and the conditions under which they are offered, as well as providing a justification for reduced corporate taxation.

Partnership is a useful device to demonstrate that the market is fulfilling its civic duty, and is not solely concerned with the maximisation of profit and the accumulation of personal wealth. Such collaborative problem-solving deflects any sectoral liability for the emergence and persistence of complex social problems. Collaboration implies that all stakeholders are concerned to address what can be defined as inevitable products of a complex world in which the concept of 'blame' or 'responsibility' is inappropriate and unhelpful in finding a solution. Partnerships do not require the active involvement of the major corporations operating within the local economy. Sectoral representation has been assigned to secondary agencies, such as Chambers of Commerce, representing small and medium size business interests, or government quangos such as the Learning and Skills Councils for whom partnership development is part of their mission and strategy. Thus, the real value of partnership for the market sector has been the appearance of sectoral commitment and engagement without a serious challenge to the local activities of the large and powerful corporations. The absence of such influential bodies continues to undermine the potential of formal partnerships.

For state-employed managers and professionals, partnership work offers benefits that go beyond the maximisation of skills, knowledge and resources to tackle complex social issues. Partnerships not only bring stakeholders together but also imply joint ownership and responsibility for decisions taken. The opportunity to share responsibility between all is a significant benefit for a sector that has faced consistent public criticism and has been undermined by governments of all persuasion over a twenty-five year period. Now all stakeholders, critics included, will come to appreciate the difficulties and complexities and take some responsibility for what is agreed. Partnerships act not only to share responsibility but also, most importantly, help to silence public service critics. Other stakeholders can no longer, as partners to an agreement, immediately condemn new initiatives or blame service providers for any failings. They too are responsible for identifying need, understanding social issues, and devising effective strategies. Over time, regular cross-sectoral dialogue will create personal and agency relationships and a commitment to their continuation will be sufficient to silence or at least modify, previously vocal, oppositional voices. Moreover partnerships, especially when dominated by professionals, help to de-politicise issues and view them as concerns requiring more sophisticated technical solutions.

Partnerships provide an opportunity for a renewed engagement and offer a way forward. Faced with intractable problems, collaboration provides a different strategy that will require investment and resources, an area of expertise to be developed and another opportunity to re-examine organisational structures and processes. However, the capacity for partnership work to fundamentally change understanding, values, and behaviour at the level of individual, organisation and sector, has still to be demonstrated. The reality has been that establishing effective collaborative relationships and processes has been elusive.

Dilemmas and challenges

Inter-agency work

From the perspective of a service user the need for a 'seamless' service is self-evident. If dependent upon two organisations for the delivery of services, it is not unreasonable for the service user to expect these public service bodies to work closely together, sharing information and communicating appropriately, coordinating provision, avoiding duplication, and working together to meet the user's needs. Unfortunately, the all too common experience is to find each organisation operating to different eligibility criteria, working to different geographic boundaries, failing to inform each other of their intended interventions, disputing respective roles and responsibilities, and duplicating or failing to provide services. Such relationships are often dominated by a deep reluctance to share information and resources and even by competitiveness or rivalry rather than collaboration. Conversely, service users regularly experience constant onward referrals and multiple agency assessments without benefiting from any direct service from any single agency.

Inter-agency work, including the 'joint management' of services originally provided by separate organisations, is meant to address such problems (DoH, 1995b). The interpretation of 'joint working' and what might be implied for each organisation is crucial to subsequent relations. A minimalist interpretation requires organisations to respond to requests for information or provide notice of their intentions. Otherwise, they remain as an independent entity with their own procedures, decision-making and accountability structures, working to their own priorities and within their professional frameworks. Other organisations are expected to take account and accommodate such data in their own actions. A more proactive approach involves each organisation sharing not only data but also how it functions and being prepared to change priorities, structures and processes in the light of what is learned in the process. Progress has been limited by the absence of the necessary commitment to organisational learning and change.

Well-established complex organisational patterns and cultures cannot be changed overnight. Yet, too often history and tradition, along with existing practices, current pressures and changes within each collaborating agency, are given insufficient attention. Similarly, as a predominantly managerial initiative, those responsible for service delivery are insufficiently consulted or are ill-informed, and consequently feel little sense of ownership or remain suspicious of managerial motivation. Inter-agency work can be an excuse to avoid or cover-up agency-specific problems or an opportunity to offload difficult service delivery problems on to other agencies and especially on those outside the collaborative forum. In other words, proactive inter-agency working, ironically, can require more openness and honesty at all levels than that prevailing within any one of the organisations involved.

Rarely is sufficient attention given to the respective strengths within each agency, the practices and procedures that had proven successful, and what can be learnt from each other. Not enough time is set aside to gain a mutual and appreciative understanding of the different agencies, professional and sectoral perceptions and approaches that help shape organisational responses to user need. The lack of a common language and understanding or complementary roles across agencies, in relation to particular user groups or specific conditions, has been a major impediment to the development of a common agenda. Rather, the continuation of traditional agency-specific procedures and processes within new inter-agency structures reinforces staff loyalties to parent agencies, creating obstacles to change and new practices.

An expectation that staff will collaborate is unrealistic while the agencies continue to work to different terms and conditions, report to different line managements, operate within different forms of supervision, and work to different budgets. Local management, often fearful of a diminished span of control or even redundancy, remain adverse to risk-taking implied by the new practices. Consequently, they fail to convey a common 'joint' approach but rather fuel staff uncertainty with inconsistent messages or simply fail to communicate. For some, the managerial requirements for effective inter-agency collaboration are beyond their skills. They lack the capacity of 'social reflexivity' to maintain and enhance team member well-being (West, 1994). Managers are charged with getting things done, through and with others, in order to achieve specific goals and objectives (Drucker, 1988; Salaman, 1995). Here, success is dependent upon possession of different leadership skills so as to win colleagues over to a new organisational vision and create an organisational environment in which it is safe to communicate openly, including one's anxieties to change. An inconsistent and faltering managerial response can leave staff lacking confidence, defensive and protective of their self-interests rather than willing to take risks, change behaviour or appreciate methods developed within a collaborating agency.

Inter-professional work

A number of major obstacles have been experienced in joint working across professional boundaries both within and between organisations or sectors. As services for a specific user group often span a number of agencies and sectors, there is necessarily some overlap with those issues raised in inter-agency collaboration. However, calls for more collaboration come at the same time as specific professions feel threatened by a loss of identity and autonomy and are struggling to maintain a professional role. Inter-professionalism can be perceived as an attempt to de-professionalise or undermine professional legitimacy. Typical problems in developing inter-professional collaboration include:

- anxiety over the continued domination of particular professions;
- the capacity to maintain a legitimate professional role within an inter-professional framework;

- an insufficient appreciation of professional roles and cultural diversity, and an absence of shared meanings and language;
- insufficient attention to the emotional aspects that are the product of professional relationships built on competition, in which other professionals have been viewed with antipathy rather than as collaborators, and generating envy, jealousy, status and resource rivalry, inferiority, fear, anger and resentment;
- competing priorities between organisational and professional imperatives;
- constant policy changes producing professional and organisational anxiety, 'initiative fatigue', and reducing the capacity to engage with the demands of collaboration.

One of the most common problems occurs over the management of inter-professional initiatives. Professionals have resisted attempts to introduce non-professional specific management, often because line management and professional supervision have been contained within a single managerial role. The 'Keys to Partnership' (DoH, 2001d) document suggests that the issue should be re-conceptualised in terms of 'accountability' rather than 'management'. Four dimensions of accountability, all of which need to be addressed, are identified:

1. To the public agency for the expected outcomes
2. To the user for delivering what is needed
3. To the professional body for standards of practice
4. To the 'manager' for 'line accountability' issues, such as absence or disciplinary concerns.

It is unlikely that all four dimensions can be addressed through one role or agency and it suggests that how they are resolved will be a matter for negotiation. However, while it is useful to acknowledge different, and sometimes competing, dimensions of accountability this approach contradicts the document's early emphasis on working with complexity. The prospect of potentially four different accountability structures could be a recipe for a protracted and exhausting process of negotiation followed by ongoing conflict at the boundary of each system.

Partnership work

Formal 'partnerships' are now found across all public sector activity and, for the current government, despite or because of their opaqueness, represent the vision of a cohesive inclusive society of collaborating citizens, organisations and sectors (Hastings, 1996; Atkinson, 1999). The language of partnership is much abused and is utilised even when what is actually being described resembles more of a traditional contractual relationship. For Snape and Stewart (1996), partnership had already begun to lose its meaning before Labour's 1997 election breakthrough. Stewart (1994) had already sounded an early warning that 'the ambition of the initiative may exceed the political will and the administrative capacity to deliver it' (p. 137).

As with other forms of collaboration, participants do not necessarily take their place at the partnership table as committed collaborators (Clarke, 1996; Local Government Association, 1997). They bring to such arrangements diverse agendas, priorities, and levels of commitment to a shared outcome and have uneven levels of awareness about the need for strategic collaboration. Participants are often reluctant collaborators, there because partnerships are rapidly becoming a statutory requirement or an essential prerequisite for government and private sector funding (DETR, 2001b). Alternatively, partners are as concerned with the partnership mechanism as a means by which to pursue a number of other interests.

For partners to espouse collaborative working, while elsewhere behaving in contrary ways, presents real problems. Thus non-profit sector representatives can find themselves simultaneously pressurised by a local authority 'partner' into organisational mergers, to abandon development activity or accept a larger service delivery role against its objectives or capacity (Miller, 1999). While some may expect greater behavioural consistency, other partners understand collaboration as a pragmatic necessity that does not imply any behavioural change in other areas of operation. Previous relationships, of hierarchy and power, can continue to dog all participants (Atkinson, 1999). Partnerships may appear to be a solution that can free participants from the past with its 'parochialism, rivalries, suspicions, complacency, and procrastinations' (Bassett, 1996: 545) but equally it is these that undermine the possibility of partnership.

For all participants, the key partnership requirements of trust, listening, networking, openness to learning and a willingness to change priorities or practice for the common good are challenging. These contrast sharply with the requirements of the traditional forms of bargaining, negotiating and conflict strategies. Switching from one mode to another takes time and, to date, some participants have yet to be convinced of the benefits that such a change would bring. The experience of partnership activity has left some stakeholders feeling that they continue to be marginalised, excluded or ignored. This has become a common lament amongst non-profit sector representatives, who have stated repeatedly that while they have much experience of successful intra-sector partnerships, these remain a rarity as far as inter-sectoral work is concerned. Partnerships are said to lack internal consistency. Invitations to the non-profit sector to participate are made reluctantly and only after sustained complaints about their exclusion. The sector regularly complains that it rarely receives additional resources to better enable it to properly fulfill the role. The introduction of the Community Empowerment Fund (SEU, 2001), as part of the strategy on neighbourhood renewal, is designed to address these concerns over sectoral capacity building. Already there are examples of the fund creating a need as well as responding to one, as monies have been secured to support work previously funded under other programmes.

Inter-sectoral cultural clashes have also been experienced over how business should be conducted, especially over issues of legitimacy, accountability and representativeness. Non-profit representatives express concern with issues of process, with how decisions are made and who is involved, and have demanded more time for sector-wide consultation (Miller, 1999). Tightly imposed funding deadlines, however unreasonable, make such expectations seem excessive to other partners. In contrast, market sector partners expect, as mandated representatives, to take decisions, initiate action in response to new opportunities, and remain focused on outcomes and end goals. Once decisions have been taken on the objectives and the direction to be followed, the construction of detailed reports can be left to designated officers who are trusted with an accurate interpretation of discussions and the practical application of general principles. Repeated failures to meet such expectations can be resolved by their dismissal from the post.

Non-profit sector participants tend to be uncomfortable with such an approach, wanting to approve all final documents. Those that do not match their expectations can be signs of betrayal or deception. For the private sector, these merely reflect pragmatic shifts introduced of necessity to meet rapidly altered circumstances. Such differing reactions are understandable given that private sector delegates are more likely to believe that their views are always taken into account.

Once decisions are taken, signatories expect all sectors to abide by the outcome. This can be difficult to realise within the non-profit sector with its history of agency and personal autonomy, little experience of speaking collectively, and with few mechanisms to do so. Thus 'managing' the sector and its individual member responses to proposals or decisions becomes a significant part of the role for any partnership participant. For some, public criticism of fellow collaborators are legitimate ways of working and extracting further concessions, especially when they are perceived to be operating in an unprincipled manner or with questionable motivations or values. Other partners can interpret such behaviour as infantile posturing, an abandonment of dialogue, a lack of commitment to change, and as undermining the partnership process by casting doubts on the capacity of sector delegates to deliver its part of the agreement.

Amongst local authority representatives the view prevails that only they as elected representatives or public servants have appropriate authority to make policy judgements and interventions. Formal partnership structures are resisted by some as representing a backdoor method to expand the influence of the market sector over local political decision-making. The need to secure government funds has countered or stifled such tendencies and ensured an opportunistic 'enthusiasm' for partnerships. Local authority attitudes also reflect the status and power of the elected members who are directly involved. Junior and opposition councillors may be enthusiastic but lack influence within the council chamber, raising anxiety amongst other partners that key decisions are made elsewhere.

There are challenges for all three sectors, as well as between them, in relation to legitimacy and accountability. Non-profit sector participants are often employees of the sector, rather than citizen-representatives from an organisation. They are, therefore, vulnerable to the charge that, as professionals, they have no legitimacy to speak as the voice of a sector that makes much of its voluntary or citizen base. Conversely, such professional backgrounds and aspirations make them easier to work with than the more unpredictable, awkward and potentially troublesome citizen-delegates. Similarly, market sector participants may not be directly involved in the world of commerce or industry. Rather, they are often employed by bodies established to be the voice of business, to represent the general interests of the market and to reflect its principles and beliefs. Direct access to corporate directors is often limited (Oatley and Lambert, 1995). While the councillor's electoral base would appear to guarantee their legitimacy, persistently low turnouts for local elections, the small size of the electorate, and the limitations of representative democracy have all undermined their position (Hambleton, 1998).

Partnerships built around specific and quite limited objectives are more likely to succeed in producing more effective policy outcomes, based on the maximisation of available resources. More ambitious initiatives are likely to be controversial, generating either fundamental conflicts of interest or impressive rhetoric but little of substance (DETR, 2000c). Central to any initiative, however limited, must be the opportunity to spend time in exploring existing cultural differences. Managing this requires skill, patience, commitment and perseverance, as well as time. Often these are in short supply especially when partnerships are constructed around specific funding requirements. Such pressing demands, the outcomes of which can be the difference between survival and closure for some agencies, prevent the emergence of sustainable strategic partnerships based on informal networking and grounded in trust, mutuality and shared vision. Instead, parties are more likely to approach the partnership with a history of mistrust and antagonism, seeking to maximise their own interests.

Partnerships need clarity of purpose and remain focused on agreed goals, as well as trusting, honest and committed relationships (DoH, 2001d). They require an appropriate balance in relation to representation, quality and skills, money and resources, innovative practice, and to be well networked with local communities. The real test is whether, on the basis of what each partner knows about the other, they are able to take risks and engage in the manner that is required. Only if all partners do so, can partnerships develop. While the feeling persists that this will prove to be yet another albeit more sophisticated mechanism to further particular interests, 'partners' will remain cautious about any committed engagement.

8

The Engagement of Service Users

The belief that those who use and benefit from services should be involved in their planning and evaluation has never been stronger (Wilson, 1998). Following the community care legislation (NHS and Community Care Act, 1990) and the Citizen's and Patient's Charters (HMSO, 1991), it is recognised that a central purpose of intervention is the 'empowerment' of service users. To this end individual users can expect to have an opportunity to contribute to the definition of need, a copy of any final assessment, the identification of appropriate responses, involvement in any review process, and be provided with, and informed about, mechanisms for complaint.

The inclusion of service users, and those organisations created to represent them, is premised on the assumption that to do so will ensure greater service diversity and sensitivity to individual needs, and therefore more effective services (Audit Commission, 2001; Brown, 2000). While the policy message is direct and forthright it can ignore the complexities and messiness of the reality. There are at least three interwoven stories to be told in relation to the changing place of service users. These are explored in this chapter and can be summarised as, how users became a central focus in service considerations, the emergence of competing models of user engagement, and the deconstruction of the homogeneous category of service user.

Users as the key to policy development

Service user involvement, especially in relation to individual 'care plans', challenges both the dominance of professional knowledge and a 'one service fits all' mentality. Labour first set out its position in the Green Paper, 'New Contract for Welfare' (DSS, 1998a):

> A modern service, like its customers (who are at the centre – not the end – of service delivery) is active in its efficiency, its support, its transparency, in tailoring its services to individual needs...it will also reclaim and reshape an ethos of public service (pp. 71–8).

Under the Health and Social Care Act (2001), every NHS body has a duty to consult and involve the public in health services. Following consultation, Labour extended user and public involvement in health by creating new structures and mechanisms to be fully operational by April 2003 (DoH, 2001b).

> We want to move away from a system of patients being on the outside to one where the voices of patients, their carers and the public generally are heard and listened to through every level of the service, acting as a lever for change and improvement (DoH, 2001b: para. 2.1).

A Patient Advice and Liaison service (PALS), offering a one-stop-shop advice service is to be established within each hospital and PCT whilst a separate Independent Complaints Advocacy Service is to be created. The latter is linked to the new Commission for Patient and Public Involvement in Health (CPPIH). This will set up local network bodies with outreach teams, employed by and accountable to the Commission, responsible for supporting community groups and promoting public involvement. Both the Commission and the local bodies are to be 'driven' by lay reference panels whose membership will be drawn from the new Patient Forums, the LSPs, the voluntary sector and local elected representatives. Patient Forums are to be established in every NHS and PCT to represent the local community views on the quality and configuration of health services. Forums will be given a place on the Strategic Health Authority Boards. Health services have also been subjected to greater democratic accountability through local authority Overview and Scrutiny Committees. These have been provided with specific powers to look at local NHS provision, as part of their role in health improvement and reducing health inequalities.

What is the model?

Labour has called for a cultural change inside public service agencies and created new lead roles, as in the Audit Commission's appointment of a Head of User Focus, with the challenge to 'change our whole culture to embrace a customer perspective' (Audit Commission, 2001). Simultaneously, the Commission announced plans to introduce a citizen-focused audit and inspection process and to undertake user-focused research on policy outcomes. However, the amount and quality of opportunities for such engagement varies across policies and provider agencies, and whether the service user 'voice' has any greater impact on policy or professional practice is a moot point.

Confusion remains over the use of language and the model of user involvement to be adopted. Labour has been reluctant to abandon the market-oriented terminology of 'customer' and 'consumer' inherited from the New Right. Both suggest an economic transaction largely absent from those public services concerned with health and welfare. These are more applicable, and used in relation to public transport or leisure services when a direct monetary transaction is involved, and in those services, such as refuse collection, when an albeit indirect payment through the Council Tax is assumed. The language of the 'consumer' when applied to health and welfare services users rarely reflects the sovereignty asserted by market models.

Labour also continues to employ those professionally derived labels, such as 'patient', 'client', 'tenant', 'pupil' and 'claimant'. These denote a particular relationship, usually one of dependency, powerlessness or supplication, with the core professionals involved. The more fashionable 'service user' is meant to convey a sense of neutrality in the social relationship between the provider and beneficiary. Its neutrality, however, conceals significant variations in the relationships and experiences surrounding different services. Such differences are significant in shaping the potential and detailed practices of user involvement across services. Nevertheless, the 'user voice' has established a legitimate place in deliberations on policy and practice, even if specific individuals or organisations continue to resist both the concept and the practice (Clarke and Newman, 1997).

When not a requirement, it is considered good practice for both strategic and provider agencies to ensure that the service user voice is heard. This expectation, described by Howe (1990) as 'reasonable' and even 'wholesome', has been embraced with enthusiasm by managers and professionals within public services (Lindow and Morris, 1995; Robson *et al.*, 1997; Harrison and Mort, 1998). It is also shared enthusiastically by academics, despite the fear that this might lead to the incorporation of oppositional voices (Forbes and Sashidharan, 1997). Yet in noting the scale of this transformation of attitude, Lewis (1998) suggests caution in that users have 'emerged from virtual invisibility to new and highly contradictory positions' (p. 56). Gilliatt *et al.* (2000) argue that there are deeper and self-defeating tendencies at work, with users:

> enlisted as responsible partners in delivering the services they receive...
> engaged in the management of reduced contact between service
> providers and users' (p. 334).

Others such as Corrigan and Joyce (1997) and Beresford (2001), representing the majority of commentators, insist that user involvement is the only secure basis for service improvement. Giddens (1984, 1989) and Hoggett (2000a, 2001) advance the concept of the service user as reflexive, knowledgeable, creative and responsible agent. Bauman (1993) and Hoggett (2001), however, insist on a critical approach to this reflexive subject, acknowledging both a negative or destructive reflexivity and a 'self' as a non-reflexive object. If reflexivity cannot be assumed then the critical interrogation of voices cannot be abandoned. The reassertion of the active and resourceful 'welfare subject', with multiple and contradictory relationships with service providers, challenged dominant images of the pathological or dependent welfare recipient implicit within the discourses of professionalism and expert knowledge. This desire to locate the welfare subject in a more progressive light has resulted in a reluctance to acknowledge that some users have no desire to engage with public service professionals or have been too traumatised to do so effectively. Service users can also be violent and intimidating, presenting a danger and a risk to those they encounter, and whose behaviour has been such that their 'right' to involvement has been severely reduced or curtailed.

Broad agreement amongst policy makers and practitioners over the legitimacy of the user voice does not imply any shared understanding on what this might mean in practice or that a commitment to user involvement is easy to implement (Barnes and Wistow, 1992). There are problems in defining the 'user', identifying the level and purpose of involvement, the appropriate mechanisms for doing so, and how to take account of the considerable variation in the scope and depth of relationships between service users and different areas of welfare provision (Taylor, 1995). Despite the rhetoric, in no area of public provision can it be said that the user voice is particularly robust or that user organisations have been satisfied with the outcomes (Barnes, 1999). Provider agencies need to reorientate themselves so as to have a more grounded relationship with their multiple user constituencies. Clarity in the politics of user involvement can only be achieved through ongoing dialogue between professionals, agencies and service users.

The emergence of the user voice

Despite a growing awareness of the legitimate role for service users they have until recently been a neglected stakeholder in the policy process (Beresford *et al.*, 1997). As was explored in Chapter 1, a cornerstone of the post-war settlement was the centrality of the welfare professional. It was the professional experts, properly trained, qualified and educated, who would apply their acquired knowledge and expertise to both the identification of need and an appropriate response for their satisfaction (Glennerster, 1983). Where necessary they would also be responsible for making judgements in any conflict of interest between individual and social needs or requirements. Service users had no part to play. Not only were they considered insufficiently insightful to correctly identify how best their own needs could be met, but they did not have the overall understanding or detachment to make informed comparative judgements between their own circumstances and those of others. Within the emergent welfare state a consciousness of citizenship remained weak.

Users were excluded because they lacked the necessary expertise acquired only after lengthy intensive training, or because they were too vulnerable or too preoccupied with their own personal concerns and lacked reflexivity. Alternatively they were too self-interested or had crossed some line in socially acceptable behaviour so that they had forfeited any right to comment. Professional knowledge and detachment, coupled with an overriding commitment to the public good, would ensure not only appropriate individual responses but also equity and fairness in resource distribution.

A model of the passive but ultimately grateful subject, too preoccupied with their own personal circumstances, or of someone whose behaviour had precipitated a controlling intervention, could not be sustained. Increasing numbers of users grew angry as they experienced inadequate or inappropriate services or no services at all, and as material and economic expectations rose among the post-war generation so it became more confident and articulate. Evidence began to appear that welfare professionals were unable to deliver what had been promised. The welfare state had not significantly reduced levels of poverty or inequality and large parts of the country's old industrial areas were stagnating. Professionals came under criticism for the circumstances experienced by particular groups of service users, such as the elderly, the mentally ill and children growing up in poverty. Unanticipated social patterns and formations developed bringing new challenges and concerns, such as the instability of the traditional nuclear family and rise in single-parent households or the social impact of an increasing number of women joining the labour market. Professionals were caught between those who condemned such trends as the cause of current and future social problems, and those who saw them as either inevitable or wished to actively promote them. For some, welfare professionals appeared unwilling to account for social problems by reference to such trends, except as an 'excuse' for the behaviour and a plea for better understanding. For others, professional interventions were at odds with social and economic trends.

Major service areas, for example public housing, were exposed by pressure groups, voluntary bodies, and through academic research, for their poor standards and rapid deterioration. New groups of service users emerged, including domestic violence victims, and previously unacknowledged needs were articulated, such as the health needs of black and ethnic minority citizens, and HIV and Aids sufferers. These created evermore differentiated but organised voices, demanding recognition and appropriate services. In response to the failure of state provision, or in order to highlight an as yet unrecognised need, an increasing number of users returned to the traditions of self-help and began to provide their own services, thereby challenging the belief that only trained professionals could do so. Others argued that not only were there areas where there was either no or inappropriate provision, but that existing services failed to recognise the individuality and diversity of the service user and were equally unacceptable as a consequence.

Finally, across a wide area of welfare provision service users voiced their complaints about the user experience, the nature of the 'state welfare–client relationship', especially the regulatory aspects, and the overall quality of provision. The dissatisfaction with being a second class citizen in receipt of a second class service grew louder. Protest over the level and quality of provision, and its absence in other areas, led to the articulation of ideas and experimentation within women's groups and labour movement activists, about more progressive approaches to the satisfaction of needs (Coates, 1978; London-Edinburgh Weekend Return Group, 1980; Mitchell, 1984; Collective Design/Projects, 1985; Gorz, 1985). Such voices of protest, often chaotic and disorganised, combined with more critical thinking amongst public sector professionals. Derived from marxism, feminism and anti-racist struggles, these helped create the conditions for a different relationship within the professional–user encounter (Brake and Bailey, 1980; Jones, 1983; Ben-Tovim *et al.*, 1986; Hanmer and Statham, 1988; Langan and Lee, 1989).

What users have to offer

The current enthusiasm for service user involvement is explained in relation to three connected issues:

1. successful lobbying on the part of user organisations in particular policy areas;
2. professional failure and the need to ensure greater accountability;
3. the need for legitimacy in service provision.

Not an insignificant part of the explanation lies in the success of user and carer organisations themselves. They have demanded the right to be heard and argued that services should be reshaped in such a way to reflect their new found identities (Barnes, 1999). The challenges arising from critical accounts of the experience of being

a user, the subsequent contributions made to theoretical development, and specific policy demands generated by user organisations,
have all been powerful influences in persuading those responsible
for provision. There has also been a growing perception amongst
policy makers and politicians that welfare professionals have failed
to deliver the 'right' answers in relation to how specific services are
provided but have through their interventions made some situations worse. Moreover, they appear unlikely to fare any better in
the future, as intervening in the social world is increasingly characterised by complexity and ambiguity. Consequently, it is argued
that only by listening to the service user and establishing a relationship
of partners or co-producers, can professionals hope to provide a
useful service. Disenchantment with professional failure has also
contributed to a growing level of mistrust between users, politicians
and service providers. Hence there is an urgent need to secure a
renewed sense of legitimacy for service provision through greater
and more transparent accountability. The construction of a 'user
dialogue' can supposedly provide this.

If it is not to remain marginal and done with reluctance, the
motivation to engage with service users must go beyond defensive
modes of operating. Professionals need to know what it is that
service users can add to their understanding and their ability to
deliver effective services. Beyond making users *feel* more involved
and, therefore, they have less need to adopt a conflict strategy,
what is the added value of such engagement? Five key reasons are
highlighted here:

1. A recognition that users have a direct interest in the quality of
   the service they receive and thereby a right to have a voice in the
   design, implementation and impact of provision.
2. A belief that knowing the user experience, from the inside,
   contributes to more effective provision, especially when the
   purpose of a service is often to change the behaviour of the
   service user.
3. A view that service users can provide immediate and evaluative
   feedback on services, identifying unintended consequences of
   unanticipated complexities.
4. A hope that users might offer constructive comments on future
   services.
5. A belief that a stronger user voice will enhance the democratic
   accountability of public service provision.

It can be argued that the mere fact that service users have an immediate and real interest, although not necessarily the same interest, in the production of welfare is sufficient in itself to justify their inclusion in service planning, implementation and evaluation. Ovretveit (1997), in questioning the appropriateness of the term 'user', along with other common descriptors such as client, patient or customer, suggests that the concept of 'co-service' captures the purpose of the welfare relationship. Similarly, Wilson (1998) argues that users are often, in fact, 'co-producers' and that without such input some services would simply not function. While it is important to recognise each contribution made to meeting the user's needs, it is also important to retain clarity around roles and expectations in respect of different inputs. The blurring or dissolution of the user/producer role boundary sharpens our awareness of the interdependency in the relationship and the need for communication and mutual respect. Beyond that, such a 'dissolution' can conceal structural differences between formal service providers with roles and responsibilities and a 'subject' engaged in meeting their own needs.

The 'gap' between the knowledge of the reflexive subject and that of the provider who observes, listens, engages in dialogue, and reflects upon their cumulative experience and theoretical knowledge may not be significant in relation to professional interventions. Nevertheless, no provider, however empathic, can 'know' in the same experiential way as the service user or carer what it means to be in that role. They have a unique experience of being in need of and receiving services in a particular area of provision. That experience may have a long history and involve a variety of services, agencies and professionals, to address a number of quite different needs, and covering several individuals from within the same immediate social network. Consequently, users have a unique and rich story to tell. They can comment on their own personal encounter with a provider and suggest how it might be enhanced, thereby contributing invaluable data for those responsible for provision. Valid comparisons can be made between their own and other service users' experience based on their own local research. However, users are not always able to reflect upon, evaluate, or are aware of what might be in their own best interests. Further, the uniqueness of the story may not be required in order to deliver an appropriate or good enough service.

Not everyone has, or can express, insight about themselves, their circumstances or condition. Not everyone can see the wood for the trees or think clearly beyond the immediate satisfaction of their needs as they define them. Not all users can distinguish between felt needs or wants or preferences, and what they need as defined by others. Not all users are aware of what is possible and thus cannot include unknown possibilities amongst their own potential needs (Doyal and Gough, 1991). As is contested concept the definition of 'need' is dependent upon who is making the judgement (Bradshaw, 1972; Sanderson, 1996) how it is negotiated, and who is involved, although attempts have been made to construct the basis of universal human needs (Doyal and Gough, 1991; Plant, 1992). While it is appropriate for users to articulate their perception of need, it may not be for them to make the ultimate judgement.

The definition of need and its satisfaction are both contestable. The user's story will be based on different experiences and knowledge, and these insights should be heard and should receive a response, as spelt out in the policy on community care (DoH, 1991b). The sharing of each of these partial knowledge bases, experiential and professional, offers new opportunities for change and mutual benefit (Barnes, 1999). The individual comments of many service users could, if collected and analysed in an organised manner, reveal many useful insights into the commonalities and differences between the individual experiences.

In each individual encounter what both the service user and provider do share is the experience of a relationship based on their respective roles. Both have an interest in making that relationship work and each is dependent on the other for it to succeed. A successful relationship can be the cornerstone of an effective future engagement, especially when a change in the behaviour of the user is the desired outcome of the relationship. Intervention goals need to be clear and shared, and strategies to realise these agreed. Without the active agreement of service users not only will goals be more likely to be sabotaged, or at least remain unfulfilled, but the costs of pursuing them will increase significantly.

Identifying the user and acknowledging difference

The first challenge in extending service user involvement is that of clarifying the meaning of the term 'service user' as it applies to a particular context (Taylor, 1995). Is the 'user' to be conceived as an individual consumer or citizen, a collective body of users with an identity and general interests, local residents affected by provision, or the more atomised 'general public'? If our concern is the primary direct service user, how should we relate to anyone involved as a carer, or to other members of the social network occupied by the primary user? Is it important to distinguish between passive and active users and to invest resources to enable the passive to become active? Can service users be treated as a homogeneous body or should distinctions be made to identify potentially excluded users as defined by structural factors such as class, age, disability, ethnicity or gender? If the latter is adopted, does this categorical approach both deny individual differences and prescribe a victim identity equivalent to the discredited pathological approaches? Should a distinction be made between actual and proxy users as well as between current and future or potential users. While it might be appropriate and desirable to engage with all categories, it is important to be clear as how particular objectives of engagement and the mechanisms used relate to each category.

Distinctions do need to be made in respect of individual users. To the extent that one service does not fit all, so one approach to user involvement is inadequate. Individual users have different relationships to social welfare provision, ranging from the transitory to a deep engagement over many years. Such relationships influence how providers approach the task of 'user engagement', and how users respond. For some, a single encounter in relation to one service offered by a single agency that carries no implications for the user's personal identity or sense of self is the limit of the relationship. For others, prolonged and intensive levels of contact combined with the particular reason for such engagement, mean that their self-identity is profoundly and permanently shaped by the experience (Beresford, 2001). All service users should have an opportunity to be heard but some may not wish to pursue this, or to invest much energy in it. For others, the need and desire to engage can be overwhelming given the meaning and personal impact of being a user of a particular service. The balance between offering appropriate opportunities and responding to need is difficult to achieve. The engagement with the user about their experience of the role becomes part of the intervention, part of the recovery process.

A variety of mechanisms for user engagement should be available to 'capture' as many of those who wish to engage as possible. Whatever the mechanism, it should be free from any immediate association with the service unless the purpose is specifically to review the individual experience of that particular user. In other words, to engage as a service user in an evaluation of the delivery of services should be distinct from the relationship created by virtue of being a user. This is especially so when the relationship is of a therapeutic nature or when rewards and sanctions are involved. Service users, as citizens or consumers, must be distinguished from the user conceived as a mental health patient or an abusing parent so as to avoid the professional temptation to listen and interpret as they would in their patient or client relationship (Davis and Ellis, 1995).

Many users are reluctant or involuntary users, required by law or the fear of it to engage with services with potentially serious consequences, such as the placement of their children into care, if they fail to do so. For some, this involuntary status, found across a range of services, such as probation and the criminal justice system, mental health, and aspects of education, need not be a barrier to the expression of voice nor reduce its significance (Broussine and Wakefield, 1997). What remains in doubt is whether such users are entitled to inclusion and at what level. Amongst voluntary users, there can remain powerful feelings of ambiguity and reluctance about their user status. They may prefer to be free of the condition that triggered the user role or disassociate themselves from the dependency that accompanies the label, and reject the potential stigmatisation and negative self-perception (Thomas, 1997).

The absence of any negative connotations associated with a particular service does not guarantee that all users will be willing at all times to engage with service providers. User involvement is constrained by access to resources, including time and knowledge, but also by personal interest and self-perception. Users are often dependent upon professionals for access to scarce and desirable resources and fear of being denied such access may well inhibit the exercise of voice, especially when this is a critical voice. The nature of the contact itself may affect their willingness to become involved beyond their immediate requirements. Parental involvement in a child's schooling will vary, for example, according to whether they perceive an injustice against the child, are enquiring about his/her educational progress, are responding to a request to discuss curriculum, approaches to learning or an educational policy, or when being asked to make a financial contribution, or stand for election to the school's governing body.

For multiple and often complex reasons many individual users will opt for an essentially passive relationship with the provider agency. The desire to engage service users, to hear their voice, raises the question of whether resources should be devoted to enabling this group of passive users to become active. There is evidence that an individual's relationship to a service can change over time if they are encouraged, become more confident about their needs or entitlements, more convinced that they have suffered an injustice and believe that something can be done to correct it. However, this developmental approach requires yet another professional intervention, albeit one that is committed to user autonomy (O'Keefe and Hogg, 1999). To accept a definition of users as independent consumers and citizens who are able to choose how and when they become actively engaged is always likely to exclude some users who could and would become involved with some support. More problematically, for universal services, such as education or health care, some social categories, relative to their economic and social disadvantage, are more likely to engage in dialogue about the quality and appropriateness of the services available while others remain effectively excluded.

Active voices may simply promote the interests of an already advantaged group in resource-related discussions (Wilson, 1998). This could be at the expense of other users, for example, in respect of decisions concerning resource allocations between geographic areas or between subcategories of service user within the same unit of provision. Such subdivisions might be based either on the type of service received, for example post-sixteen educational resources against special needs provision, or between different social categories. There are then dangers in listening to the 'user voice' without ensuring that all interests have been identified and efforts taken to overcome barriers and engage them. To address such barriers requires not only confronting the negativity or stigma that is part of many welfare transactions but also providing practical support to enable participation. This might include, 'dependant' care, payment for sustained involvement, or other practical resources such as language support. In addition, it requires ensuring that it is easy to gain access to the process, that it is conducted in a facilitative manner, and that all reports or information are communicated in an accessible language.

The most basic understanding of what is meant by the individual 'user' is that of the direct recipient of any service. A single name on a case file may resolve the agency's dilemma when there is any doubt about who the user might be. Yet, conflicts of interest are often apparent when services are identified with one primary individual but are in reality offered within a social system, particularly the family. For example, important differences could be expected between parents and children over what is the appropriate educational content or priority for school-based religious or sex education, as well as between them and educational providers.

Of greater significance are those potential differences of interest or need when social workers intervene within a dysfunctional family and specifically where there are issues of child-protection at stake (Parker *et al.*, 1991). The needs of an individual might initiate an intervention and subsequently shape the form it takes, but meeting these needs can depend upon securing changes in the behaviour of others that cannot occur without their needs also being addressed. The primary concern might be to protect the child, with its implicit meaning of 'protect it *from* someone else' and other interests can then become secondary, if not entirely discounted. The reality is that the child's development or protection is dependent upon some desired change in parental or adult behaviour that will not occur without skilled intervention. Consequently, they too are service users. Moreover, the parents, whatever their shortcomings, do not lose their right to intervene in relation to or on behalf of their children, unless that right is specifically removed from them through a legal process. As parents they too have an interest in how their children's needs are defined and met. The 'rights' of others such as step-parents, common-law partners or other significant relationships are even less clearly defined in relation to users involvement.

The desire to focus on the often-vulnerable primary user can be reinforced by an anxiety that his/her needs may be neglected, ignored or abused by stronger more powerful members from within his/her social system. Such protective instincts can lead professionals to act as advocate for the primary user whose interests are now pitched against those immediate to them. This may clarify who is the user but confuse other members of the primary social group. Yet, it may still be appropriate to prioritise the individual whose circumstances and needs have triggered the intervention and where a future positive assessment in respect of that same person will bring that intervention to an end. In other words, regardless of the degree of inter-dependency between the primary user and other members of the social system, the voice of the relatively most vulnerable should be heard independently and not simply subsumed within the voices of the more articulate.

The user's social system will contain complex sets of dependent and inter-dependent relationships that can be neglected or damaged by inappropriate attempts to focus on a primary user. There are also occasions when it is the primary user who is the more intimidating and powerful in relation to those around them. In such cases it may be more important to hear the needs of the carers. There are issues to be resolved in relation to the capacity of and degree to which some groups of highly dependent users can engage meaningfully in service delivery issues. Age and mental infirmity may both inhibit what can be achieved. While such users should not be denied opportunities for engagement, there is a danger that the emphasis on user involvement will lead to the creation of what are little more than participatory rituals so the agency can demonstrate its commitment.

Proxy users

There are useful distinctions to be made between actual and 'proxy' users and current and potential users. In this context, 'proxy' is used somewhat loosely to mean those who speak on behalf of actual or immediate users. However, not all those who claim a proxy status have been authorised by users, either singly or collectively, to represent their interests. Professionals may be convinced that as a consequence of accumulated experience they are able to act in this proxy role, speaking for and anticipating user needs or views, especially in relation to agencies other than their own. More commonly, proxy users will be personal advocates bringing their skills and resources in the interests of the user. They will inevitably find themselves on occasions having to interpret such interests.

When acting regularly on behalf of a number of users in respect of the same service provider, such advocates need to develop and nurture their own relationships with the provider. To be successful they must ensure that these remain intact and functioning appropriately for the next time they interact. If they work within a restricted environment with a small number of providers, they must retain respect and credibility within the role. Central to this is to ensure that judgements in respect of the user and the environment in which they are functioning are perceived to be sound. Consequently, the proxy user's interpretations of the needs or interests of any specific user are mediated by a sense of what is needed to maintain the advocate–provider relationship.

In addition to the individual advocate as proxy user is the collective proxy user, third parties – usually community or non-profit organisations – that claim to speak for all those users within their specified area. The views of such organisations on current user experience are legitimised because of their allegedly closer proximity to the real user than the provider bodies seeking information. Yet such organisations might not contain any current or previous users, nor have good links with user groups. Often such organisations are effectively professional bodies with little of their own user involvement to offer as a model of good practice. Where the organisation is a membership body, its political stance may not reflect that of the individual or user subset it seeks to represent. Nevertheless, they claim to have user interests at heart and provide a convenient channel through which dialogue with public bodies can be established. Engaging proxy users, especially those organisations that have developed formal structures and processes, represents a less demanding challenge for service providers and avoids having to deal directly with 'difficult' people. However, user groups and individual users may be either unaware of the role played by such organisations, may have little direct contact with them, or may disagree strongly with what is being said 'on their behalf'. To use proxy organisations is at best a poor alternative and at worst indicative of a lack of commitment in the work of engaging immediate users. Provider organisations should at least enquire closely into processes of governance and accountability. Aware of the mounting concern about the role played by voluntary or non-profit organisations, their own service users must be involved and support given to the development of independent user groups. They too must expose themselves to the criticisms of users and their organisations (Robson *et al.*, 1997).

Finally, there is the distinction between current and potential or future users. Although the immediate pressure for engagement is likely to come from current users, service providers cannot ignore potential or future users although their direct engagement is more difficult to achieve. For example, health care providers must anticipate and prepare for the likely needs of the future elderly population. This may involve a reduction in provision for current users. Understandably, it is difficult to engage either future or current users in such forward planning. Consequently, decisions are taken when the benefits will be felt some time in the future although there may be an immediate but less tangible impact for current users.

Papering over the complexities

Too often advocates of user involvement pay too little attention to the complexities involved in defining the service user or appear to want to speak only about a small minority whilst retaining a universal language (Beresford, 2001). Should all those who use public services have equal rights and opportunities to engage, either as individuals or part of an interest group, in shaping the policy and delivery of services? If this is unrealistic then what is appropriate and possible at any time will involve dialogue, assessment, and ultimately will require professional judgements about the level and processes of engagement. Some service users either through circumstances or condition do not have the same capacity or entitlement to engage – they are too dependent, too much at risk, too vulnerable, too hostile, or are a user as a consequence of their own wrongdoing. Here some continuing level of mediation between the service user, or their 'responsible other', and the professional is necessary. A balance has to be found between the role of the provider as a 'container' of the service user's anxiety, dependence or rehabilitation, and the 'right' of the user to have an autonomous voice. To have a 'voice' in this context is quite different from the expectation that the provider would, as a matter of good practice, always listen to what the service user has to say, although they might not act on the basis of what the user wants. Where a third party mediates the relationship, other challenges need to be resolved. The role could be undertaken by either independent professional mediator/advocates or current or former service users who are able to take a detached but knowledgeable view. A judgement would still be required by the provider agency, that was open to scrutiny by an independent ombudsman, as to how far and in what ways they were prepared to engage.

User organisations

A number of user organisations have emerged recently, especially in mental health, disabilities and learning difficulties. Those most successful in securing recognition, for example in the areas of disabilities and mental health, have done so following consistent pressure and advocacy, better self-organisation, and some public sympathy based on a sense of past injustices (Hoyes *et al.*, 1993; Penna and O'Brien, 1996). Other user groups, such as families seeking advice and support in relation to childcare, in which there is considerable ambiguity about the welfare relationship, such that stigma and the apportionment of blame continue to be in evidence, have fared much worse in generating an organisational base. Often they are at best reluctant users.

Such groups have found it difficult to apply collective pressure, face considerable barriers to self-organisation or collective identity and receive less public sympathy. Social categories, such as children or the elderly, who have not fared well in establishing their social rights generally find their status mirrored in relation to public service users although this pattern may be changing (Carter and Nash, 1995; Butler, 1997). Creative strategies and support are needed to enable such users to form and sustain user groups. Similarly, agencies need to avoid talking only with the more articulate or better organised.

User organisations are not 'representative' bodies but are rather an example of direct democracy involving a subset of the overall user group who come together to pursue a set of interests. They provide an indicative insight into the likely concerns of the broad category of the unorganised users. User organisations are not equally prominent, well organised locally or nationally, or effective in communicating their message. Those positioned so as to build a broad-based programme are more likely to gain a wider membership and a stronger voice. Such voices are often privileged, especially if they are determined and challenging, and when they represent the only organised body with whom to speak. Successful user organisations, for example in the areas of mental health and disabilities, and their advocates in academia have effectively shaped the nature of the user debate (Beresford, 1997). This has resulted in a generalised 'user' experience being defined by the experience of specific service users. For example, a perceived power relationship between mental health service users and psychiatry is frequently portrayed as the dominant feature of all professional service user relationships.

Such undifferentiated user projections can be shaped by the nature of the 'service' they receive, as in mental health 'survivors', by a social category with which they identify, such as 'women users', or by both such as people with disabilities. Such categories tend to crowd out other considerations that might suggest quite different experiences. Thus the shared experience of being a mental health service user, is less important than the reasons for accessing the service, whether one is a voluntary or involuntary user, for what length of time, whether treatment is institutional or community based and the treatment outcomes. Understandings defined by membership of a social category are often inappropriately applied to services and social circumstances. Those derived from a particular service can produce organisations that reflect the assumed specific experiences of that social category, for example black and ethnic minority mental health users. Local policy responses often only reinforce such categorical thinking. Subsequent outcomes are perceived as 'tokenistic', do not capture the complex internal differentiations, imply that these categories embody different ways of being, and are based on a dubious assumption that service provision by someone assigned to the same category produces a more user sensitive service.

As with all organisations, user groups seek to establish a niche with a defined platform or agenda. Not all will be effective in doing so and consequently will be in competition with others for the same resources or attention. User groups both help to shape a new identity for their actual and potential members, often in opposition to one seemingly imposed or reinforced by service providers, and seek to ensure that the implications of such identities are translated into policy. To succeed they must first secure the limited attention available from those influential in the shaping of policy, if necessary by 'nudging out' others pursuing similar ends. Some areas of provision have as yet no matching user organisation. Some, such as social service clients, appear too unwieldy to offer an easy reference point for organisation. For others, becoming a service user does not offer a positive identity, such as a 'failing parent' in cases of child protection, and potential members remain reluctant to identify themselves collectively and publicly.

It is important that providers are clear about the basis on which the relationship is to be constructed, in particular whether the group claims and can defend some broader user representational role or seeks to speak only for its members. Groups do not need to claim to be 'representative' in order to offer a valuable contribution and providers do not need to elevate a group's status in order to appreciate its input. The commitment to user organisations is likely to lead, quite appropriately, to provider agencies offering financial and organisational support. With sufficient resources user organisations can employ staff, who may or may not be qualified professionals or have been a service user. The recruitment of former service users potentially creates a 'professional user', a user whose employment legitimises action based on generalisations from their personal experience.

There is a tendency in voluntary organisations for those who occupy formal roles, either in a paid capacity or as full time volunteers, to be repeatedly called upon to undertake representational tasks. From the provider's perspective, such accumulated experience of the structures and processes and familiarity with the other participants may justify this practice. Moreover such individuals are likely to be amongst the most vociferous or committed of 'users', forever calling for greater involvement. Such critical voices may be more manageable if they are part of the decision-making processes, to draw upon their ideas, engage their energies, and secure their commitment to specific decisions as well as to the process itself.

Repeatedly engaging the same 'representatives' and the status this bestows also results in a process of 'professionalisation'. They become experts, user spokespeople, with opportunities to develop a personal 'career' on the basis of such claims. This may of course suit all concerned, if the primary object is to demonstrate to a third party that users are consulted. User organisations, like any other, can become set in their ways, routinised, less energetic or out of touch. Long-standing and established groups can lose touch with the immediate reality of current users.

Three models of user involvement

Consumerist models

The pressure exerted by service user voices and the shortcomings of the professional providers go some way to explaining the priority given to involve service users in the policy process. However this is not the whole story. The emergent user voices of the pre-Thatcherite period wanted better quality, more extensive public services, both in range and volume. They sought user-sensitive services with increased professional and provider accountability.

The New Right argued that governments could no longer afford to pay for the seemingly endless demand for new services and they could never correctly anticipate and respond to individual needs. Welfare users were, as a consequence of too much mollycoddling, too dependent upon the state. It was only in either the market, through the workings of the law of supply and demand, or from charity and self-help, that needs could be met and users, or more appropriately 'customers', could exercise choice whilst at the same time acting as responsible citizens. Moreover, it was argued that with the virtual monopoly of state provision welfare professionals and bureaucrats would maximise any opportunity to advance their own 'market' interests by expanding their organisational size and span of control. The subsequent promotion of user or customer 'choice' as part of the marketisation of social welfare was a useful device by which to maintain pressure on welfare professionals, but more fundamentally as an opportunity to remove services whenever possible from the public to the private sector.

The public choice (Niskanen, 1971) or 'exit' model of service user involvement drew heavily and directly from the popular image of the high street customer seeking 'value for money' products and the 'best buy'. In a competitive market with multiple providers, service quality would be driven upwards by informed customers, exercising personal choice and seeking an alternative provider when dissatisfied. In this way providers would become more sensitive to customer needs or lose their customers, and would tend to seek to be economic, efficient and effective (Shaw, 1997). However, there are limits to the high street analogy as prices cannot be posted or services inspected prior to purchase, nor returned if unsatisfactory (see Chapter 3). The model ignored or dismissed the fact that often users acted as indifferent, not active, citizens, staying with what is familiar or not so bad as to necessitate a move elsewhere.

The internal 'quasi' market, in which purchasing agencies were separated from those providing services, was to provide a quality regulating mechanism (Le Grand and Bartlett, 1993). To strengthen this, and ensure an orientation towards consumer needs and satisfactions, a new inspection regime was introduced, through such bodies as the Audit Commission and Social Services Inspectorate, and performance standards were set within central government departments. A customer-orientated agency, lead by a generic management, offering quality products became the 'mantra' whenever any difficulties, including efforts to push down the cost of provision, were encountered.

Implicit within the consumer model is the assumption and encouragement to dissatisfied public service users to seek satisfaction elsewhere within the private sector. Since economically rational individuals, intent on securing the best value at a price they are willing to pay, would make a similar decision if they had the necessary resources, there could be no argument against those who opted for this route. Through a process of consumer drift, as more private sector providers emerged to meet demand while public services were resource squeezed, public services would be 'residualised', utilised only by those who for whatever reason had little opportunity to purchase elsewhere. The reluctance of the private sector to offer anything other than the most profitable services, meant that the neo-right was required to restructure public services through the introduction of market principles rather than reform them through direct privatisation (Clarke and Newman, 1997).

This re-commodification of welfare legitimised the existence of differential welfare markets each designed to provide services of a quality equated to the purchasing power of the consumer. Moreover, it would depoliticise social welfare by undermining the principle of common needs met collectively through public funding and support. The elevation of the user as consumer under neo-liberalism was an attempt to undermine the concept of citizenship built around a series of social rights secured in the political sphere. What it also did was to draw attention to the details of the relationships and mechanisms of welfare in ways that the traditional social democratic models had not.

For those less sanguine about the expansion of the market economy, the concept of the sovereign customer in social welfare able to exercise informed choice and holding the ultimate 'exit' card had a number of fundamental flaws. 'Involuntary' users, required by law and sanction or other circumstances, have no choice but to receive a 'service' with no exit option, irrespective of the quality of provision. The inclusion of those who perceive they have no choice is contested by the neo-right. For the unemployed, single parents or social housing tenants, there have always been choices to be made. Rather, the widespread provision of universal welfare services, and the assumption of social rights in relation to these, has meant that such people made the 'wrong' choices or sought to avoid the responsibilities that flowed from such 'choices'. For social democrats, at the point when users most need services they are unable to exercise choice. They may be too poor, too frail or vulnerable, too ill, too desperate, too ill-informed or lacking in personal insight to act in the manner of the enquiring, demanding, reflective consumer and to take advantage of services provided by other providers. For those requiring specialist services, or living outside urban centres, there may be no alternative providers, unless contract funded by the state or through private provision.

In many areas of public service, the 'service' *is* the relationship between the provider and user and its quality or effectiveness cannot be judged until during or even after the experience. Indeed the impact of such a relationship may not be felt for some considerable time after it has been terminated. Service users have few sanctions to apply if they are dissatisfied with either the quality or level of provision available. This is in the nature of the relationship, irrespective of the provider.

To be truly successful the exit model depends on two key assumptions that do not apply for the majority of those in receipt of public services. The first is that the consumer commands a place in the labour market such that the economic rewards are sufficient to allow for any appropriate mobility, or that market skills are transferable so that relocation is possible, in order to gain access to particular providers. The second is that service users either as individuals or 'units' such as families are willing to construct their social lives around multiple decisions taken in respect of public services. The assumption is that choices made in relation to housing, childcare, schools, leisure, hospitals, primary health and social care, are unrelated to employment patterns, extended families, friendship networks, or social and cultural patterns. For some these assumptions may hold true. Thus some parents will either relocate or send their children away in order to secure access to a particular school. The majority either lack the resources for this to be an option or would not choose it.

Such criticisms do not deny the value of multiple providers or initiatives to ensure that the service user is better informed about the nature of the service, the alternatives offered, and what is available elsewhere. Opportunities should be available for service users to provide evaluative feedback on the service they have experienced, to make suggestions about how services can be improved, comment on what they see as future priorities, and have an accessible, effective and responsive complaint procedure at their disposal. Regulatory mechanisms are essential to both evaluate and compare services offered by different providers. In applying a fully-fledged consumerist approach to public services one might expect to find a range of features including:

- The provision of accessible services both in terms of proximity and ease of understanding, and users aware of their entitlements and the available services.
- Multiple and diverse providers, flexible in response to individual needs and circumstances, working to service performance targets known to service users.
- Service quality checks, including monitoring of reception and user interviews, and regular, independent service evaluation research, including the use of users as researchers, customer satisfaction surveys or end of contact interviews.
- Transparency in relation to professional practice, including user involvement in inspections and audits, the disclosure of personal information held by any public service agency, and the introduction of an effective complaints process.
- The creation of specific vehicles for the expression of user voices such as, suggestion boxes, user committees, fora or conferences.
- Consultation with service users on the development of new services, prioritisation between services and opportunities to access and participate in the management of specific services.

The introduction of such processes backed by additional resources to respond to the outcomes generated would contribute to improved services and provide users with a sense of meaningful involvement.

The democratic model

The voices of those demanding a more inclusive, responsive, accountable, and quality driven public sector were not silenced during the period of neo-liberal dominance. During the 1980s an alternative democratic model was actively promoted amongst Labour-held, metropolitan, local councils (Lansley *et al.*, 1989). In the context of service user engagement, the democratic model re-emphasises the relationship between service user and citizenship, on the assumption that services should reflect both our citizenship rights and our inter-dependence. In addition, since there is some evidence to suggest that service users are less involved in local democratic processes and are non-participants in public affairs, becoming more active in respect to a specific public service can be the means to wider engagement (Parry *et al.*, 1992).

The citizenship model reminds us that if we value our membership of the polity, it behoves us to ensure that appropriate mechanisms are in place for democratic dialogue, including between service users and providers, and that any collectively agreed provision is both accountable and offered to the appropriate standard. In determining such standards our inter-dependence, alongside a recognition that we are all both potentially service users as well as the beneficiaries of the availability of services to others, is a powerful driver in ensuring that they are of the highest quality. However, a lack of confidence in the capacity of traditional representative democracy to manage the increasing complexity associated with the differential needs of a diverse and articulate user population, require that as well as strengthening existing mechanisms, new forms of democracy must be developed (Burns *et al.*, 1994). Labour has recognised the citizenship-based model through its inclusion of the 'public' in the user discourse, but this has not yet been accompanied by a commitment to strengthening and extending direct and participatory forms of democracy. The introduction of Foundation Hospitals does, however, hold out the promise of 'community' ownership, including the involvement of hospital employees as well as users.

The democratic model argues for additional features to those found in the consumerist approach, including:

• Investment in forms of direct democracy and community or neighbourhood membership organisations, to enable user groups to emerge, survive and thrive, including support for individual users who wish to become more actively involved.
• User access to provider decision-making structures and explicit forms of collective accountability through executive 'user and patient councils', functioning in every provider agency.

- An extension of representative democracy through street or neighbourhood elected delegates, service-related elected bodies, and the creation of neighbourhood boards with financial control and decision-making powers for local public services.
- Support for inclusive general public fora, that is, non-user specific, to facilitate discussion about public concerns, including citizen focus groups, citizen juries, deliberative opinion polls, citizen panels, conferences, teach-ins and so on.
- Regular dialogue on policy development, priorities, and service delivery between local politicians, policy makers, front-line service providers through their collective organisations, users and the public.
- The negotiation of local mandates for policy and practice in particular circumstances that could, for example, acknowledge cultural differences or locally sensitive issues.

User empowerment

In addition to both 'voice' and 'exit' models a third related approach has been developed concerned with the immediate relationship between professionals and service users. This has been constructed on the concept of 'user empowerment', which has gained increasing usage across all public services (Simon, 1990). It has been especially prominent within social work (Darvill and Smale, 1990) replacing earlier ideas of a radical practice (Corrigan and Leonard, 1978; Langan and Lee, 1989). Although imprecise and ambiguous and concealing a range of political philosophies, 'empowerment' focuses attention on the relationships of power between providers and users (Ward and Mullender, 1991; Beresford and Croft, 1993).

Empowerment directs attention both to the desired outcomes of any intervention, giving emphasis to the ultimate autonomy of the user, and to the micro-politics of the transactions between user and professional. It is concerned with how these relationships are established, maintained, and developed in ways that are respectful, confirming, inclusive and non-exploitative. For Rodwell (1996), to empower a service user so that they are more able to control their own lives, it is necessary to pay attention to the user's self-esteem. This can best be achieved by working in partnership, with mutual decision-making, respect, trust, and by giving authority and resources including advocacy support to make real choice possible.

Such choices may initially be confined to the particular public service around which the relationship is constructed, but the intention
is that the user will be able to transfer this increased capacity to
other aspects of their lives.

An empowering practice is concerned with facilitating user self-
determination by building confidence and assertiveness, raising
expectations, and increasing knowledge and skills (Beresford and
Croft, 1993). It implies reflecting critically upon and changing the
ways in which the professional welfare relationship or the structures and procedures dis-empower or oppress the user. In turn this
can lead to supporting the development of collective organisation
amongst users. Taken together the desired outcome is both a more
engaged, reflective user with a greater sense of personal agency,
and a service that is more humane and accountable, built on the
principles of equity, respect, and negotiated relationships between
service providers and users (Braye and Preston-Shoot, 1995).

Whilst the concept of empowerment has become firmly lodged
within the discourse of social welfare practice, its lack of conceptual clarity has tended to de-politicise its meaning. Within the
immediate provider–user relationship, empowerment has extended
the context in which that exchange is properly understood. Yet the
implicit association between empowerment and the relationship of
social welfare professionals to progressive social movements
remains under-theorised and lacking sound practice models.

Agency dilemmas

Provider agencies face considerable challenges in defining what
they mean by service user in a particular context and how they
intend to respond to the range of user constituencies. Agencies
need to be aware of and explicit about the frameworks within
which they have to operate, and of the room for manoeuvre. Not
all will be able to respond to the same degree to user demands:
some are more closely regulated by statute and have less flexibility.
Not surprisingly, user organisations may perceive such a response
as a defensive tactic to 'manage' the pressure or criticism.

Many of the potential benefits of user involvement have yet to
be realised and indeed only a few aspects of service delivery that
might benefit from a user perspective have been identified. None
of those involved can claim expertise in this area. Service users are

not always in a position to know what they need, or whether particular agencies are able to meet their needs, but providers can no longer assume that as 'professionals' they are necessarily in any better position. Consequently, the capacity to identify need, both for individuals and social categories, must form an important part of the provider–user dialogue. Yet, this must be conducted in the recognition that previous encounters have been fraught with difficulty, have favoured one party over the other, and were a significant motivation in the drive to establish the user's right to speak with authority.

Current policy encourages providers, increasingly with the threat of sanctions, to demonstrate their engagement with service users. Subsequent action is then driven by this imperative rather than a real acceptance of the benefits to be gained in terms of improvements to service quality. It reinforces a feeling amongst professionals of having to be on the defensive. Without a sense of policy ownership it is unlikely to generate sufficient attention to the detail of the engagement, the appropriate mechanism for doing so, and a spirit of dialogue. It is just as likely to result in 'spoiling mechanisms' to undermine the process. Expecting agencies concerned primarily with delivering services, to create structures for user engagement in order to improve more abstract democratic processes is unlikely to be greeted with much enthusiasm by hard-pressed professionals. Ensuring sufficient resources are available over a sustained period of time to enable effective and inclusive mechanisms and processes to be developed is essential if agencies are to move beyond a mere tokenistic response. What is as important is that provider organisations and professionals adopt a different relationship to users at the point of delivery.

Provider agencies need to work simultaneously with service users at different levels applying a variety of engagement strategies. These are required for engagement with both individual service users and their immediate social systems, as well as with the collective interests and concerns. Some features have already been suggested as characteristic of the two models of engagement. In addition the following points are offered as suggestions for moving the agenda forward in a way that avoids the early pitfalls identified in the politics of user engagement.

In relation to individual service users:

• Access to or ownership of all personal files and the further development of contract-based engagement with service providers.

- Access to independent service-based mediation/advocacy provision and complaints process.
- Engagement with individual users and user organisations on the organisation and delivery of services, covering: accessibility and responsiveness; organisation ambience and culture; working practices; user and service information systems; collaborative practices with other agencies.

In relation to service user organisations:

- Stronger links between service user organisations and those collective bodies, such as trade unions, representing those responsible for the direct provision of services. These could provide an opportunity to move beyond traditional professional–client relationships and gain a better understanding of the contexts, the opportunities and constraints, in which both parties are expected to operate. This would require trade unions and professional organisations to change the balance of their focus more towards service quality.
- Further research, undertaken in partnerships between user organisations, service providers and academics, to identify user and worker perspectives on what constitutes effective professional intervention.
- The employment of development workers within local agencies tasked with developing sustainable links with user communities and enabling the latter to engage more effectively.

In relation to provider agencies:

- The creation of local decentralised agencies each with management boards comprising substantial user representation, including direct users and citizens, as well as worker representatives. Such boards could be responsible for such matters as the formulation and review of local policy and practice, staff recruitment and development, and financial management.
- The extension of a 'Best Value' system to each local agency, involving users and other agencies, for their accreditation and review.
- Neighbourhood and client-based dialogue between providers and user/citizens on current, especially complex problems and needs, how these are best managed, and the potential roles of the respective parties.

- The introduction and publication of clearly stated agency policies in respect of such matters as service delivery philosophy, comprehensive and timely processes for service user need and preferences identification, record keeping, risk management for users, workers and agency, and case reviews that are carefully analysed.

The introduction of such measures aim to bring together both consumer and democratic models of user engagement. In moving the dialogue forward what cannot be abandoned is the critical interrogation of all participating voices, including the diverse and contradictory perspectives of the service user.

9

A Community Focused Approach

Previous chapters have argued that collaboration within and between agencies, professionals, service users, and across sectors is an essential ingredient for any contemporary system of social welfare. A further plank in the reconstruction of welfare practice has been the focus on the relationship between the state and 'community', those intermediary sites between family and the state (Bulmer, 1986). This chapter examines the pre-eminence given to 'community' as a site of and for policy-making and implementation. It explores the contested nature of community and whether it continues to have value as a working concept. Finally, it examines the potential of a community-focused approach and identifies some of the requirements if this is to be successful.

The current emphasis given to community marks a revival in the life of a concept that over thirty years ago had been written off as a meaningless area of study (Stacey, 1969). Over a decade ago the UK Local Government Commission (1992) was urged to seek a closer relationship between local authorities and identifiable communities (Department of Environment, 1991). The Commission on Social Justice (1994) emphasised the need for investment in community capacity building, whilst the Local Government Association (1997) and the Association of Metropolitan Authorities (1989, 1991) called for a democratic renewal, wider citizen participation and community development. In the introduction to a Labour Party (1995) consultative document Tony Blair states, 'individuals prosper when backed by strong communities'. Once in office, Labour's SEU argued:

Communities need to be consulted and listened to, and the most effective interventions are often those where communities are actively involved in their design and delivery, and where possible in the driving seat. Often this applies as much to 'communities of interest'... as it does to geographical communities (SEU, 2001, para. 1.19).

Such trends have been strengthened during Labour's second term of office, for example, in both the Local Government Act (2000) and the Health and Social Care Act (2001). The latter places a duty on the NHS to involve the public in the planning and development of services whilst the discussion document, 'Involving Patients and the Public in Healthcare' (2001) states:

We are determined to increase public involvement as much as public investment; to reform the way we engage the public as much as to reforming the way we deliver public services... (p. 6).

The Local Government Act (2000) places a new duty on local authorities to 'promote the economic, social and environmental well-being' of their areas, and a power 'to do anything which they consider is likely to achieve' this objective. It also requires authorities to take the lead in the development of a 'community strategy' as part of an exercise in 'community planning partnership'. These are closely linked to both the reforms in local political management, including directly elected mayors, and to the duty of Best Value. The Draft Guidance to local authorities on the preparation of community strategies (DETR, 2000c) makes clear that three objectives have to be met:

1. Local communities have to be able to articulate their aspirations, needs and priorities.
2. Actions undertaken by local authorities must be coordinated with other public, voluntary organisations, the community and local private sector agencies.
3. Existing and future activities have to be refocused to more effectively meet local needs.

Although 'community' is here used in different ways, for example to include whole areas served by local authorities, it also acknowledges smaller distinctive communities. Community strategies must be produced in partnership with other stakeholders and are expected to contain a long-term vision for the area, an action plan, a shared commitment to implementation, and a mechanism for monitoring and evaluation. Direct community engagement is central to the whole process:

> Community strategies should be grounded in the views and expectations of local communities (DETR, 2000: para. 42).

This view was later echoed by the Head of the SEU, who noted:

> One of the biggest oversights...has been the failure to involve local communities. Nobody knows the problems of an area better than the people who live there ... (Wallace, 2001).

Community as a focus for policy

Community is now seen as the site of service provision, a key place where both individual and collective needs are defined and met (Butcher *et al.*, 1993). It is also the basis for which services are provided, by whom they are evaluated, and with whom they are developed. Community is thus the provider and recipient of services and is the context in which much of the provider collaborative work will take place (PAT 17, 2000). Because of the characteristics associated with it, such as 'neighbourliness', and the assumed behaviours that are said to flow from these characteristics, community is also the basis on which policy is constructed. Community provides a basis for those responsible for the planning and provision of services to engage with the citizen, individually and in their collectivities, in respect of strategic service planning and more wide ranging open-ended democratic dialogue.

Central government has acknowledged that in order for communities to play such a role they must have the appropriate resources, economic and social infrastructure, and contain and be able to mobilise the necessary capacities (Active Community Unit, 2001). Further, communities need to be experienced both by their members and to outsiders as sustainable and rewarding, contributing positively to individual and collective well-being. Such goals, if they are achieved, are the product of ongoing processes that cannot be taken for granted but require constant attention if communities are not to decline or lose their meaning. Government policy has long recognised that many spatial communities have been in serious decline over a sustained period and are far from having the necessary requirements or in a position to take on the positive role as outlined above (SEU, 1998, 2001; Miller, 2001). Hence the need for investment in neighbourhood regeneration, and to build sustainable social, economic and political capital.

An early decision in 1997 was the creation of the SEU to coordinate and develop 'integrated and sustainable' policies to tackle the inter-related issues of unemployment, poor health, housing, education, crime and neglected neighbourhoods. The SEU recommended the development of a National Strategy for neighbourhood renewal. Eighteen Policy Action Teams were established to report on the detail of specific issues such as locally co-ordinated or 'joined-up' work. It is claimed that 85 per cent of the 569 recommendations have been fully accepted, and a further 10 per cent partially so (SEU, 2001). Following a wide-ranging consultation process on the consequent framework for a national strategy, an Action Plan was published in 2001 (SEU, 2001). Another initiative, the New Deal for Communities (NDC), focused on thirty-nine disadvantaged English neighbourhoods, was announced in 1998 as a pathfinder programme. For the government, the key findings highlighted by the NDC were:

> It is possible for partnerships whose boards have a majority of community representatives to run a major neighbourhood renewal programme successfully... true community involvement takes time, and that if programmes are to deliver they must focus on delivery and need people with strong skills in programme management (SEU, 2001: para. 2.14).

Community in policy and practice

A community orientation in social welfare is not new. Since the late 1960s there have been numerous examples when community has been used in relation to specific services, for example in area-based housing management or in response to young offenders. In personal social services, both the Seebohm Report (1968) and the Barclay Report (1982) advocated a 'community'- or 'patch'-based approach as a way of obtaining a better understanding of the presenting problem and developing preventive work. Both highlighted the need for community involvement, greater awareness of local needs, closer physical and emotional proximity between professionals and service users, and the recruitment of community development workers.

A community orientation was clearly articulated in the adoption of community care policies as central to the de-institutionalisation in the care of both the elderly and mental health patients. These now cover a much larger group of service users, including those with disabilities and special learning needs, as well as being at the heart of contemporary approaches to health care. The concept's slipperiness is also well illustrated in this area. Initially, the policy was understood in terms of 'care in the community' then 'care by the community' which became 'care by the family' and finally 'care by women in the family' (Bornat *et al.*, 1993). A broader community orientation has also been adopted in relation to what were first seen as marginal and disadvantaged areas that had failed to benefit from post-war prosperity. Both the Urban Programme (1968–94) and the twelve experimental Community Development Projects (CDP) (1969–75) were designed to address these concerns through a range of strategies. These included:

- bringing mainstream service providers closer to the neighbourhoods they served;
- improving communication between elected members, local authority officers, and neighbourhood residents and organisations;
- developing more effective coordination between services;
- initiating local research to gain an understanding of the nature of neighbourhood problems;
- providing information and advice to local residents about service availability;
- supporting local initiatives, and facilitating the development of community organisations to address local concerns.

Neither the CDP analysis that such neighbourhoods were suffering from the costs of industrial change and capital's unfettered global search for increased profits, rather than internal 'community' shortcomings, nor the conflict strategies many adopted were well received (Loney, 1983). The experimental projects were terminated but the community-based method survived as a way to address social and economic disadvantage and manage those who had either lost out through economic restructuring or had become marginalised. During the 1980s, the emphasis shifted to encouraging private sector initiatives, discouraging welfare claimants and increased law enforcement (Atkinson and Cope, 1997; Miller, 2001). A significant number of local authorities did launch a number of initiatives to decentralise local authority services (Burns *et al.*, 1994; Miller, 1996). As well as an attempt to improve local services decentralisation provided an opportunity for a number of radical Labour authorities to build a local alliance of opposition to a central government intent on dismantling public provision and hostile to local democracy. The majority were more pragmatically concerned with improved efficiency in the management of service delivery (Dale, 1987). The London Borough of Islington's Labour Party 1982 Manifesto summed up the broad orientation,

> There is a need to give fresh impetus to breaking down the bureaucratic isolation of much of the Council's activity. Involving more people will lead to services that more closely reflect needs, are better run, and have stronger support in the community (p. 1).

Across the political spectrum the 1990s saw a revival of interest in community initiatives. The short-lived Community Challenge (1991–93) and its successor, the Single Regeneration Budget (SRB) (1993), were based on a competition between invited bidders, so that success was not automatically related to need. Labour has retained the SRB but reasserted the prioritisation of need in determining funding. Support was also more firmly linked to evidence of collaborative inter-sectoral partnerships and community involvement. Under the NDC (1998), the seventeen relatively small pathfinder districts each focused on areas of some 4000 households, and selected on the basis of need, are able to benefit from an £800m investment over a ten-year period. The New Deal stresses the importance of rebuilding the social fabric through developing local leadership, investing in people and 'mainstreaming' – ensuring that key services adapt to meet the needs of disadvantaged areas – alongside neighbourhood safety and economic development. New Deal for Communities complements other neighbourhood-directed initiatives such as Sure Start, which provides support services for families with children under three and 'Action Zones' in health and education.

The principles and philosophy of a community orientation are no longer marginal to mainstream service delivery mechanisms or state–citizen relationships but are expected to infuse each initiative and mainstream provision. There is a growing consensus that modern nation states have no option but to invest in building sophisticated and sensitive relationships with its increasingly diverse and articulate citizenry especially where there are few unambiguous answers to complex social issues. This it must do if it is to maintain 'order within diversity' and to ensure it can both compete and collaborate with other nation states. From a perspective of extending and strengthening democracy along with the capacities and opportunities of all citizens, a broad-based and proactive community orientation is essential (Butcher and Mullard, 1993).

An ambiguous and contested concept

If a community focus is to be a central feature of any contemporary system of social welfare it should not obscure the fact that it remains a highly ambiguous and deeply sentimental concept. Bauman (2001) suggests it is but

> another name for paradise lost – but one to which we dearly hope to return, and so we feverishly seek the roads that may bring us there (p. 2).

Despite its 'motherhood' status (Donnison, 1993), to work with or within communities in all their complexity and heterogeneity provides no easy solution for the effective basis of social policy. Indeed it is only possible to understand the shifting meanings, workings, and symbolic significance of any community by capturing the experience of its members. Further, it cannot be assumed that particular meanings ascribed to community by some members will be shared by all. At one level, communities are simply 'imagined' constructs that help us make sense of the immediate world around us and of our relationships to that world.

Meaningful communities are broadly characterised by a variety of human sentiment, such as those of belonging, mutuality, connectedness, solidarity, and emotional cohesion but also fear, jealousy and anger (Bornat, 1993; Hoggett, 1997). Yet while such emotions may be imagined, desired, exaggerated or misplaced, communities can also be the containers of actual shared experience, reciprocity, and sometimes bitter conflict, a living reminder of our inter-subjectivity, and an expression of the significance attached to such experiences. Thus regular and meaningful face-to-face interaction, active, durable rather than episodic, and dense social networks are central to thriving dynamic communities. Multiple networks can coexist together in an uneasy and hostile relationship. Such characteristics form what Bauman describes as 'the epistemological foundation of the experience of community' (Bauman, 2001: 48), rarely experienced in their totality, but accumulated over time, creating and then reinforcing a sense of continuity and history, through changing experiences that are imbued with meaning and significance.

Communities as containers of these interactions, emotions and beliefs are, according to Anderson (1991), imagined, but no less important for that. Such characteristics, actively pursued and sought after by their members, are always in the making and, if realised, then reformulated and remade. Many of these valued sentiments and especially that sense of belonging and solidarity are often articulated or become lived experiences only during times of crisis or adversity and in response to some perceived external threat. The extent to which they survive in any active way beyond such moments is highly variable and uncertain, as is the extent to which they can be sustained during prolonged periods of crisis. Communities can be the basis for social and cultural practices or rituals through which collective histories are created, stored, and handed-on. The commitments and obligations that flow from such continuous interaction can be powerful and contribute to the construction of self-identity and a sense of the stranger or the 'other'. While community may signify inclusion and belonging, it is also about exclusion and division (Crow and Allan, 1994). Bauman (1997) suggests that in this postmodern age with its 'ambient fear', strangers are:

> vexing, unnerving, off-putting and otherwise a problem...(with a) tendency to befog and eclipse boundary lines which ought to be clearly seen...(pp. 25–6).

Within the policy discourse community is often presented in its idealised form with little reference to the relations of power or the inequalities within communities, unless it is to illustrate the depth of decline in a particular community. Yet communities are sites of internal conflict and struggle, as well as the basis for conflict with others, around age, gender, ethnicity, religion or housing tenure (Southall Black Sisters, 1989; Campbell, 1993; Danziger, 1996;

Hoggett, 1997). Current policy debates pay little attention to the management and resolution of such conflicts (SEU, 2001). Not everyone will experience the same reaction to the same event or have their experience acknowledged, nor are the costs and benefits of membership necessarily shared equally. The experience of community for particular groups, such as women, the elderly, young people, or minority groups can also differ significantly as can their contribution (Williams, 1993). Thus while community might be the source of mutuality and support it can also be experienced as intrusive, regulating, resistant to change, introspective, parochial, conservative and restrictive, or violent and abusive – frightening places from which to escape. This has led some writers to argue that in a world of increasing differentiation, community inappropriately privileges 'sameness' or unity as well as acting as a barrier to understanding the 'other's' perspective and experience (Young, 1990).

Bauman (2001) sympathises with Dench (1986) who suggests that the community-derived obligation to share benefits amongst members regardless of any sense of 'merit' or 'desert' makes community a 'philosophy of the weak' – designed for those unable to succeed as individuals within a meritocracy. In contrast, the powerful and successful who seek the freedom to act as individuals unconstrained by allegiances or obligations deny the value of community, even though they too occasionally feel the 'need to belong' in an increasingly risk-defined society (Beck, 1999). Community then is a shifting, complex, contradictory and contested phenomenon. These very real difficulties that make for less certainty and much caution should not, in themselves, prevent its use as a vehicle for policy, provided that idealised or fantasy communities do not blur our judgement. However, the contradictions and messiness of community may lead to a reassertion of the ultimate centrality of 'professional' dispassionate judgement as the only sound basis for intervention.

Meanings of community

Spatial communities

Community is most commonly associated with territory: a relatively small bounded geographical place, a locality, neighbourhood, or village, in which its members are able to easily identify fellow members, as well as denoting the physical demarcations between it and other communities. However, other and often much larger types of spatial, or even virtual, areas are increasingly defined as a community – cities, nation states, the European Community, the global village, cyber space. Clearly the scale of such geographical spaces make it more difficult for them to act, beyond a relatively high level of abstraction, as a basis for policy intervention and evaluation, as well as for political dialogue or face-to-face interaction. It also becomes more complex and less meaningful for members to either recognise or acknowledge other community members or define clear boundaries.

In themselves, place or territory signifies little or nothing (Pahl, 1966), although Sennett (1996) argues that there exists a fundamental need to 'belong' to a particular localised place and that it is this that leads to the construction of commitments and loyalties. Bauman (2001) too suggests that it is the creation of social patterns and roles built upon shared biographies over a long period of time within a locality that creates and sustains a sense of community identity. Sociological 'community studies' have explored the relationships between inter-generational stability and shared material circumstances. Key influences on community have been identified as restricted sources of employment; housing tenure; social class, ethnic or religious homogeneity; stable gender-based roles, kinship networks and cultural life (Dennis *et al.*, 1957; Young and Willmott, 1957; Rex and Moore, 1967; Bulmer, 1975; Abrams in Bulmer, 1986).

Conversely, the disintegration of 'community' has been analysed in terms of the impact of any significant change in any combination of these factors, whether evolutionary in nature, the result of policy intervention, or a consequence of some other external effect (Willmott and Young, 1960; Seabrook, 1984; Campbell, 1993). Recent attention has focused on the rapid evolution and contested nature of social roles, the uncertainty of material life, increasing social diversity, and the significant movement in and out, both between generations and social groups. In response the question has been raised as to whether such socially and culturally diverse localities can still be the basis of belonging and identity, albeit of a different nature (Gilchrist and Taylor, 1997).

Just when 'community' or locality is understood to be central to modern welfare, so new technology and communications, transport, growing social diversity and mobility, as well as changes in family structures, lifestyles, leisure patterns, consumerism and housing, reduce its centrality as a locus for social interaction (Crow and Allan, 1994). Globalisation raises additional challenges, as well as new possibilities, for traditional notions of identity, suggesting that relationships to those immediately around us will be transformed as new forms of communication and a different sense of space dissolve previous boundaries. Yet, a stronger self-identification as an equal but inter-dependent member of the human species does not prevent the simultaneous continuation of an even more powerful association with people and places much closer at hand. Alternatively, anxiety over the uncertainties of the times may generate defended or 'gated' communities in an attempt to construct tighter, inflexible or restrictive boundaries, whilst consumerism and free global markets demand few social obligations. Indeed, those able to operate as global consumers may find little need for community (Bauman, 2001).

Boundaries are crucial to the definition and meaning of community (Cohen, 1985). Communities are thus in large part defined in relation to the 'other' (Elias and Scotson, 1994). Yet defining the 'other' in terms of 'we belong here and they don't' is far from straightforward. Those most likely to be excluded, for example, sex workers, 'anti-social families' or mental health service users, may well insist upon their right to belong, refusing to place themselves, physically and socially, somewhere else. Equally some of those amongst the included, such as young Asian women or teenage mothers, may well reject membership if it implies adherence to unacceptable norms or codes of behaviour. Boundaries are never fixed, as new emergent communities, for example, refugee or asylum seekers, struggle for acknowledgement and thus a shift in boundaries.

The meanings and boundaries given to a particular community can also come from outside, ascribed to it either by those excluded or by those responsible for policy interventions. Communities are far from immune to what goes on beyond their imagined boundaries, although their members may wish otherwise and may resist such externally imposed definitions, for example, through active campaigning against the perception of an area being a 'sink estate'. Neighbourhoods are more likely to be shaped by external social, political, and economic forces and interventions, including the movements in and out of people, than they are by any internal structures or values. Those with significant levels of both inward and outward mobility rarely acquire the features of community. However, other factors especially those posing a threat may be sufficiently powerful to bind members together and generate a feeling of togetherness for that period necessary to respond to the circumstances. Such experiences can, in turn, form the foundations of more long-lasting relationships and sense of place.

Communities of interest

Alongside geographical communities are those constructed around perceived common interests or identities, acting according to Bauman (2001) as a 'surrogate of community', such as those based on 'race', ethnicity, gender, sexuality, occupation or leisure pursuits. Perception is again crucial, since objectively members may not have common interests, or at least fewer than they would like to assume or proclaim. Indeed, there may be no essential core to the social categories commonly utilised for such purposes (Mayo, 2000). Moreover, those interests that divide them may be ultimately more significant than those that bring them together, at which point the sense of community may be undermined, especially if expectations are high and much has been invested in its potential.

People have not one but many identities and learn to move between them as is socially appropriate. Occupying such different identities is not always comfortable and tensions, such as being a western-born female Muslim, or gay working class male, have to be carefully negotiated. When this proves impossible, individuals may face the consequences of rejecting one identity, or find themselves facing rejection and exclusion. While identities are not fixed, others may want to fix us. We may carry the essential characteristic, such as skin colour, but may feel this to be of little significance, while all around the message is that this is indeed the defining feature. Except at the level of crime and anti-social behaviour, Labour appears to lack any serious determination to confront the complexities and conflicts that lie within community. It shows little awareness of how internal tensions and divisions are to be negotiated or of the skills and capacities required of those whose responsibility it is to do so.

Communities of attachment

A third related category of 'community' is that derived from a shared attachment to a set of values or beliefs, the strength of which is conditional on whether the beliefs are all-encompassing or specific and how central they are in the lives of its members. Bauman (2001) points to the proliferation of 'aesthetic communities' constructed either around celebrities, either as idols or figures of fear, or the pre-occupations with fads and fixations. Such 'communities', created without any basis of reality, may generate a sense of emotional attachment but remain superficial and transient. Here membership has no consequences in terms of either ethical responsibilities or long-term commitments.

These different sources of community – spatial, identity or attachment – are not exclusive but often overlap and it is common for individuals to identify with and negotiate a number of different and potentially conflicting communities at any given moment. Over time, membership is likely to change as people move into or away from, or feel a decline in the meaning and significance of a particular community to a point where it can evaporate completely. This is not an uncommon occurrence amongst those who successfully negotiate a place within the mainstream, moving beyond 'victim' communities.

The mobilisation of community

'Community' is most regularly summoned by those claiming membership or by the state to illustrate a set of desirable relationship, behaviour and feelings. Conversely, it is rolled out as a benchmark when behaviour and attitudes suggest that something essential has been lost, or is found to be unacceptable and an affront to those who wish to preserve or build community. To successfully lay claim to the definition of 'community' is a powerful resource in local intra-group politics. Cochrane (1986) suggests that community has been used as a prefix, aerosol spray paint, to make policy interventions more appealing and progressive. As Williams noted (1983) it has this 'warmly persuasive' characteristic.

Butcher and Mullard (1993) argue that community policy can be mobilised by those adopting quite different views on citizenship, and is available both as a controlling mechanism and as a vehicle for advancing or protecting positive attributes. Community encompasses desirable, but ambiguous and abstract, outcomes. Its lack of precision is its strength. What is usually of greater concern is where the responsibility is located for any failure to reproduce such self-evident outcomes and the suggested means to these ends: what lies beneath the surface of any policy when community is the rallying cry. Once defined, the meanings of such interventions become part of the dialogue of engagement.

Community is typically mobilised from within for a number of purposes, including:

- to secure or preserve, through the maximisation of collective effort, a larger – fairer, more equitable or privileged – slice of some scarce and desirable resource; or
- to gain public recognition and generate a policy response in support of a particular group; or
- to defend members against a perceived or real threat to anything essential to their collective economic, social or political well-being; or
- as an alternative to institutions and values for which members have little sympathy; or
- a regulatory mechanism against those who claim membership but defy its social norms or conversely to place exclusionary barriers in the face of non-members; or
- a rallying point to reclaim, often through retrospective idealisation, seemingly lost values, institutions and social relations; or
- a vision for something better than what is otherwise available.

Conversely, the state, at national or local level, can utilise community as a vehicle for an equally diverse set of purposes including:

- to inform people of its intentions, or acquire information or knowledge;
- to gain endorsement or legitimacy for current policies or previous interventions or engage in dialogue about potential developments;
- to regulate expenditure by withdrawing existing services or resisting the call for additional services on the grounds that the 'community' itself is or should be responsible for meeting a particular need or dealing with a social concern;
- as partners in local problem-solving, with an acknowledged contribution and a shared interest in the outcome;

- as regulator of, and alternative to other public service providers through service evaluation or the creation of new locally managed service delivery organisations;
- to build better state–community relationships through dialogue and being more accessible, responsive, and accountable to local needs, concerns and priorities;
- to increase involvement in civic life, expanding the opportunities for the expression of democratic participatory 'voice';
- where active communities do not, or no longer exist, promote and facilitate the emergence of new communities, support vulnerable ones, and contribute to the sustainability of existing communities;
- in response to the actual or potential breakdown in public order.

Community is thus a suitable vehicle for intervention in relation to:

- service specific issues;
- broad social concerns;
- local governance and public order;
- the shifting state–citizen relationship in what is an uncertain, and complex environment.

The relationship between state and community is dynamic. How each responds to the initiative of the other depends on a number of quite nebulous considerations. These might include, the dominant characteristics of the relationship as experienced over time, each how initiative is understood and relates to other agendas, its potential to mobilise a number of diverse interests, the respective organisational and resources capacity at the time, and how competing demands are prioritised. All interventions, taken by either party, take place within an existing narrative and are influenced by past experience and mythology and in turn become a part of that process.

A community focused approach for social welfare

What then is the potential for a community-focused approach in relation to social welfare? Two key ideas are the recognition of differences within and between social groups and the value in actively seeking local solutions to social problems (SEU, 2001).

This requires a careful and sustained attempt to understand how community members understand such needs and how these can be met most effectively. Implicit in such an approach is the recognition, subsequently reinforced by the community members themselves, of the knowledge and understanding contained within that community. A significant shift in Labour's approach, culminating in the introduction of Community Strategies under the Local Government Act (2000), has been to move away from looking at communities through the lens of unfulfilled needs – a deficit model – to one that identifies collective assets and reasserts the concept of 'agency'. People not only have an understanding of local issues but they can act to change things. Building and supporting this local capacity, by strengthening social capital, understood as those features of social organisation such as networks, norms and social trust, is central to reviving a commitment to existing social and political processes and institutions (Gittell and Vidal, 1998). It also serves to ensure that disadvantaged citizens retain a belief in the possibility of individual achievement (Northern Ireland Office, 1993). With this comes a concomitant diminution in the elevation of professional or other formal systems of knowledge. Service planning and evaluation is to be enhanced by an evaluation of those directly affected by it for its appropriateness, potential or actual effectiveness, and suggestions for immediate improvement.

The new duty on local authorities to draw up community strategies is part of the wider requirement to promote local social, economic and environmental well-being. The Act makes clear that the central aim of the community strategy is to 'allow local communities to articulate their needs and priorities' (Local Government Act, 2000: para. 38). The process of compiling the strategy, using a bottom-up model, is seen as being as important as the outcome (para. 16). The Act states emphatically:

> Community strategies must give local people a powerful voice in planning local approaches to economic, social and environmental well-being and in holding core public services and local politicians to account (para. 16).

A community-orientation presents the possibility for community members to provide different but equally creative and effective solutions to social issues to what might be offered by external agents or elected members, some of which could be delivered from within the community itself. Hilary Armstrong, then minister with responsibility for local government, stated (2000) in relation to the New Deal for Communities:

> The NDC is very different from previous regeneration programmes, in giving the community a key – and in many cases a leading role – in determining the programme to turn around some of the most disadvantaged neighbourhoods in the country.

A community approach also involves a degree of risk especially as it can lead to a loss of control over the policy agenda and the direction of the dialogue. This requires a capacity for flexibility and responsiveness rarely developed amongst those training for professional roles. However, the downgrading of professional knowledge suggests that community solutions will be perceived as intrinsically superior to those of 'experts' leading to a withdrawal of formal services. This would leave disadvantaged communities even more vulnerable but with the additional expectation that they provide for themselves. Community-based solutions raise issues about the role of local community organisations in relation to the management and deployment of resources, human or otherwise, necessary to address a particular need or social problem. This presupposes that community organisations would want to invest their own resources (labour, time, knowledge and skills, even finance) into providing a service or tackling a social problem, and have the capacity to do so.

The assumption that working in partnership, perhaps as part of a neighbourhood management scheme as set out in the regeneration Action Plan (SEU, 2001), will increase the sense of ownership and therefore the desire to tackle local issues is as yet unproven. Service users may not be satisfied with public provision but this may not be a sufficient enough incentive to convert them into 'active citizens' providing their own services. Local willingness and capacity cannot be taken for granted nor can such reluctance be dismissed under pressure to devolve responsibility. Involvement in a LSP might be appealing for community organisations but the differential command over resources, and therefore influence, held by each of the partners will need to be addressed. Community organisations are just as likely to expect the more powerful collaborators to provide the resources and deliver the services at an appropriate level.

It also raises the more fundamental question of whether it is appropriate to delegate such authority. A critical test will be how such locally determined community strategies address what have previously been universal criteria for the allocation of welfare resources, such as equity of access to those eligible and transparent criteria for service allocation. On what basis do communities provide services or respond to social issues? How are individual rights and freedoms to be protected? How are communities to be held to account? Historically, the resolution of need assessment and resource distribution has been left to the state and its professionals. Within a community model the relationship between individual 'contributions' and the benefits received is more explicit, immediate and subject to local preconceptions. When such judgements and responsibility for intervention lie elsewhere with a formal body invested with that power they draw less attention and can carry less local significance.

Given the ambiguous, contradictory and complex nature of communities, any effective strategy must be one that is truly sensitive to local circumstances, and to do so it must be willing to enter into a sustained and critical dialogue. As stated in government guidelines (DETR, 2000c), 'Authorities will need to be alive to these layers of complexity...' (para. 44). The first major hurdle is in defining the boundaries of any community and identifying non-exclusionary ways of communicating with its membership, especially those groups that have been either excluded from local political processes or reluctant to participate. Within a spatial community it may not be appropriate to engage all those who have some relationship to it. Strategic decisions would have to be made, for example, in respect of the business sector. It might be appropriate to draw in small-to-medium local businesses but not larger enterprises that simply have an outlet in the area. Conversely some major companies do take, or might be persuaded to take, a particular interest in their local neighbourhood, backed by financial or human investment. It may also be important to engage to change employment practices in relation to recruitment policy, investment or purchasing strategies.

Similarly, priority might be given to work through existing community organisations, the already-participating members of the community. This does assume that such groups exist, are relevant, and are dynamic and active relative to their goals and potential membership. Moreover, active engagement may either tip them over the edge of what they can effectively manage or change their nature and original purpose. Government has recognised that engaging community organisations will require additional resources. Support is to come through the creation of the Community Empowerment Fund and the Community Chests, within the Action Plan of the Neighbourhood Renewal Fund, alongside the proposed development of a better neighbourhood-focused database and an online 'knowledge management system', a

> systematic and comprehensive guide to the information available on what works in tackling the various problems of deprived neighbourhoods (SEU, 2001: para. 6.23).

Whatever the level and vitality of existing organisations, it is likely that some will be undeveloped, gaps will exist across significant areas, and new needs or interests will emerge for which new organisations will be required. Thus, as well as having an engagement strategy for existing groups, there must also be a second one, run in parallel, focused on the sustainability and development of existing organisation and the facilitation of new ones. Organisations would need to be distinguished in terms of whether they were member serving or public serving bodies. Another refinement would be to think in terms of 'how' an organisation works – through mutual self-help, campaigning or education, direct service provision to others, or development work.

Not all citizens are 'joiners' and opportunities still have to be found to engage people on an individual basis. A number of relatively successful engagement techniques are now available to capture individual perspectives. These include, 'planning for real', profiling, social audits, listening surveys, citizen juries, and focus groups, as well as the more traditional public meeting, postal questionnaire, neighbourhood fora or informal networking (Chanan, 1999; Barr and Hashagen, 2000; Chanan *et al.*, 2000). The use of any single method is unlikely to be effective. Whatever techniques are utilised they will need to reflect the circumstances and capacities of the targeted groups, and some 'mapping' between the techniques, the targeted group and the policy objectives, is required.

One approach is to identify all those concerned with the overall well-being and development of a locality or community of interest. Another is to combine this with dividing the target community into subgroups. Potential organising categories might include those focused on:

- particular services (e.g. housing tenants, health service users, childcare, public transport users and disability services);
- groups based on cross-cutting bio-social categories, such as women, young people, black and ethnic minority communities and the elderly;
- more fluid social categories related to current issues or interests, such as refugees, school girl mothers, drug abuse, cultural development, victims of domestic violence or local economic development.

Whatever single or multiple approach is adopted, and a version of the latter is more likely to succeed, the outcome is likely to generate a complex structure (Chanan *et al.*, 2000). Some core and transparent principles should underpin any community engagement. For example, those individuals or organisations claiming to represent the community need to be able to substantiate such claims and are not simply hollow shells with little active membership. In establishing legitimacy clarity is required as to whether this is measured against the principles of representative, participatory or direct democracy (Burns *et al.*, 1994). To expect full representativeness is too demanding and hard to justify given local voting patterns. It is more reasonable to think in terms of community organisations as indicative of sectional rather than universal interests. Matching existing groups against an awareness of the complex nature of a community would indicate whether there were significant absences in the community voices.

In making sense of any engagement the material interests of those voices need to be disentangled, even if only at the conceptual level, from what they have to say. To repeatedly recruit the same individuals or organisations, to each engagement may make for a more comfortable relationship but diminishes the likelihood that the complexity of the community will be captured. Minority or sectional voices need to be identified and heard, and questions of whose interests or needs are being served or denied have to be asked in relation to any proposal or initiative. Conversely, those drawn from the community to participate must guard against their own seduction or co-option by the processes of patronage or derived status as a valued community 'leader'.

Community-generated policy proposals need to be evaluated in terms of how, and to what extent they acknowledge social and cultural diversity, without assuming the validity of such differences, or whether a solution for one community simply creates problems for another. Local perspectives or solutions must also be explored in the context of national policy goals and objectives. The goal should be to build communities that are experienced as open systems that welcome and are in dialogue with others. A balance has to be struck, and be open to renegotiation, between the rights, freedoms, choices, and responsibilities of the individual, groups or subcategories, and those of the wider collective. These are challenging and demanding requirements and it might be tempting for service providers to find a resolution independently of any community engagement. However, welfare state professionals have themselves been found lacking in an awareness of the complexities involved. Change has often occurred only in response to pressure exerted by community organisations. Indeed, there is no once-and-for-all solution to social issues but only constant evaluation and renegotiation with those directly affected.

The requirement to put aside existing assumptions about service delivery and the relationships between providers and recipients presents the greatest challenge. Within a community-oriented approach these need to be reformulated in a dialogue involving professionals, elected representatives, service users and citizens. To acknowledge the complexity and messiness of community is but the first step towards creating services that are responsive to diverse needs and that the rationale behind such differences is the product of dialogue. It brings closer the possibility that collective interventions in relation to broad policy objectives will also be subject to locally sensitive dialogue.

10

Capacity Building and Civic Engagement

The previous chapter highlighted the growing importance given to a 'community-focused' approach in policy design and implementation, in which 'community' is both an object of policy and a basis for the delivery of policy. The priority afforded to this, alongside partnership working, can be located within a wider context in which there is mounting concern about the level of public or civic engagement. Not for the first time have governments expressed anxiety about the level of confidence in and commitment to existing political processes as demonstrated by the disadvantaged or socially excluded. Fear about the potential for political disaffection has never been far from urban policy and has led repeatedly to the introduction of 'special measures' targeted at such groups or the places they are said to inhabit.

Such positive discriminatory measures may indeed generate real, albeit limited, material gains for those targeted, for example, in the form of improved employment opportunities, housing, environment or transport, reduced crime levels or increased social mobility. However, there is usually another, sometimes more important, purpose. This is to bind participants more closely and ensure that they feel sufficiently confident in the 'fairness' of existing structures such that they believe they too can reap more benefit by participation than they can by political conflict or withdrawal. The value of 'public participation', as instituted by the state, is often less in the concrete outcomes that might be secured, although these might be uppermost in the motivations of the participants, as in reinforcing the belief that progress can be secured through legitimate democratic processes. Thus in reviewing community development, the Community Development Review Group for

Northern Ireland, later endorsed by the Northern Ireland Department of Health and Social Services (1991), suggested its value lay in 'reassuring local communities and groups that social and economic change is both possible and achievable'.

The 'social inclusion' strategy adopted by the Labour government is more ambitious and goes beyond an anxiety about social disorder. Social exclusion, or the failure to achieve citizenship (Bergham, 1995) has replaced Labour's traditional goal of poverty eradication. It reflects a concern about public legitimation in the political process, specifically at local level but also in relation to the direction and implementation of policy, especially where local intelligence can be harnessed to make for more successful outcomes (DETR, 1998b; Foley and Martin, 2000). This has been fuelled by low voter turnout in local elections, limited participation in consultative bodies, and the desire for greater public accountability following criticism over the management and professional leadership in core policy areas (Giddens, 1998). Citizen involvement in their communities is seen as a benchmark of a healthy democracy and the basis of social inclusion and solidarity (Beck, 1998). There have been a growing number of voices advancing the merits of a vibrant associational activity and a participatory society (Young, 1990; Putnam, 1993a, 1995; Beck, 1998; Giddens, 1998; Barnes, 1999). Fragmentation within local communities thus represents a particular challenge (Chandler, 2001). Self-help and volunteering are actively promoted (SEU, 2001). Participatory structures and a deliberative and inclusive culture, what Clarence and Painter (1998) describe as a 'collaborative discourse', are prerequisites to success. However, a commitment to enhancing local democracy and realising such goals as 'active citizenship' brings its own problems in the management of involvement. It is easier to create deliberative structures than it is to control or manage the agenda, the content of debate, or the subsequent actions.

If 'communities' are to be involved in strategic and policy specific planning, implementation and monitoring, they need as a prerequisite the capacity to do so. Labour has accepted the need to intervene to promote involvement where it does not already exist (DETR, 1998b), or as Chandler (2001) notes, 'to involve the uninvolved, to create and promote the model of the "active citizen"' (p. 8). The mainstreaming of 'capacity building', long advanced by community development professionals, has occurred in response to the supposed dependency inducing tendencies of state welfare.

Labour seeks what Giddens (1998) describes as 'positive welfare', characterised by autonomy, active health, life-long learning, initiative and risk-taking as well as protection from risk. This requires self-confident, socially aware citizens with the skills and attributes to participate effectively in public life. Thus capacity building for civic engagement, a once marginal activity, becomes a key instrument underpinning the success of other service-related measures, both in the UK and globally (AMA, 1991; Craig and Mayo, 1995; Miller and Ahmad, 1997). Its success is dependent upon the acquisition by other social welfare professions of values, skills and methods practiced within community development.

State and civil society

Social democratic systems survive to the extent that they secure popular legitimacy demonstrated by at least some form of symbolic participation in the democratic process. A significant and/or consistent decline in voting levels, poor quality and low numbers amongst those willing to be candidates in such elections, or the membership levels of political parties, are all indicators of a potential crisis of political legitimacy. However, it is the perceived weakness of civil society, that public space between state and family, that has come to act as a barometer for political and economic stability (Beck, 1998). Indicators of a vibrant and dynamic civil society include:

- Participation rates in non-profit organisations, community organisations and social movements, levels of active neighbourliness and mutual self-help, or conversely evidence of neighbourhood conflict, resident anti-social behaviour, or a high visibility of groups displaying socially challenging behaviour, such as rough sleepers, school truants, those involved in drug and alcohol and substance abuse.
- The number of volunteers offering themselves in pursuit of 'good causes' and the volume of financial contributions to charitable and public interest issues.
- The quality of local environments and public spaces, the degree to which these are utilised and for what purposes, evidence of vandalism and excessive litter, perceptions of public safety and neighbourhood crime.

- The strength and diversity of local cultural life, the degree of involvement and multiple expressions of voice and identity by minority groups.
- Levels of civil unrest.

The extent to which state-led participatory initiatives are genuine attempts to strengthen civil society and extend local democracy is debatable. Arnstein's (1969) well-referenced 'ladder of participation', extending from manipulation and therapy to citizen control, illustrates the potential range of motives and potential outcomes behind such state initiatives. Chandler (2001) considers current initiatives to be symbolic exercises concerned with individual engagement and subsequent feelings in relation to the social world, rather than ensuring greater democratic accountability over decision-making. Without strong, independent and countervailing civic associations, and opportunities for public discourse, involvement in state constructed efforts to increase public involvement, however sophisticated, is likely to leave participants vulnerable to state incorporation.

Behind current concerns about civic health lies a challenge, first highlighted by the New Right, to the limits of governmental capacity to meet rising social expectations when issues appear ever more complex and there are few unambiguous answers about the nature of the problem or the remedy. Social complexity and governmental uncertainty or incapacity are powerful drivers to maximise involvement, thereby lowering expectations and reducing the responsibility of any single party. The emergence of new provider agencies makes governance more complex, generating a renewed interest in their accountability. Community organisations, user and interest groups have demanded that their voices be heard in the new structures. There is also a growing perception that beyond a certain point, state intervention, resourcing and orchestrating society's response to social issues, produces negative outcomes for both society and individuals. For neo-liberals this is often expressed in terms of the suffocating effects of state regulation on free market competition and a 'over-dependency' in individuals and families with a consequent decline in personal responsibility, initiative and morality. For the left, the issue has been less to do with the level of state involvement, except that it is inadequate, and more with the nature of the involvement itself, especially the extent to which it enhances or diminishes local democracy and citizenship.

Labour and responsible citizenship

Labour has produced a number of measures designed to address its anxiety about civil society, public behaviour and responsible citizenship. Taken together they suggest a five-pronged 'joined-up' approach aimed at:

1. increasing individual opportunities
2. combating anti-social behaviour
3. focusing on priority groups
4. reforming local governance
5. strengthening local communities.

Adopting the slogan of 'education, education, education' for the 2001 general election, Labour has maintained a belief that a sound education provides the best opportunity for personal advancement and social inclusion. Under the all-encompassing heading of 'life-long learning' the government has committed itself to raising the level of basic skills, for both children and adults, introducing 'citizenship' teaching, and widening participation in higher education. In launching the SEU (1997), it identified rough sleepers, teenage mothers, and drug users as priority targets for special attention. Its approach to anti-social behaviour has at times appeared hasty and unclear with policy intentions such as the proposal for on-the-spot fines for drunken or noisy behaviour, withdrawn almost as quickly as they appear. Youth offending and anti-social behaviour has been the primary target. Curfew schemes for under-tens have been introduced along with anti-social behaviour orders, targeting thirteen- to sixteen-year-olds thought to be at risk of offending, fines and imprisonment for the parents of persistent truants, streamlining the youth justice system and the introduction of community wardens.

Concern has also grown about the levels of activity within both the formal political process and associational activity. Episodic involvement through voting is no longer considered sufficient for democratic legitimation. Greater public participation is required and Labour has attempted to strengthen local governance through a number of initiatives including:

• The introduction of elected mayors, changing voting procedures, and reforming the role of local councillors and the organisation of council business through the separation of powers between executive and representative functions.

- The introduction of a variety of participatory or consultative mechanisms, such as citizens' juries, youth councils or neighbourhood forums and neighbourhood management.
- Placing a duty on local authorities to promote the economic, social and environmental well-being of their areas, and the power to do anything they consider is likely to achieve this objective, along with an expectation that it will develop its 'community leadership' role.
- Imposing a duty on local authorities to consult with the public both under Best Value and the development of community strategies.
- Creating new structures of governance and participation, as in LSPs and Patient Forums in health care (DoH, 2001b).
- The introduction of a variety of local initiatives, each with a requirement to engage and consult, such as Health Action Zones, Employment and Education Zone's, NDC, while also strengthening the consultative requirements of existing programmes.

Strengthening communities

Labour has placed public engagement at the heart of its strategy for tackling social exclusion, particularly in relation to disadvantaged neighbourhoods. The NDC (1998) initiative that seeks to 'bridge the gap between these neighbourhoods and the rest of the country' (DTLR, 2001), represents some continuity with previous efforts to address the contentious issues of deprived neighbourhoods with short-term experiments. In assessing the lessons based on the initial round of the nineteen pathfinder areas, the DTLR stated, 'communities must be at the heart of the regeneration process'. An amount of £1.9b, committed over ten years, is to be invested in thirty-nine 'pathfinder' partnerships, identified on the basis of deprivation, as measured by the Index of Local Deprivation and regional spread. Five key features are offered as evidence of a distinctive approach within the NDC that addresses earlier shortcomings (Armstrong, 2000). These are:

1. community involvement and ownership;
2. joined up thinking and solutions;

3. action based on 'what works' pragmatism;
4. a long-term commitment to deliver real change; and
5. a partnership between local communities and key agencies.

The NDC is located within the wider strategy designed to address neighbourhood deprivation and implemented in parallel to the existing SRB, geared to areas greater in size to those envisaged under NDC. A feature of the approach has been the desire to learn from previous policies and to bring together in a coherent framework, the three strands of urban policy, community development and citizen engagement. The initial programme, as outlined in 'Bringing Britain Together: A national strategy for neighbourhood renewal' (SEU, 1998), adopted a three-pronged joined-up approach designed to tackle 'deep-seated' problems over a ten to twenty year period. It was promoted as a comprehensive approach that linked together a number of policy areas, including 'New Deals' for the unemployed, the disabled and single parents, changes to local government representation and management, and a crime and drugs strategy. It was to provide, 'a backdrop that has been missing in past regeneration efforts' (SEU, 1998: 54).

Effective coordination was the third element within the strategy. The SEU was to symbolise the new approach, with its remit to break the 'vicious circle' caused by the 'combination of linked problems' and 'shifting the policy and practice of mainline departments' (SEU, 1998). The SEU would encourage inter-agency and inter-professional collaboration, and identify and disseminate 'best practice'. The staffing of SEU mirrored this process by bringing together workers from a wide range of government departments, local authorities, and non-profit organisations, while supported by a 'ministerial network' from the key government departments.

Following publication of the 'Bringing Britain Together' report, eighteen Priority Area Teams (PAT) were established (1998), each with the task of exploring a specific aspect of the renewal strategy. PAT membership was drawn from external experts as well as ten central government departments, and the teams were responsible for producing a consultation 'national strategy' framework document (SEU, 2000), to drive subsequent policies. PAT 9 stressed the importance of volunteering as contributing to personal development and skill acquisition, self-confidence, and improved social networks, as well as ensuring that volunteers were better prepared for employment and felt socially included (DETR, 2000d). In 2001 the Chancellor,

Gordon Brown, suggested a target of at least two hours of voluntary activity per week for all adults by 2005. The Active Communities Unit (ACU) produced a code of practice for promoting volunteering and announced a new Development Fund, to support the recruitment and training of volunteers (ACU, 2001). The ACU had initially been established within the Cabinet Office but within a year was relaunched and relocated to the Home Office. Its remit is to engage with the voluntary and community sectors, strengthen community leadership, promote citizenship and public involvement, and take the lead on community development.

The SEU national strategy action plan (SEU, 2001) focuses on the 10 per cent most deprived wards (i.e. 841 electoral wards, with 82 per cent concentrated in 88 local authority districts). It re-emphasises the need to revive local economies, rebuild communities, provide quality services, and develop local leadership and collaborative working. It highlights the need to build social capital and to address the loss of faith in the political process. It proposes combining national policy initiatives with local collaboration, to develop joint ownership, underpinned by national and regional support, stretching over a ten- to twenty-year period. At the local level, LSPs, proposed in the 'Joining it up locally' PAT 17 report, and introduced under the Local Government Act (2000), are identified as the key mechanism to bring together local authorities, residents, private, voluntary and community sector organisations (see Chapter 9). Two new funding mechanisms were also established, the Community Empowerment Fund and Community Chests, to support community involvement. The primary task of the LSPs is to produce a local neighbourhood renewal strategy and to prepare community and neighbourhood strategies.

Capacity building and community development

Capacity building is a relatively new term to describe the resources, processes and support needed to enable citizens and community-based organisations to become and remain involved in participative initiatives. More generally, when applied to organisations, it describes a developmental process for greater effectiveness. It also encompasses an earlier stage of persuading people that engagement is both worthwhile and likely to produce desirable outcomes (Anastacio *et al.*, 2000).

The application of capacity building is largely dependent upon the core skills and knowledge acquired within the practice of community development. The potential of community development as a practice or method of working has been steadily accorded increasing recognition as a mechanism to facilitate the citizenship and social inclusion agenda (Miller and Ahmad, 1997). Since the late 1960s community development projects have been funded by, and qualified practitioners employed within, various local government departments, as well as in voluntary organisations. It was until recently of marginal interest in the policy debate despite a small number of high profile initiatives, a steady increase in the numbers employed, and the emergence of national representative bodies (AMA, 1989, 1991). Today its methods and values are now recognised as invaluable in the context of public engagement. However, community development has not simply been a method of practice, but has also been associated with a political project concerned with equity and social justice in which the state was constructed both as an obstacle and potential facilitator (Miller and Ahmad, 1997).

Community development methods can be utilised to achieve diverse and conflicting political objectives. It should not be forgotten that its first deployment by the state was in the former colonies in preparation for an independence designed to ensure a continuing and deferential association with the 'mother country' (Mayo, 1975). Since its early application in the UK, some thirty-five years ago, it has been used as a mechanism for:

- Mobilising and organising to address social injustice and inequalities – social, economic, political, environmental – and dominated by conflict and bargaining strategies targeted at the powerful.
- Strengthening representative and participatory democracy – building a culture that reinforces the belief that being involved makes a difference, enabling citizens to gain their 'voice', strengthening relations of accountability with formal structures.
- Building and strengthening intermediate structures within and between neighbourhoods and external institutions.
- Enabling local identities, cultures, social processes, rituals and institutions to be created, maintained, developed or curtailed, to generate social recognition and dignity.
- Generating a capacity for local need identification, problem-solving and service provision.

- Extending individual and collective capacities by providing informal educative opportunities.
- The management of public dissent through the incorporation of local leadership and the creation of symbolic and impotent local structures.

Community development can be a resource for a variety of political traditions. Within a pluralist consensual model of politics, it is focused on strengthening threatened core values, institutions or social behaviours. In radical pluralism with its recognition of conflicting and unequal interests, it is an organising tool to address excessive inequities. Within a structural conflict model those advocates of radical change adopt it as a means of political mobilisation or conversely for those who seek to maintain existing hierarchies of privilege it can ensure tighter state control (Popple, 1995). The introduction of the language of 'capacity building' suggests an attempt to distance the method from the associated overtly conflict-based politics. Whereas the dominant theme once was to be working 'in and against the state', the message today is to be working 'in and on the state, and certainly 'with the state'.

The espoused values and methods of community development as identified in the literature (Thomas, 1995; SCCD, 2000) that closely mirror ideas on capacity building can be summarised as:

- Working *'with'* and not *'on'* people to focus on individual and community assets and capacities – that ultimately people have the capacity to bring about change, to make a difference, to be more in control of their own lives.
- Citizens should be at the centre of policy initiatives, able to define their own needs and how these should be met.
- Practitioners start from people's current experience and knowledge, with a view to developing collective/individual knowledge, expertise and skill.
- An emphasis on how things are done – the means are ends in themselves, as important as any other material outcomes – and as far as possible mirror objectives.
- People should participate/engage freely and voluntarily, working within local organisations that are independent and autonomous. Local organisations retain control – they do what they decide needs to be done; decision-making is in their hands along with the organisation's strategic direction.

- A respect for and promotion of difference and diversity – we have different, histories, cultures, and needs; there are multiple perceptions of the nature of the problem and what should be done; that a solution for one group may be a problem for another; and the various individual contributions should all be valued.
- An emphasis on collaboration and working across and beyond boundaries, to find holistic solutions.

Such idealistic values, for example working 'with' as opposed to 'on' or 'for' people, have been contrasted with the traditional approaches of social welfare professionals. Indeed, there has always been a strong anti-professional tendency amongst community development practitioners (Miller and Bryant, 1990). Applying these values to the provision of welfare services requires practitioners to act in the face of contradictory pressures and to demonstrate sophistication in managing these boundaries. There is, for example, a tension between identifying and building upon people's assets or capacities, and responding to their needs, which implies a deficit model. To acknowledge current experience or knowledge is a positive personal validation but can be of little utility when based on narrow or limited experience, or where the range of alternative possibilities is unknown, or when it has left a legacy of negativity towards self and others.

Practitioners need to manage complex individual and group emotions. In prioritising collective needs, individual needs cannot be ignored. Indeed if they are left unattended, collective needs are unlikely to be addressed, sabotaged by the pressing claims of individual members. Matching the pace and urgency of individual needs with the achievement of collective goals is a skilled process. Individuals are often in distress, due either to the weight of other people's problems or to the personal impact of their own activism. Practitioners are often ill-equipped to be working with those various forms of mental distress that are only too widespread in distressed neighbourhoods (Jarman *et al.*, 1992).

Practitioners are also likely to encounter anger, fear and jealousy focused on new and emergent social divisions – producing targets for 'out group' hostility. The exchange of milder hostilities between neighbourhoods and networks as they compete for scarce resources can undermine community cohesion and deflect groups away from common problems. While it may seem appropriate to argue for the autonomy of local organisations, the impact of funding, the employment of professional workers, participation in partnership mechanisms, and becoming a service delivery agency, all have a profound effect on that autonomy. To speak of the importance of 'means' as 'ends in themselves' can neglect the fact that people are usually motivated to secure some material difference in their life situation and not to have an experience in collective learning. The process by which material outcomes are achieved can be of less interest. The educative processes may not be what participants have consciously signed up for, although some may come to appreciate it and ultimately to see it as a valuable outcome. Finally, valuing diversity and difference, whilst it may inform a judgement, cannot be allowed to prevent action and some actions will at least imply that not all views or behaviours are equally valued or respected.

The application of capacity building (Key Idea 12, SEU, 1998) within the context of Labour's modernisation agenda poses an additional set of dilemmas for practitioners. For example, there is already anecdotal evidence of 'activist exhaustion' and 'consultation fatigue' (Purdue *et al.*, 2000). Practitioners must manage the tension between what is a developmental approach and the pressure to respond quickly to each new output-driven initiative. Immediate and tangible results are expected but these might not produce sustainable outcomes. Again the collaborative practices of developmental activity sit uncomfortably with the need to compete for resources. Practitioners and activists may well be aware of the opportunities presented by current essentially short-term initiatives, but are also likely to be conscious of the deeper and intractable structural disadvantages that underpin social exclusion.

Theorising citizen engagement

Previous efforts to 'theorise' public participation as a policy measure have highlighted its ambiguous, confused, and sometimes dangerous objectives. Arnstein's (1969) eight-rung ladder of citizen participation drew attention to the possibilities of participation being used as a tool for citizen manipulation and duplicity as much as for citizen influence and control. Contemporary writers concerned with the participatory approaches to third world development emphasise the tyrannical aspects of the now dominant participatory methods

(Cooke and Kathari, 2001). They identify three tyrannies: of decision-making and control, of the oppressive tendencies of the collective, and the tyranny of one dominant methodology and approach. Writing in relation to the UK a number of writers (Beresford and Croft, 1993; Burns *et al.*, 1994) have adopted, critiqued and extended Arnstein's approach. Distinctions are made between those strategies designed for citizen control, citizen participation and non-participation while recognising that the experience of any citizen or community will not be uniform across policy areas. Moreover, varying degrees of involvement and control are quite appropriate and it would be a mistake to 'read-off' from a 'ladder of participation' that the object is always to move from the bottom to the top.

Labour has adopted the language of social exclusion from continental European partners, where the relationships between the economic, political and social dimensions of citizenship have continued to be part of strategic policy. This tension between a social democratic inclusiveness and a market-oriented North American model, no doubt, reflects conflicts within the party. The Labour leadership has more closely identified with those arguments emerging from the US. Labour's approach to engagement and social exclusion, has been influenced by the divisive effects of neo-liberal policies. Local authorities now have a major role in building and managing new relationships between individuals, communities and the institutions of governance. Nolan (1998) and Chandler (2001) argue that these current strategies, found in both the US and UK are much more concerned with therapeutic purposes and the subjective feelings of those who participate, rather than strengthening democratic accountability. Writing about phase two of the 'Third Way', Tony Blair stated:

> democracy needs to respond to people's demand that they have a right to be listened to *even if decisions do not always go the way they want* (Blair, 2001: 12, emphasis added).

The objective is to ensure that individuals and communities feel involved and validated that their voices have been heard, and the act of participation is the vehicle by which this is accomplished. There are elements of this approach within the Action Plan on neighbourhood renewal (SEU, 2001). Yet, if this was the primary purpose it could only be sustained by a high degree of gullibility amongst the participants.

Social capital

Within the discourse of community engagement the North American concept of 'social capital' has grown in influence (Gittell and Vidal, 1998; Kubisch and Stone, 2001). The existence of high levels of social capital is correlated with the achievement of a number of current government policy objectives (Putnam, 2000; Woolcock, 2001). The World Bank argues that social capital is, 'critical for societies to prosper economically and for developments to be sustainable' (World Bank, 1999). Social capital is defined by OECD as 'Networks together with shared norms, values and understandings that facilitate cooperation within or among groups' (Cote and Healy, 2001). Currently, the Office for National Statistics is developing a framework for the measurement and analysis of social capital and eighteen national surveys include some measure of social capital (ONS, 2001). The ONS review suggests that five themes can be identified across the eighteen surveys: participation, social engagement and commitment; control and self-efficacy; perception of community level structures or characteristics; social interaction, networks and social support; and trust, reciprocity and social cohesion.

Social capital was popularised through the work of Putnam (1993b, 1995), although others such as Jacobs (1961), Granovetter (1974) and Coleman (1988) first introduced the terminology. Schuller (2000) suggests that the speed of popularity and application to such diverse aspects has turned it into 'a promiscuous parvenu in our intellectual world' (p. 1). Putnam's concern is the decline in associational activity within the US, and the subsequent impact on governance. Since de Tocqueville, associational activity has been represented as a core characteristic of American pluralism. Putnam defines social capital as:

> features of social organisation such as networks, norms, and social trust that facilitate co-ordination and co-operation for mutual benefit... Networks of civic engagement foster sturdy norms of generalised reciprocity and encourage the emergence of social trust...facilitate co-ordination and communication, amplify reputations, and thus allow

dilemmas of collective action to be resolved...embody past success at collaboration which can serve as a template for future collaborations... broaden participants' sense of developing the 'I' into the 'we'... (Putnam, 1995: 67).

It is these features of social life that Putnam suggests:

enable participants to act together more effectively to pursue shared objectives (Putnam, 1995: 664)

Bourdieu (1986) defines social capital more broadly. He sets it alongside other forms of capital such as economic or cultural capital and includes all the resources generated through durable, trusting and collaborative ties. Most significantly, Bourdieu sees social capital not simply as the attributes of a healthy community but as a resource that can be used to extract additional resources from other more privileged groups or converted into other forms of capital. In other words, social capital is related to relations of power, both in the sense that its relative 'volume' is a measure of inequality and a means by which existing relationships are challenged or reinforced. The concept of 'linking social capital' (Cote and Healy, 2001; Woolcock, 2001) that refers to relations between groups located in different positions on a hierarchy of power and resource distribution reconnects with Bourdieu's understanding of social capital as leverage.

Social capital is both a way of analysing the attributes of a healthy community from a social perspective and the primary determinant in predicting neighbourhood stability (Kubisch and Stone, 2001). Those neighbourhoods exhibiting high levels of social capital are said to be less likely to decline when other factors are held constant. It is seen as a non-exclusive private and public good, in which the benefits are unrestricted (Putnam, 2000). The current embrace of social capital within the policy domain with its focus on 'healthy' communities neglects relationships of power both within and between social groups. Moreover by emphasising spatial communities it ignores networks based on interest-based groups such as social class, gender, or race that cross spatial boundaries.

CONSCISE, a European-funded research project, identifies six elements within social capital with trust, a very fragile concept that is easily destroyed and painstakingly long to develop, as the most important along with well-established social networks, shared values, belonging, joint working and reciprocity (www.mdx.conscise. ac.uk). It also suggests that social capital is stronger between individuals rather than between organisations and that the departure of key individuals can weaken relationships between organisations. It also highlights the detrimental impact on health levels within a community following a decline in social capital. As argued in the earlier discussion on community (Chapter 9), communities that exhibit high levels of social capital may utilise it for negative purposes (Walker *et al.*, 2000; ONS, 2001).

Sampson *et al.* (1997) refer to the significance of what they describe as 'collective efficacy' – the informal mechanisms by which local residents achieve public order – suggesting that this depends in large measure on conditions of mutual trust and solidarity among neighbours. Temkin and Rohe (1998) highlight the overall sense of attachment and loyalty amongst neighbourhood residents, along with the ability of residents to convert a strong 'socio-cultural milieu', underpinned by institutional infrastructures, into effective collective action. The socio-cultural milieu is understood as comprising a number of elements. Key to these are the degree to which a neighbourhood is experienced as a distinct space, the interaction between neighbours (its nature, scope and depth), the degree to which work and socialising is conducted in the neighbourhood, and the utilisation of local facilities.

Two types of social capital are identified: bonding capital to strengthen the ties that bind those who already know each other, and bridging capital to build links between those who previously did not know each other. Elliot (2001) notes that strong bonding capital can be exclusive and can be the basis for reactionary politics such as sectarianism. Bridging capital can be applicable both for strengthening intra-neighbourhood relations and between a neighbourhood and its external environments. It is thought to be especially important in respect of those links between neighbourhood-based institutions and those external to it but able to influence and shape the lives of both the neighbourhood as a whole and the individuals within it. Keyes *et al.* (1996) stress the importance of these institutional networks between government, philanthropic, educational and other institutions that are able to channel financial, technical, political, and other types of support. For these to be effective requires long-term relationships of trust and reciprocity, a shared vision, mutual interests, and a capacity for reciprocity, adaptability and flexibility. Such features are all to be headlined amongst the desirable outcomes of current partnership work.

Thus 'connectedness' between citizens in neighbourhoods and communities of interest, as well as between them and wider social, political and economic institutions, is increasingly identified as the key to ensuring self-sustaining healthy communities, to attracting additional resources, and to increasing the opportunities of community members. Burt (1992) warns of missed opportunities or what he calls, the 'structural holes' or 'gaps between non-redundant contacts', where the failure to connect with more appropriately resourced individuals results in an inability to take advantage of opportunities that could make a difference. Granovetter (1974) made a different point by highlighting the potential strength of 'weak ties', that is, the power of non-familial or primary relationships in making possible opportunities for personal advancement.

Communitarianism

More popular than the proponents of social capital are those advancing the cause of communitarianism (see Chapter 2). Although it has its academic advocates (Tam, 1998), its key public spokesperson, Etzioni, aims to reach a public rather than academic audience and seeks a social movement for change. Feted by both former US President Clinton and Prime Minister Blair, Etzioni identifies an emergent social crisis, the product of both new social rights established during the 1960s, and the economic liberalism of the 1980s. As a consequence key institutions, such as the family and community, have been undermined. Too much attention has been devoted to securing 'rights' and too little given to duty and social responsibility. The result has been an increasingly atomised world with a declining sense of civic virtue and moral purpose. Etzioni sees 'community' as the central organising vehicle to re-establish a sense of belonging, underpinned by a strengthened ethical and moral base, in which individuals can

> act rationally and on their own, advancing their self or 'I', but their ability to do so is deeply affected by how well they are anchored within a sound community and sustained by a firm moral and emotive personal underpinning – a community they perceive as theirs, as a 'we', rather than as an imposed, restraining, 'they' ... (Etzioni, 1988).

Communitarians, like social capital theorists, see networks and 'connectedness' as central but primarily as regulatory devices

> social webs of people who know one another...and have a moral voice...draw on interpersonal bonds to encourage members to abide by shared values (Etzioni, 1995: ix).

For Etzioni, people act without any consideration for one another when they are without any moral commitments. By maintaining a civic, social and moral order, communities are key policy sites but to be effective they too need support, legitimation and guidance by a set of overarching values expressed by government (Etzioni, 1993). Driver and Martell (1997) suggest that communitarian ideas have had a powerful influence on Labour's approach and indeed can be found in Blair's own pre-election position,

> For myself, I start from a simple belief that people are not separate economic actors competing in the marketplace of life. They are citizens of a community. We are social beings, nurtured in families and communities and human only because we develop the moral power of personal responsibility for ourselves and each other (Blair, 1996: 3).

In an effort to popularise their ideas, communitarians have carefully avoided some of the more complex issues that arise. For example, if communities are to reflect a morality generated by their members they need to be sufficiently autonomous. This poses some interesting issues of how individuals manage their relationships with the numerous communities to which they belong, and how they act between a single community and wider political bodies. Communitarianism provides few answers as to how cultural and social diversity within and between communities is to be expressed, legitimised, protected and nourished. Similarly, neither intra- nor inter-community conflict is adequately addressed and the inequalities between different social groups are largely ignored. While the importance of meeting individual responsibilities is stressed, much less attention is given to how powerful institutions should exercise their responsibilities to the community. At a fundamental level there are limitations to any project that attempts to re-establish a fixed universal morality in a rapidly changing and complex world. Attempts to define core or essentialist values must be placed alongside a capacity to live with difference, change, ambiguity and uncertainty. Communitarian desires to secure, and some suggest impose, agreement on a common set of ethics divorced from social rights, social justice or without making significant inroads into existing inequities, are likely to remain frustrated.

Governance and local regime theory

As part of its modernisation programme, Labour has introduced new forms of governance at the centre of which is partnership working (see Chapter 7), closely associated with public participation and the role outlined for a reformed local authority. Another North American concept, regime theory (Stone, 1986, 1989; Stoker, 1995) has addressed the question of how 'a capacity to govern' can emerge, 'in the midst of diversity and complexity' within a social democratic capitalist society (Stoker, 1995). The influence of regime theory is apparent within Labour thinking and indeed Stoker has acted as a government advisor.

New processes of governance are needed when nation states struggle to function in the face of powerful global forces, cities compete for inward investment, and there is anxiety over the consequences of social exclusion (Clarke, 1996). Not unlike social capital theorists, Judd and Parkinson (1990), writing from within regime theory, refer to the need for 'leadership capacity', the 'range, stability and durability of local mechanisms and alliances...' (p. 21). Regime theory stresses the need for long-term collaborative coalitions that acknowledge mutual inter-dependencies in order for certain interests to govern (Stone, 1989). Such coalitions need to be constructed and maintained through co-operative networking, solidarity, loyalty, trust and mutual support. The need for such coalitions, especially between governmental and non-governmental forces, is paramount in a world characterised by change, diversity, fragmentation and a lack of consensus. In themselves formal arrangements will be insufficient and more extensive and informal opportunities must be opened up if local regimes are to flourish. Resources and authority must be shared as no one institution can identify and deliver solutions to contemporary economic and social problems (Bryson and Crosby, 1992). Regime theory suggests that neither traditional command power nor short-term bargaining can meet the requirements for contemporary governance.

In words reminiscent of Labour, the local state is perceived in regime theory as the agency through which these inter-dependencies are coordinated and appropriate resources, organisations and sectors mobilised (Stone, 1986). Participants commit themselves to a set of objectives but offer different contributions but with no expectation or requirement to marshal the same level of resources. Within such collaborative arrangements, Stoker highlights the role of the community and non-profit sectors, trade unions, and professionals employed within the local state and non-departmental government bodies (Stoker, 1995). Stone (1993) too argues that to be effective, governments 'must blend their capacities with those of various non-governmental actors' (p. 6). However, collaborative practice cannot be imposed but must be felt by the participants to be necessary and effective.

Managing participation

The various arguments as presented by communitarians, social capitalists and regime theorists have influenced Labour's broad thrust in relation to capacity building and civic engagement. However, it has remained anxious about the potential consequences of a truly participatory society, cautious about local variations, and reluctant to address other economic aspects of social cohesion. This has resulted in a set of policies designed to 'manage' or orchestrate such participatory processes. Typically, this has been achieved by ensuring that any new mechanism works to centrally determined outcome targets, linking funding to 'approved' collaborative arrangements, introducing highly prescriptive procedures for engagement, and giving legitimacy only to those new mechanisms which it then uses as evidence of engagement.

Labour's desire to exercise control over the nature of public engagement could result in the decline of democratic accountability. While it remains fixated on control, more imaginative and innovative ideas, such as those of Holman (2000) calling for the provision of substantial funding to local organisations to be administered by local trusts with members elected by their localities, are unlikely to be heeded. Despite its desire to learn from the past, Labour remains resistant to the lesson that in order for state-lead mechanisms of engagement to succeed they have to be matched by a vibrant, dynamic and independent civic society, one that enables the full range of political voices to flourish. Democratic engagement cannot be imposed. Associational activity cannot be managed in the way Labour would like although it does require substantial support and recognition. Current policy aims to create top-down participatory structures in which everyone speaks but in a language that connects with the framework developed by government. It seeks a 'managed dialogue', with one not multiple communities, in which conflict is perceived as dysfunctional rather than a creative source of energy and ideas. Having recruited skilled advisors and generated policies based on a careful analysis of existing problems and past failings, it appears as though Labour has nothing more to learn from grassroots voices except for their feedback on policy implementation.

Yet this is a high-risk strategy precisely because participation cannot be managed. The employment of experienced advisors and practitioners, both centrally and locally, who are also committed and prepared to take the policy at face value will inject a tension with and resistance to centralised control. It is very difficult to manage and control what happens on a day-to-day basis within neighbourhoods and communities, especially from central but also local government. Once people engage and work together within their own organisations it is difficult to predict or influence how they understand the issues that dominate their lives, what they prioritise for action, how they organise, with whom, and how they respond to government. Equally, those concerned that current approaches only focus on individual feelings and perception do not fully appreciate the powerful impact that collaborative and collective work can have as a dynamic force for change. Labour's strategy does provide an opportunity to explore how democratic life within dynamic and complex societies can be extended. Disagreements about what might be the underlying agenda should not prevent the exploitation of opportunities for public engagement. This includes maximising the potential within the methods and values of community development adopted to facilitate such engagement.

References

Abrams, P. (1986) 'From analysis to facts: The problem of community', in Bulmer, M. (eds) *Neighbours: The work of Philip Abrams* (Cambridge: Cambridge University Press).

Active Community Unit (2001) Funding community groups – a consultation document issued by ACU on behalf of the Inter-Departmental Working Group on Resourcing Community Capacity Building (London: ACU, Home Office).

Anastacio, J., Gidley, B., Hart, L., Keith, M., Mayo, M. and Kowarzik, U. (2000) *Reflecting Realities: Participants' perspectives on integrated communities and sustainable development* (Bristol: Policy Press).

Anderson, B. (1991) *Imagined communities: Reflections on the origin and spread of nationalism* (London: Verso).

Argyris, C. (1993) 'Education for leading – learning', *Organisational Dynamics* **21** (3): 5–17

Argyris, C. and Schon, D. (1978) *Organisational learning: A theory of action perspective* (Reading MA: Addison-Wesley).

Armstrong, H. (2000) 'Communities first – delivering local democracy', speech given at Centre for Local Democracy Conference, Bristol, February.

Arnstein, S. (1969) 'A ladder of participation in the USA', *Journal of the American Institute of Planners* (July), **35**.

Association of Metropolitan Authorities (AMA) (1989) *Community development: The Local Authority role* (London: AMA).

Association of Metropolitan Authorities (AMA) (1991) *Local Authorities and community development: A strategic opportunity for the 1990s* (London: AMA).

Atkinson, R. (1999) 'Discourses of partnership and empowerment in contemporary British', Urban regeneration *Urban Policy*, **36** (1): 59–77.

Atkinson, R. and Cope, S. (1997) 'Community participation and urban regeneration in Britain', in Hoggett, P. (ed.) *Contested communities: Experiences, struggles, policies* (Bristol: Policy Press).

Audit Commission, Local Government Management Training Board, Institute for Local Government Studies (1985) *Good management in local government – Successful practice and action* (Luton: Local Government Training Board).

Audit Commission (1992) *Community care: managing the cascade of change* (London: HMSO).

Audit Commission (1993) *Practices make perfect the role of the Family Health Services Authority* (London: HMSO).

Audit Commission (1998) *A fruitful partnership: Effective partnership working* (London: Audit Commission).

Audit Commission (2001) *Appointment of 'Head of User Focus', Information Pack* (London: Audit Commission).

Bains Report (1972) *The new local authorities: Management and structure* (London: HMSO).

Baldock, J. and Ungerson, C. (1996) 'Becoming a consumer of care: Developing a sociological account of the "new community care"' in Edgell, S., Hetherington, K. and Warde, A. (eds) *Consumption matters* (Oxford: Blackwell/Sociological Review).

Baldwin, S. (1997) 'Charging users for community services', in May, M., Brunsdon, E. and Craig, G. (eds) *Social Policy Review 9* (London: Social Policy Association).

Ball, A., Bowerman, M. and Hawksworth, S. (2000) 'Benchmarking in local government under a central government agenda', *Benchmarking: An international Journal*, 7 (1): 20–34.

Ball, R., Heafey, M. and King, D. (2001) 'Private Finance Initiative – a good deal for the public or a drain on future generations?' *Policy and Politics*, 29 (1): 95–108.

Banks, S. (1998) 'Professional ethics in social work: What future?', *British Journal of Social Work*, 28: 213–31.

Barclay, P. (1982) *Social workers: Their roles and tasks* (London: Bedford Square Press).

Barnes, M. (1999) 'Users as citizens: Collective action and the local governance of welfare', *Social Policy and Administration* (March), 33 (1): 73–90.

Barnes, M. and Wistow, G. (eds) (1992) *Researching user involvement* (Leeds University Nuffield Institute for Health Services Studies).

Barr, A. and Hashagen, S. (2000) *ABCD Handbook: A framework for evaluating community development* (London: Community Development Foundation).

Barry, N. *et al.* (1984) *Hayek's serfdom revisited* (London: Institute of Economic Affairs).

Bass, B. (1981) (ed.) *Stogdill's handbook of leadership* (New York: Free Press).

Bass, B. and Avolio, B. (1994) 'Transformational leadership and organizational culture', *Public Administration Quarterly* (Spring), 17 (1): 112–21.

Bassett, K. (1996) 'Partnerships business elites and urban politics: New forms of governance in an English city', *Urban Studies*, 33: 539–55.

Bauman, Z. (1993) *Postmodern Ethics* (Cambridge: Polity Press).

Bauman, Z. (1997) *Postmodernity and its discontents* (Cambridge: Polity Press).

Bauman, Z. (2000) 'Am I my brother's keeper?', *European Journal of Social Work*, 3 (1): 5–11.

Bauman, Z. (2001) *Community: Seeking safety in an insecure world* (Cambridge: Polity Press).

Beck, U. (1992) *Risk society: Towards a new modernity* (London: Sage Publications).

Beck, U. (1998) *Democracy without enemies* (Cambridge: Polity Press).

Beck, U. (1999) *World risk society* (Cambridge: Polity Press).

Ben-Tovim, G., Gabriel, J., Law, I. and Stredder, K. (1986) *The local politics of race* (Basingstoke: Macmillan).

Bennington, J. (1976) *Local government becomes big business* (London: Home Office, Community Development Projects, Information and Intelligence Unit).

Beresford, P. (1997) 'The last social division? Revisiting the relationship between social policy, its producers and consumers', in May, M., Brunsdon, E. and Craig, G. (eds) *Social Policy Review 9* (London: Social Policy Association).

Beresford, P. (2001) 'Service users, social policy and the future of welfare', *Critical Social Policy*, **21** (4): 494–512.

Beresford, P. and Croft, S. (1993) *Citizen involvement: a practical guide for change* (Basingstoke: Macmillan).

Beresford, P., Croft, S., Evans, C. and Harding, T. (1997) 'Quality in personal social services: The developing role of user involvement in the UK', reproduced and abridged in Davies, C., Finlay, L. and Bullman, A. (2000) (eds) *Changing practice in health and social care* (London: Sage Publications).

Berghman, J. (1995) 'Social exclusion in Europe' in Room, G. (ed.) *Beyond the threshold* (Bristol: Policy Press).

Beveridge, W. (1942) *Report of the Committee on Social Insurance and Allied Services*, Cmd 6404 (London: HMSO).

Beveridge, W. (1948) *Voluntary action: A report on methods of social advance* (London: Allen & Unwin).

Blair, T. (1996) *New Britain: My vision of a young country* (London: Fourth Estate).

Blair, T. (1997) 'The will to win', speech at the Aylesbury Estate, Southwark, 8 May.

Blair, T. (1998) *Compact on Relations between Government and the Voluntary and Community Sector in England* (London: HMSO Cm 4100, p. 1).

Blair, T. (1998) *Leading the way: A new vision for local government* (London: Institute for Public Policy Research (IPPR)).

Blair, T. (2001) Third way, phase two, *Prospect* (March), pp. 10–13.

Blair, T. (2002) 'The courage of our convictions: Why reform of the public services is the route to social justice', *Fabian Ideas* 603 (London: Fabian Society).

Blake, R. and Mouton, J. (1964) *The managerial grid* (Houston: Gulf).

Blau, P. and Scott, W. (1963) *Formal organisations: A comparative approach* (London: Routledge & Kegan Paul).

Boateng, P. (2002) Speech to the New Economics Foundation, May, reproduced at [www.hm-treasury.gov.uk/Spen . . . ntary_emergingthemes]. Downloaded 10/12/02.

Boateng, P. and Stowe, K. (1998) 'The state we're in', *The Guardian*, 11 November.

Bolger, S., Corrigan, P., Docking, J. and Frost, N. (1981) *Towards socialist welfare work* (Basingstoke: Macmillan).

Boddy, M. and Fudge, C. (1984) (eds) *Local socialism* (Basingstoke: Macmillan).

Bornat, J. (1993) Representations of community in Bornat, J., Pereira, C., Pilgrim, D. and Williams, F. (eds) *Community care: A reader* (Basingstoke: Macmillan in association with the Open University).

Bourdieu, P. (1986) 'The forms of capital', in Baron, S., Field, J. and Schuller, T. (eds) (2000) *Social capital – critical perspectives* (Oxford: Oxford University Press).

Bovaird, T. and Halachmi, A. (2001) 'Learning from international approaches to Best Value', *Policy and Politics*, **29** (4): 451–63.

Bradshaw, J. (1972) 'The concept of social need', *New Society*, 30 March: 640–3.

Bradshaw, Y., Kendall, I., Blackmore, M., Johnson, N. and Jenkinson, S. (1998) 'Complaining your way to quality: Complaints, contracts and the voluntary sector', *Social Policy and Administration* (September), **32** (3): 209–25.

Brake, M. and Bailey, R. (eds) (1980) *Radical social work and practice* (London: Edward Arnold).

Braverman, H. (1974) *Labor and monopoly capital* (New York: Monthly Review Press).

Braye, S. and Preston-Shoot, M. (1995) *Empowering practice in social care* (Buckingham: Open University Press).

Broussine, M. (2000) 'The capacities needed by local authority chief executives', *International Journal of Public Sector management*, **13** (6): 498–507.

Brown, H. (2000) 'Challenges from service users', in Brechin, A., Brown, H. and Eby, M. (eds) *Critical practice in health and social care* (London: Sage Publications).

Brown, H. (2000) 'Challenges from service users', in Brechin, A., Brown, H. and Eby, M. (eds) *Critical practice in health and social care* (London: Sage Publications).

Brown, P. and Sparks, R. (1989) (eds) *Beyond Thatcherism: Social policy, politics and society* (Milton Keynes: OUP).

Bruce, I. and Raynor, A. (1992) *Managing and staffing Britain's largest charities* (London: VOLPROF, City University).

Bryman, A. (1992) *Charisma and leadership in organisations* (London: Sage Publications).

Bryson, C., Budd, T., Lewis, J. and Elam, G. (2000) *Women's attitudes to combining paid work and family life* (London: The Women's Unit, The Cabinet Office).

Bryson, J. and Crosby, B. (1992) *Leadership for the common good: Tackling public problems in a shared power world* (San Francisco: CA: Jossey Bass).

Bryson, L. (1992) *Welfare and the state: Who benefits?* (Basingstoke: Macmillan).

Bulmer, M. (1975) 'Sociological models of the mining community', *Sociological Review*, **23**: 61–92.

Bulmer, M. (1986) *Neighbours: The work of Philip Abram* (Cambridge: Cambridge University Press).

Butler, I. (1997) *'Used and abused: Engaging the child in child protection'* in Pithouse, A. and Williamson, H. (eds) *Engaging the user in welfare services* (Birmingham: Venture Press).

Burchardt, T. and Propper, C. (1999) 'Does the UK have a private welfare class?', *Journal of Social Policy* (October), **28** (4): 643–66.

Burns, D., Hambleton, R. and Hoggett, P. (1994) *The politics of decentralisation: Revitalising local democracy* (Basingstoke: Macmillan).

Burns, J. (1978) *Leadership* (New York: Harper & Row).

Burns, T. and Stalker, G. (1961) *The management of innovation* (London: Tavistock).

Burrell, G. and Morgan, G. (1979) *Sociological paradigms and organisational analysis* (London: Heinemann Educational Books).

Burt, R. (1992) *Structural holes: The social structure of competition* (Cambridge MA: Harvard University Press).

Butcher, H., Glen, A., Henderson, P. and Smith, J. (1993) (eds) *Community and public policy* (London: Pluto Press).

Butcher, H. and Mullard, M. (1993) 'Community policy, citizenship and democracy', in Butcher, H., Glen, A., Henderson, P. and Smith, J. (eds) *Community and public policy* (London: Pluto Press).

Butler, I. (1997) 'Used and abused: Engaging the child in child protection', in Pithouse, A. and Williamson, H. (eds) (1997) *Engaging the user in welfare services* (Birmingham: Venture Press).

Cabinet Office (1999a) *Modernising Government*, Cm 4310 (London: HMSO).

Cabinet Office (1999) *Report to the Prime Minister from Sir Richard Wilson, Head of Home Civil Service* (London: Cabinet Office).

Cabinet Office (2001a) *Strengthening leadership in the public sector: A report by the Performance and Innovation Unit* (March) (London: Cabinet Office).

Cabinet Office (2001b) *A new commitment to neighbourhood renewal* (London: Social Exclusion Unit, Cabinet Office).

Campbell, B. (1993) *Goliath: Britain's dangerous places* (London: Methuen).

Carter, T. and Nash, C. (1995) 'Pensioners' forums – a voice for older people', in Jack, R. (ed.) *Empowerment in community care* (London: Chapman & Hall).

Chamberlayne, P. (1992) 'New directions in welfare? France, West Germany, Italy and Britain in the 1980s', in *Critical Social Policy* (Winter), Issue 33, 1991–92, pp. 5–21.

Chanan, G. (1993) 'Local voluntary sectors: The hidden dynamic', in Saxon-Harrold, S. and Kendall, J. (eds) *Researching the voluntary sector*, 1st Edition (Tonbridge: Charities Aid Foundation).

Chanan, G. (1999) *Local community involvement: A handbook for good practice* (Dublin: European Foundation for the Improvement of Living and Working Conditions).

Chanan, G., Garratt, C., West, A. (2000) *The new community strategies: How to involve local people* (London: Community Development Foundation).

Chandler, D. (2001) 'Active citizens and the therapeutic state: The role of democratic participation in local government reform' (January), *Policy and Politics*, **29** (1): 3–14.

Chemers, M. (1993) 'An integrative theory of leadership', in Chemers, M. and Ayman, R. (eds) *Leadership theory and research: Perspectives and directions*, pp. 293–319 (San Diego, CA: Academic Press).

Clapham, D. (1985) 'Management of the local state: The example of corporate planning' *Critical Social Policy* (Winter), Issue 14.

Clarence, E. and Painter, C. (1998) 'Public services under New Labour: Collaborative discourses and local networking', *Public Policy and Administration*, **13** (3): 8–22.

Clarke, J. (1996) 'The problem of the state after the welfare state', in May, M., Brunsdon, E. and Craig, G. (eds) *Social Policy Review 8* (London: Social Policy Association).

Clarke, J., Gewirtz, S. and McLaughlin, E. (eds) (2000) *New managerialism: New welfare?* (London: Sage Publications).

Clarke, J. and Langan, M. (1993) 'The British welfare state: Foundation and modernization', in Cochrane, A. and Clarke, J. (eds) *Comparing welfare states: Britain in international context* (London: Sage Publications).

Clarke, M. (1996) 'Urban policy and governance', *Local Government Policy Making* (July), **23**: (1).

Clarke, M. and Newman, J. (1997) *The managerial state* (London: Sage Publications).

Clarke, M. and Stewart, J. (1997) 'Handling the wicked issues', reproduced in Davies, C., Finlay, L. and Bullman, A. (eds) (2000) *Changing practice in health and social care* (London: Sage Publications in association with The Open University).

Clegg, S. (1990) *Modern organisations: Organization studies in the postmodern world* (London: Sage Publications).

Cloke, P. (1992) (ed.) *Policy and change in Thatcher's Britain* (London: Pergamon Press).

Coates, K. (1978) (ed.) *The right to useful work: Planning by the people* (London: Spokesman Books).

Cochrane, A. (1986) 'Community politics and democracy', in Held, D. and Pollitt (eds) *New forms of democracy* (London: Sage Publications).

Cockburn, C. (1977) *The local state: Management of cities and people* (London: Pluto Press).

Cockburn, C. (1980) *The local state: Management of cities and people* (London: Pluto Press).

Cohen, A. (1985) *The symbolic construction of community* (London: Tavistock).

Coleman, J. (1998) 'Social capital in the creation of human capital', *American Journal of Sociology*, 94 Supplement S95–S120, University of Chicago.

Collective Design/Projects (1985) *Very nice work if you can get it: The socially useful production debate* (London: Spokesman Books).

Commission on Social Justice (1994) *Social justice: Strategy for national renewal* (London: Vintage/Institute for Public Policy Research (IPPR)).

CONSCISE Project: The contribution of social capital in the social economy to local economic development in Western Europe, unpublished [www.mdx.conscise.ac.uk].

Cook, S. and Yanow, D. (1993) 'Culture and organisational learning', *Journal of Management Inquiry*, **2**: 373–90.

Cooke, B. and Kothari, U. (2001) 'The case for participation as tyranny', in Cooke, B. and Kothari, U. (eds) *Participation: the new tyranny?* (London: Zed Books).

Coote, A. and Hunter, D. (1996) *A new agenda for health* (London: Institute of Public Policy Research).

Corrigan, P. and Joyce, P. (1997) 'Reconstructing public management: A new responsibility for the public and a case study of local government', *The International Journal of Public Sector Management*, **10** (6): 417–32.

Corrigan, P. and Leonard, P. (1978) *Critical texts in social work and the welfare state: Social work practice under capitalism – A Marxist approach* (Basingstoke: Macmillan).

Cote, S. and Healy, T. (2001) *The well-being of nations: The role of human and social capital* (Paris: Organisation for Economic Co-operation and Development (OECD)).

Craig, G. and Manthorpe, J. (1999) 'Unequal partners? Local government reorganisation and the voluntary sector', *Social Policy and Administration* (March), **33** (1): 55–72.

Craig, G. and Mayo, M. (eds) (1995) *Community empowerment: A reader in participation in development* (London: Zed Press).

Craig, G., Taylor, M., Szanto, C. and Wilkinson, M. (1999) *Developing local compacts: Relationships between local public sector bodies and the voluntary and community sectors* (York: Joseph Rowntree Foundation).

Craig, G., Taylor, M., Wilkinson, M., Bloor, K., Munro, S. and Syed, A. (2002) *Contract or trust? The role of compacts in local government* (York: Joseph Rowntree Foundation).

Croft, S. and Beresford, P. (1996) 'The politics of participation', in Taylor, D. (ed.) *Critical Social Policy* (London: Sage Publications).

Crook, S., Pakulski, J. and Waters, M. (1992) *Postmodernization: change in advanced society* (London: Sage Publications).

Crow, G. and Allan, G. (1994) *Community life* (Hemel Hempstead: Harvester Wheatsheaf).

Crozier, M. (1964) *The bureaucratic phenomenon* (London: Tavistock).

CSE State Group (1979) *Struggles over the state: Cuts and restructuring in contemporary Britain* (London: CSE Books).

Cutler, T. and Waine, B. (1994) Managing the welfare state: The politics of public sector management (Oxford: Berg).

Cutler, T. and Waine, B. (2000) 'Managerialism reformed? New Labour and public sector management', *Social Policy and Administration*, **34** (3): 318–32.

Dale, J. (1987) 'Decentralisation: Grounding the debate', *Community Development Journal* (April), **22** (2): 150–6.

Danziger, N. (1996) *Danziger's Britain: A journey to the edge* (London: Flamingo).

Darvill, G. and Smale, G. (eds) (1990) *Partners in empowerment: Networks of innovation in Social work* (London: National Institute for Social Work).

Davies, C. (2000) 'Improving the quality of services', in Brechin, A., Brown, H. and Eby, M., *Critical Practice in Health and Social Care* (London: Sage Publications and Open University).

Davis, A. and Ellis, K. (1995) 'Enforced altruism in community care', in Hugman, R. and Smith, D. (eds) *Ethical issues in social work* (London: Routledge).

Deacon, A. (1997) 'Welfare to work: Options and issues', *Social Policy Review*, **9**: 34–49.

Deacon, B., Hulse, M. and Stubbs, P. (1997) *Global social policy: International organisations and the future of welfare* (London: Sage Publications).

Dench, G. (1986) *Minorities in the open society: Prisoners of ambivalence* (London: Routledge & Kegan Paul).

Dennis, N., Henriques, F. and Slaughter, C. (1957) *Coal is our life* (London: Eyre & Spottiswoode).

Department for Education and Employment (1998a) *Public private partnerships: A guide for school governors* (London: DfEE). [www.dfee.gov.uk/ppp/intro.htm].

Department for Education and Employment (1998b) *Practice progress and value. Learning communities: assessing the value they add* (Sudbury: DfEE).

Department of the Environment (1991) *City Challange* (London: HMSO).

Department of the Environment, Transport and the Regions (DETR) (1998a) *Modern local government – In touch with the people*, Cm 4014 (London: DETR).

Department of the Environment, Transport and the Regions (DETR) (1998b) *Guidance on enhancing public participation in local government* (London: DETR).

Department of the Environment, Transport and the Regions (DETR) (1999) and the Audit Commission, *Best Value and local authority performance indicators for 2000–2001* (London: DETR).

Department of the Environment, Transport and the Regions (DETR) (2000a) PAT 17 (2000) *Joining it up locally, Report of Policy Action Team 17*, National Strategy for Neighbourhood Renewal (London: DETR).

Department of the Environment, Transport and the Regions (DETR) (2000b) *Local compact guidelines* (London: DETR).

Department of the Environment, Transport and the Regions (DETR) (2000c) *Preparing Community Strategies: Issues and advice* (London: DETR).

Department of the Environment, Transport and the Regions (DETR) (2000d) PAT 9 (1999), *Report of Policy Action Team 9, Community Self Help*, National Strategy for Neighbourhood Renewal (London: DETR).

Department of the Environment, Transport and the Regions (DETR) (2001a) *Local Strategic Partnerships: Government Guidance* (March) (London: DETR).

Department of the Environment, Transport and the Regions DETR (2001b) *Accreditation Guidance for Local Strategic Partnerships, Neighbourhood Renewal Unit* (October) (London: DETR).

Department of Health (DoH) (1991a) *Working together under the Children Act 1989: A guide to arrangements for inter-agency co-operation for the protection of children from abuse* (London: HMSO).

Department of Health (DoH) (1991b) *Assessment systems and community care* (London: HMSO).

Department of Health (DoH) (1995a) *An introduction to joint commissioning* (London: HMSO).

Department of Health (DoH) (1995b) Building Bridges: a guide to arrangements for inter-agency working for the care and protection of severely mentally ill people (London: HMSO).

Department of Health (DoH) (1997) *The New NHS: Modern, Dependable*, Cm 3807 (London: Stationery Office).

Department of Health (DoH) (1998a) *Modernising Social Services*, Cm 4169 (London: Stationery Office).

Department of Health (DoH) (1998b) *Quality protects: Frameworks for action, Local Authority Circular LA*(98)28 (London: DoH).

Department of Health (DoH) (1998c) *A first class service: Quality in the new NHS, a consultation paper* (London: DoH).

Department of Health (DoH) (2001a) Shifting the balance of power (London: Stationery Office).

Department of Health (DoH) (2001b) *Involving patients and the public in Healthcare: Responses to the learning exercise* (London: HMSO).

Department of Health (DoH) (2001c) *Heath and Social Care Act* (London: HMSO).

Department of Health (DoH) (2001d) *Keys to partnership*, Community Care Development Centre (London: DoH).

Department of Social Security (DSS) (1998a) *New contract for welfare* (London: HMSO).

Department of Social Security (DSS)(1998b) *New ambitions for our country* (London: Stationery Office).

Department of Social Security (DSS)(1999) *Opportunity for all: Tackling poverty and social exclusion*, Cm 4445 (London: Stationery Office).

Department of Trade and Industry (2000) *Work and parents: Competitiveness and choice* (London: DTI).

Department of Transport, London and the Regions (DTLR) (2001) *New Deal for Communities*, Neighbourhood Renewal Unit (London: DTLR).

Dixon, J., Kouzmin, A. and Korac-Kakabadse, N. (1998) 'Managerialism – something old, something borrowed, little new', *International Journal of Public Sector Management*, **11** (2/3): 164–87.

Dixon, N. (1992) 'Organisational learning: A review of the literature with implications for HRD professionals', *Human Resource Development Quarterly* (Spring), **3**: 88–115.

Donnison, D. (1993) 'Listen to the voice of the community' (Manchester: *The Guardian*, 10 November).

Doyal, L. and Gough, I. (1991) *A theory of human need* (Basingstoke: Macmillan).

Driver, S. and Martell, L. (1997) 'New Labour's communitarianisms', *Critical Social Policy*, **17** (3): 27–44.

Driver, S. and Martell, L. (1998) *New Labour: Politics after Thatcherism* (Cambridge: Polity Press).

Drucker, P. (1988) 'Management and the world's work', *Harvard Business Review*, Sept.–Oct., pp. 75–6.

Drucker, P. (1992) 'The new society of organisations', *Harvard Business Review*, Sept.–Oct., **5** (4).

Du Gay, P. (1994) 'Colossal immodesties and hopeful monsters: Pluralism and organizational conduct', *Organization*, **1** (1): 125–48.

Easterby-Smith, M. (1997) 'Disciplines of organisational learning: contributions and critiques', *Human Relations*, **50** (9): 1085–113.

Ekins, P. (1992) 'Towards a progressive market', in Ekins, P. and Max-Neef, M. (eds) *Real-Life economics: Understanding wealth creation* (London: Routledge).

Elias, N. and Scotson, J. (1994) *The established and the outsiders* (London: Sage Publications), 2nd Edition.

Elliot, I. (2001) *Social capital and health: Literature review*, Institute of Public Health in Ireland, unpublished.

Etzioni, A. (1969) (ed.) *The semi-professions and their organisations* (New York: Free Press).

Etzioni, A. (1988) *The moral dimension. Towards a new economics* (New York: Free Press).

Etzioni, A. (1993) *The spirit of community: Rights, responsibilities and the Communitarian agenda* (New York: Touchstone books).

Etzioni, A. (1995) *Spirit of Community: Rights, responsibilities and the Communitarian agenda* (London: Fontana Press).

Faith in the City (1985) *Report of the Archbishop of Canterbury's Commission on urban priority areas* (London: Church House).

Farnham, D. and Horton, S. (1999) 'People management reform in the UK public services since 1979: Learning from the private sector or learning to cope with change?', *International Journal of Public–Private Partnerships* (February), **1** (2): 153–76.

Farnham, D. and Horton, S. (1993) 'Managing private and public organisations', in Farnham, D. and Horton, S. (eds) *Managing the new public services* (Basingstoke: Macmillan).

Fiedler, F. (1967) *A theory of leadership effectiveness* (New York: McGraw-Hill).

Fiedler, F. (1978) 'The Coutingency Model and the dynamics of the leadership process', in Berkowitz, L. (ed.) *Advances in experimental social psychology* (New York: Academic Press).

Flynn, N. (1993) (2nd Edition) *Public sector management* (London: Harvester Wheatsheaf).

Foley, P. and Martin, S. (2000) 'A new deal for community? Public participation in regeneration and local service delivery', *Policy and Politics* (October), **28** (4): 479–92.

Forbes, J, and Sashidharan, S. (1997) 'User involvement in services – Incorporation or challenge?' *British Journal of Social Work*, **27** (4): 481–98.

Foster, P. and Wilding, P. (2000) 'Wither welfare professionalism?' *Social Policy and Administration* (June), **34** (2): 143–59.

Fournier, V. (1999) 'The appeal to "professionalism" as a disciplinary mechanism', *The Sociological Review*, pp. 280–306.

Freeman, J. (1973) *Informal elites and the tyranny of structurelessness* (London: Second Wave, Rising Free Bookshop, November).

French, R. (1999) 'The importance of capacities in psychoanalysis and the language of human development', *International Journal of Psychoanalysis* (December), **80** (6): 1215–26.

Friedman, A. (1977) 'Responsible autonomy versus direct control over the labour process', *Capital and Class*, **1** (1).

Friedman, M. and Friedman, R. (1980) *Free to choose* (London: Penguin).

Friedson, E. (1976) 'The division of labor as social interaction', *Social Problems*, **23** (3): 304–13.

Friedson, E. (1994) *Professionalism reborn: Theory, prophecy and policy* (Cambridge: Polity Press).

Gaster, L. (1995) 'Quality in welfare services', in Gladstone, D. (ed.) *British social welfare: Past, present and future* (London: UCL Press).

Gaster, L. and Deakin, N. (1998) 'Quality and citizens', in Coulson, A. (ed.) *Trust and contracts: Relationships in local government, health and public services* (Bristol: Policy Press).

Gewirtz, S., Ball, S. and Bowe, R. (1995) *Markets, choice and equity in education* (Buckingham: Open University Press).

Giddens, A. (1984) *The constitution of society* (Cambridge: Polity Press).

Giddens, A. (1989) 'A reply to my critics', in Held, D. and Thompson, J. (eds) *Social theory of modern societies: Anthony Giddens and his critics* (Cambridge: Cambridge University Press).

Giddens, A. (1994) *Beyond Left and Right* (Cambridge: Polity Press).

Giddens, A. (1998) *The Third Way: The renewal of social democracy* (Cambridge: Polity Press).

Gilchrist, A. and Taylor, M. (1997) 'Community networking: Developing strength through diversity', in Hoggett, P. (ed.) *Contested communities* (Bristol: Policy Press).

Gilliatt, S., Fenwick, J. and Alford, D. (2000) 'Public services and the consumer: Empowerment or control?', *Social Policy and Administration* (September), **34** (3): 333–49.

Gillies, P. (1998) 'The effectiveness of alliances and partnerships for health promotion', *Health Promotion International*, **13**: 2.

Gilmore, T. and Shea, G. (1997) 'Organisational learning and the leadership skill of time travel', *Journal of Management Development* (4 April), **16**: 302–8.

Gittell, R. and Vidal, A. (1998) *Community organizing: Building social capital as a development strategy* (London: Sage Publications).

Glennerster, H. (1983) *Planning for priority groups* (Oxford: Martin Roberston).

Glennerster, H. (1995) *British social policy since 1945* (Oxford: Blackwell).

Goleman, D. (2000) 'Leadership that gets results', *Harvard Business Review*, March–April.

Good Housekeeping (2000) 'Good Housekeeping Timesaver Campaign', *Good Housekeeping*, September, 54–58.

Gorz, A. (1985) *Paths to paradise: On the liberation from work* (London: Pluto Press).

Gorz, A. (1999) *Reclaiming work: Beyond the wage-based society* (Cambridge: Polity Press).

Goss, S., Hillier, J. and Rule, J. (1988) *Labour councils in the cold: A blueprint for survival* (London: Labour Co-ordinating Committee).

Gough, I. (1983) 'Thatcherism and the welfare state', in Hall, S. and Jacques, M. (eds) *The politics of Thatcherism* (London: Lawrence and Wishart).

Granovetter, M. (1974) 'The strength of weak ties', *American Journal of Sociology*, **78** (6): 1360–80.

Grint, K. (1995) *Management: A sociological introduction* (Cambridge: Polity Press).

The Guardian (25/11/02) 'Footsie 100 givers donate 0.95 per cent of pre-tax profits, in The Giving List' (London: *The Guardian*).

Gutch, R. (1992) *Contracting lessons from the US* (London: National Council of Voluntary Organisations).

Hague, G., Malos, E. and Dear, W. (1995) *Against domestic violence: Inter agency initiatives*, Working Paper 127, School for Advanced Urban Studies (Bristol: University Press).

Hall, S. and Jacques, M. (1989) (eds) *New times* (London: Lawrence & Wishart).

Hambleton, R. (1998) 'Strengthening political leadership in UK local government', *Public Money and Management*, January–March, 1–11.

Hambleton, R., Essex, S., Mills, L. and Razzaque, K. (1995) *The collaborative council: A study if inter-agency working in practice* (London: Joseph Rowntree Foundation and LCC Communications).

Hambleton, R. and Hoggett, P. (1984) *The politics of decentralisation: Theory and practice of a radical local government initiative*, SAUS Working Paper 46 (Bristol: School of Advanced Urban Studies).

Hambleton, R. and Hoggett, P. (1987) 'Beyond Bureaucratic paternalism', in Hoggett, P. and Hambleton, R. (eds) *Decentralisation and democracy: Localising Public Services*, Occasional paper 28 (Bristol: School for Advanced Urban Studies).

Handy, C. (1989) *The age of unreason* (London: Business Books).

Handy, C. (1994) *The empty raincoat* (London: Hutchinson).

Handy, C. (1995) 'Trust and the virtual organisation', *Harvard Business Review*, **73** (3): 40–55.

Hanmer, J. and Statham, D. (1988) *Women and social work: Towards a woman-centred practice* (Basingstoke: Macmillan).

Harris, R. and Seldon, A. (1979) *Over-ruled on welfare* (London: Institute of Economic Affairs).

Harris, R. and Seldon, A. (1987) *Welfare without the state: A quarter century of suppressed public choice* (London: Institute of Economic Affairs).

Harrison, S. and Mort, M. (1998) 'Which champions, which people? Public and user involvement in health care as a technology of legitimation', *Social Policy and Administration* (March), **32** (2): 60–70.

Hart, S. and Quinn, R. (1993) 'Roles executives play: CEOs, behavioural complexity and firm performance', *Human Relations*, **46** (5): 543–74.

Harvey, C. and Denton, J. (1999) 'To come of age: The antecedents of organisational learning', *Journal of Management Studies*, **36** (7): 897–917.

Hastings, A. (1996) 'Unravelling the process of partnership in urban regeneration policy', *Urban Studies*, **33**: 253–68.

Hawtin, M. and Kettle, J. (2000) 'Housing and social exclusion', in Percy-Smith, J. (ed.) *Policy responses to social exclusion: Towards inclusion?* (Buckingham: Open University Press).

Hendry, C. (1996) 'Understanding and creating whole organisational change through learning theory', *Human Relations*, **49** (5).

Heron, E. and Dwyer, P. (1999) 'Doing the right thing: Labour's attempt to forge a new welfare deal between the individual and the state', *Social Policy and Administration* (March), **33** (1): 91–104.

Hersey, P. and Blanchard, K. (1982), *Management and organisational behaviour: Utilizing human resources* (Englewood Cliffs, NJ: Prentice Hall).

Hill, M. (1997) (3rd Edition) *The policy process in the modern state* (London: Prentice Hall/Harvester Wheatsheaf).

Hirschorn, L. (1988) *The workplace within: Psychodynamics of organisational life* (Cambridge, MA: MIT Press).

HM Treasury (2000) *Public private partnerships: The Government's approach* (London: the Stationery Office).

HM Treasury (2002) *The cross cutting review of the role of the voluntary sector in public service delivery* (London: HM Treasury).

Hochschild, A. (1983) *The managed heart* The Commercialisation of human feeling (Berkeley: University of California Press).

Hodkinson, P. and Issitt, M. (eds) (1995) *The challenge of competence* (London: Cassell Education).

Hoggett, P. (1987) 'A farewell to mass production? Decentralisation as an emergent private and public sector paradigm', in Hoggett, P. and Hambleton, R. (eds) *Decentralisation and democracy* (Bristol: School for Advanced Urban Studies).

Hoggett, P. (1990) 'Modernisation, political strategy and the welfare state', in *Studies in decentralisation and quasi-markets* No. 2, Occasional Paper 28 (Bristol: School for Advanced Urban Studies).

Hoggett, P. (1994) 'The politics of the modernisation of the welfare state', in Burrows, R. and Loader, B. (eds) *Towards a post-fordist welfare state?* (London: Routledge).

Hoggett, P. (1997) (ed.) *Contested communities: Experiences, struggles, policies* (Bristol: The Policy Press).

Hoggett, P. (2000a) *Emotional life and the politics of welfare* (Basingstoke: Macmillan).

Hoggett, P. (2000b) 'Social policy and the emotions', in Lewis, G., Gewirtz, S. and Clarke, J. (eds) *Rethinking social policy* (London: Sage Publications/ Open University Press).

Hoggett, P. (2001) 'Agency, rationality and social policy', *Journal of Social Policy* (January) **30** (1): 37–56.

Hoggett, P. and Kimberlee, R. (2001) *Going local? Area and neighbourhood governance* (Bristol: Occasional Paper 1, Centre for Local Democracy, University of the West of England).

Hoggett, P. and McGill, I. (1988) 'Labourism: Means and ends', *Critical Social Policy* (Autumn), Issue 23, 22–33.

Holman, B. (2000) 'Serious commitment to deprived areas needs serious funding', *The Guardian*, 18 January.

Hollander, E. (1993) 'Legitimacy, power and influence: A perspective on relational features of leadership', in Chemers, M. and Ayman, R. (eds) *Leadership theory and research: Perspectives and directions*, 29–47 (San Diego: Academic Press).

Home Office (1998) *Compact: Getting it right together. Compact on relations between Government and the Voluntary and Community Sector in England* (London: Cm 4100, November).

Hood, C. (1991) 'A public management for all seasons?', *Public Administration* (Spring) **69**: 5–19.

Horton, S. and Farnham, D. (2000) 'New labour and the management of public services: Legacies, impact and prospects', in Horton, S. and Farnham, D. (eds) *Public management in Britain* (Basingstoke: Macmillan).

House of Commons (2000) *Local Government Act* (London: The Stationery Office).

Howe, D. (1986) *Social workers and their practice in welfare bureaucracies* (Aldershot: Gower).

Howe, D. (1990) 'The client's view in context', in Carter, P., Jeffs, T. and Smith, M. (eds) *Social work and social welfare, Yearbook two* (Milton Keynes: Open University Press).

Hoyes, L., Jeffers, S., Lambert, C., Means, R. and Taylor, M. (1993) *Studies in decentralisation and quasi-markets* (Bristol: School of Advanced Urban Studies, Bristol University).

Hughes, G. (1998) 'Picking over the remains: The welfare state settlements of the post-Second World War UK', in Hughes, G. and Lewis, G. (eds) *Unsettling welfare: The reconstruction of social policy* (London: Routledge in association with the Open University).

Hughes, J. and Carmichael, P. (1998) 'Building partnerships in urban regeneration: a case study from Belfast', *Community Development Journal,* **33** (3): 205–25.

Huntingdon, J. (1986) 'The proper contributions of social workers in health practice', *Social Science and Medicine,* **22** (11): 1151–60.

Huxham, C. (ed.) (1996) *Creating collaborative advantage* (London: Sage Publications).

Iles, V. and Sutherland, K. (2001) *Organisational Change* (London: NCCSDO).

Institute for Public Policy Research (IPPR) (2001) *Building better partnerships: The final report from the Commission on Public Private Partnerships* (June) (London: Institute for Public Policy Research).

Isaacs, W. (1993) 'Taking flight: Dialogue, collective thinking, and organisational learning', *Organisational dynamics* (Autumn), **22** (2): 24–39.

Jacobs, J. (1961) *The death and life of great American cities* (New York: Random House).

Janis, I. (1982) *Groupthink* (Boston: Houghton Miffin).

Jarman, B., Hirsch, S., White, P. and Driscoll, R. (1992) 'Predicting psychiatric admission rates', *British Medical Journal,* **304**: 1146–51.

Jessop, B. (1994) 'The transition to post-Fordism and the Schumpeterian workfare state', in Burrows, R. and Loader, B. (eds) *Towards a post-Fordist welfare state?* (London: Routledge), 13–37.

Jessop, B. (2000) 'From the KWNS to the SWPR', in Lewis, G., Gewirtz, S. and Clarke, J. (eds) *Rethinking social policy* (London: Sage Publications/ Open University Press).

Johnson, T. (1972) *Professions and power* (Basingstoke: Macmillan).

Jones, C. (1983) *State social work and the working class* (Basingstoke: Macmillan).

Jones, S., Hodge, H. and Pearson, M. (1994) 'Primary health care and community care: Will e'er the twain meet?', *Community Care Management and Planning Journal,* **2** (3): 71–80.

Jordan, B. (1998) *The new politics of welfare* (London: Sage Publications).

Joyce, P. (1999) *Strategic management for the public services* (Buckingham: Open University Press).

Joyce, P., Corrigan, P. and Hayes, M. (1988) *Striking out: Trade unionism in social work* (Basingstoke: Macmillan).

Judd, D. and Parkinson, M. (eds) (1990) *Leadership and urban regeneration: Cities in North America and Europe* (London: Sage Publications).

Kanter, R. (1984) *The change masters: Corporate entrepreneurs at work* (London: Allen & Unwin).

Kanter, R. (1989) *When giants learn to dance: Mastering the challenges of strategy, management and careers in the 1990s* (London: Simon-Schuster).

Kendall, J. and Knapp, M. (1996) *The voluntary sector in the UK* (Manchester: Manchester University Press).

Keyes, L., Schwartz, A., Vidal, A. and Bratt, R. (1996) 'Networks and non-profits: Opportunities and challenges in an era of Federal devolution', *Housing Policy Debate,* **7** (2): 21–8.

Kirkpatrick, I. and Lucio, M. (1995) *The politics of quality in the public sector* (London: Routledge).

Klein, N. (2000) *No logo* (London: Flamingo).

Knapp, M., Hardy, B. and Forder, J. (2001) 'Commissioning for quality: Ten years of social care markets in England', *Journal of Social Policy*, **30** (2): 283–307.

Kramer, R. (1989) 'Voluntary organisations and the welfare state, reproduced as Voluntary Organisations, Contracting and the Welfare State' in Batsleer *et al.* (eds) (1992) *Issues in voluntary and non-profit management* (London: OUP).

Krantz, J. (1998) 'Anxiety and the new order', in Klein, E., Gablenick, F. and Herr, P. (eds) *The psychodynamics of leadership* (Madison, Connecticut, Psychosocial Press).

Kubish, A. and Stone, R. (2001) 'Comprehensive Community Initiatives: The American experience' in Pierson, J. and Smith, J. (eds) *Rebuilding community* (Basingstoke: Palgrave).

Labour Party (1991) *Building bridges: The final draft of Labour's policy on the voluntary sector* (London: Labour Party).

Labour Party (1995) *Renewing democracy, rebuilding communities* (September) (London: Labour Party).

Labour Party (1997) *New Labour because Britain deserves better* (General Election manifesto) (London: Labour Party).

Laffin, M. (1989) *Managing under pressure: Industrial relations in local government* (Basingstoke: Macmillan).

Langan, M. (1998) 'The contested concept of need', in Langan, M. (ed.) *Welfare: Needs, rights and risks* (London: Open University/Sage Publications).

Langan, M. and Lee, P. (1989) (eds) *Radical social work today* (London: Unwin Hyman).

Lansley, S., Goss, S. and Wolmar, C. (1989) *Councils in conflict: The rise and fall of the municipal left* (Basingstoke: Macmillan).

Larson, M. (1977) *The rise of professionalism* (California: The University of California Press, Berkeley).

Lawton, A. and Rose, A. (1991) *Organisation and management in the public sector* (London: Pitman).

Lazarus, R. and Flokman, S. (1984) 'Coping and adaptation', in Gentry, W. (ed.) *Handbook of Behavioural Medicine* (New York: The Guildford Press).

Le Grand, J. (2001) 'The provision of health care: Is the public sector ethically superior to the private sector' (London: London School of Economics and Political Science Health and Social Care Discussion Paper Number 1).

Le Grand, J. and Bartlett, W. (eds) (1993) *Quasi-markets and social policy* (Basingstoke: Macmillan).

Leat, D. (1996) 'Are voluntary organisations accountable?', in Billis, D. and Harris, M. (eds) *Voluntary agencies: Challenges of organisation and management* (Basingstoke: Macmillan).

Leathard, A. (1994) *Going inter professional: working together for health and welfare* (London: Routledge).

Leathard, A. (1997) 'The new boundaries in health and welfare collaborative care', in May, M., Brunsdon, E. and Craig, G. (eds) *Social Policy Review 9* (London: Social Policy Association).

Levitas, R. (1996) 'The concept of social exclusion and the new Durkheimian hegemony', *Critical Social Policy*, **16** (1): 5–20.

Levitas, R. (1998) *The inclusive society?* (Basingstoke: Macmillan).

Levitas, R. (2001) 'Against work: A utopian incursion into social policy', *Critical Social Policy* (November), **21** (4) Issue 69: 449–66.

Lewis, G. (1998) 'Citizenship', in Hughes, G. (ed.) *Imagining welfare futures* (London: Routledge).

Lewis, J. (1996) 'What does contracting do to voluntary agencies?', in Billis, D. and Harris, M. (eds) *Voluntary agencies: Challenges of organisation and management* (Basingstoke: Macmillan).

Lewis, M. and Hartley, J. (2001) 'Evolving forms of quality management in local government: Lessons from the Best Value pilot programme', *Policy and Politics*, **29** (4): 477–96.

Lindow, V. and Morris, J. (1995) *Service user involvement: Synthesis of findings and experience in the field of community care* (York: Joseph Rowntree Foundation).

Lipsky, M. (1980) *Street-level bureaucracy* (New York: Russell Sage Publications).

Lipsky, M. and Smith, S. (1989) 'Nonprofit organisations, government and the welfare state', *Political Science Quarterly* (Winter), New York.

Lister, R. (1997) *Citizenship: feminist perspectives* (Basingstoke: Macmillan).

Lister, R. (1998) 'From equality to social inclusion: New Labour and the welfare state', *Critical Social Policy*, **18** (2): 215–26.

Lister, R. (2001) 'New Labour: a study in ambiguity from a position of ambivalence', *Critical Social Policy*, **21** (4): 425–47.

Local Government Association (1997) *New deal for regeneration* (London: LGA).

Local Government Association (1999) *Take your partners. LGA hearing on partnerships* (London: LGA).

Local Government Association (2001) *Effective local strategic partnerships: LGA advice note for working with the community and voluntary sectors* (London: LGA).

Local Government Association (2002) *Learning from local strategic partnerships: LGA Advice note for working with the community and voluntary sectors* (London: LGA).

London Edinburgh Weekend Return Group (1980) *In and against the state* (London: Pluto Press).

Loney, M. (1983) *Community against Government: The British Community Development Project 1968–1978* (London: Heinemann Educational Books).

Loney, M., Bocock, R., Clarke, J., Cochrane, A., Graham, P. and Wilson, M. (1991) (eds) (2nd Edition) *The state or the market: Politics and welfare in contemporary Britain* (London: Sage Publications).

Lorenz, E. (1992) 'Trust, community, and cooperation: Toward a theory of industrial districts', in Storper, M. and Scott, A. (eds) *Pathways to industrialization and regional development* (London: Routledge).

Lowndes, V., Nanton, P., McCabe, A. and Skelcher, C. (1997) 'Networks, partnerships and urban regeneration', *Local Economy*, **11** (4): 333–42.

Lowndes, V. and Skelcher, C. (1998) 'The dynamics of multi-agency partnerships: an analysis of changing modes of governance', *Public Administration* (Summer), **76**: 313–33.

Lupton, C., Peckham, S. and Taylor, P. (1998) *Managing public health involvement in healthcare purchasing* (Buckingham: Open University Press).

Mackintosh, M. (1992) 'Partnerships: Issues of policy and negotiation', *Local Economy*, **7** (3): 210–24.

Mackintosh, M. (2000) 'Flexible contracting? Economic cultures and implicit contracts in social care', *Journal of Social Policy* (January), **29** (1): 21–36.

Maddock, S. and Morgan, G. (1997) 'Barriers to professional collaboration and inter-agency working within health and social care', paper presented at the Public Services Research Unit Conference.

Maddock, S. and Morgan, G. (1998) 'Barriers to transformation: Beyond bureaucracy and the market conditions for collaboration in health and social care', *International Journal of Public Service Management*, **11** (4): 234–51.

Maglacas, A. (1988) 'Health for all. Nursing's role' *Nursing Outlook*, **36** (2): 66–71.

Maile, S. and Hoggett, P. (2001) 'Best Value and the politics of pragmatism', *Policy and Politics*, **29** (4): 509–19.

Malpass, P. and Murie, A., (1990) (3rd Edition) *Housing policy and practice* (Basingstoke: Macmillan).

Mandelson, P. (1997) *Labour's next steps: Tackling social exclusion, Fabian Society Pamphlet No. 581* (London: Fabian Society).

Marshall, T. (1996) 'Can we define the voluntary sector?', in Billis, D. and Harris, M. (eds) *Voluntary agencies: Challenges of organisation and management* (Basingstoke: Macmillan).

Marsland, D. (1996) *Welfare or welfare state?* (Basingstoke: Macmillan).

Martin, S. and Davis, H. (2001) 'What works and for whom? The competing rationalities of "Best Value"', *Policy and Politics*, **29** (4): 465–75.

Marx, J. (1999) 'Corporate philanthropy: What is the strategy', *Nonprofit and Voluntary Sector Quarterly* (June), **28** (2): 185–98.

May, M. and Brunsdon, E. (1996) 'Women and private welfare', in Hallett, C. (ed.) *Women and social policy* (Hemel Hempstead: Harvester Wheatsheaf).

Mayo, M. (1975) 'Community development: A radical alternative?', in Bailey, R. and Brake, M. (eds) *Radical social work* (London: Edward Arnold).

Mayo, M. (1997) 'Partnerships for regeneration and community development', *Critical Social Policy* (August), Issue 52, **17** (3).

Mayo, M. (2000) *Cultures, communities, identities: Cultural strategies for participation and empowerment* (Basingstoke: Palgrave).

McArthur, A. (1996) 'The active involvement of local residents in strategic community partnerships', *Policy and Politics*, **23** (1): 61–71.

Menzies, I. (1988) *Containing anxiety in institutions, selected essays* (London: Free Association Books).

Merton, R. (1969) 'The social nature of leadership', *The American Journal of Nursing*, **69**: 315–36.

Metcalfe, L. and Richards, S. (1990) *Improving public management*, 2nd Edition (London: Sage Publications).

Miliband, R. (1969) *The state in capitalist society: An analysis of the Western system of power* (London: Weidenfeld & Nicolson).

Miller, C. (1996) *Public service trade unionism and radical politics* (Aldershot: Dartmouth).

Miller, C. (1998) 'Canadian non-profits in crisis: The need for reform', *Social Policy and Administration* (December), **32** (4).

Miller, C. (1999) 'Partners in regeneration: Constructing a local regime for urban management?', *Policy and Politics*, **27** (3): 343–58.

Miller, C. (2001) 'Community regeneration and national renewal in the United Kingdom', in Pierson, J. and Smith, J. (eds) *Rebuilding community: Policy and practice in urban regeneration* (Basingstoke: Palgrave).

Miller, C. (2002) 'Towards a self-regulatory form of accountability in the voluntary sector', *Policy and Politics* (October), **30** (4): 551–66.

Miller, C. and Ahmad, Y. (1997) 'Community development at the crossroads: A way forward', *Policy and Politics* (July), **25** (3): 269–84.

Miller, C. and Bryant, R. (1990) 'Community work in the UK: Reflections on the 80s', *Community Development Journal*, **25** (4): 316–25.

Mitchell, J. (1984) *What is to be done about illness and health? The crisis in the eighties* (London: Penguin).

Morgan, G. (1988) *Riding the waves of change: Developing managerial competencies for a turbulent world* (San Francisco, CA: Jossey-Bass).

Morgan, G. (1997) (2nd Edition) *Images of organization* (London: Sage Publications).

Monbiot, G. (2000) *Captive state* (Basingstoke: Pan).

Mori (2002) 'Company reputation', in *The Guardian*, The Giving list, 25 November.

Mullen, J. (1997) 'Performance-based corporate philanthropy: How "giving smart" can further corporate goals', *Public relations Quarterly*, **42** (2): 42–9.

Murray, C. (1990) *The emerging British underclass* (London: Institute of Economic Affairs, Health and Welfare Unit).

Murray, S. (2000) *Appendix C, The evidence base, (p. 17) in Joining it up Locally, Policy Action Team 17*, National Strategy for Neighbourhood Renewal (London: Department of the Environment, Transport and the Regions).

National Council for Voluntary Organisations (1996) *Meeting the challenge of change* (The Commission on the future of the voluntary sector) (London: NCVO).

Newman, J. and Clarke, J. (1994) 'Going out of business? The managerialization of public services', in Clarke, J., Cochrane, A. and McLaughlin, E. (eds) *Managing social policy* (London: Sage Publications).

NHS Executive (1999) Quality and Performance in the NHS: High level performance indicators (Leeds: NHS Executive).

Niskanen, W. (1971) *Bureaucracy and representative government* (New York: Aldine-Atherton).

Nolan, J. (1998) *The therapeutic state: Justifying government at century's end* (New York, NY: New York University Press).

Northern Ireland Office (1993) *Strategy for the support of the voluntary sector and for community development in Northern Ireland, Efficiency Scrutiny of Government funding of the Voluntary Sector* (Dept. of Health and Social Services, Belfast, Northern Ireland Office).

O'Brien, M. and Penna, S. (1998) *Theorising welfare: Enlightenment and modern society* (London: Sage Publications).

O'Keefe, E. and Hogg, C. (1999) 'Public participation and marginalised groups: The community development model', *Health Expectations*, December, **2** (4): 245–54.

Oatley, N. and Lambert, C. (1995) 'Evaluating competitive policy: The city challenge initiative', in Hambleton, R. and Hughes, T. (eds) *Urban policy evaluation* (London: Paul Chapman).

Offe, C. (1984) *Contradictions in the welfare state* (London: Hutchinson).

Office of the Deputy Prime Minister (ODPM) (2001 Strong local leadership. Quality public services (London: ODPM).

Office of National Statistics (ONS) (2001) 'Social capital: A review of the literature', *Social Analysis and Reporting Division* (October) (London: ONS).

Organisation for Economic Co-Operation and Development (OECD) (2001) Public sector leadership for the 21st century (Paris: OECD).

Ovretveit, J. (1997) 'How patient power and client participation affects relations between them and professionals' in Ovretveit, J., Mathias, P. and Thompson, T. (eds) (1997) *Interprofessional working for health and social care* (Basingstoke: Macmillan).

Pahl, R. (1966) *Whose City: And further essays on urban society* (London: Penguin).

Palmer, I. and Hardy, C. (2000) *Thinking about management* (London: Sage Publications).

Parker, R., Ward, H., Jackson, S., Aldgate, J. and Wedge, P. (1991) *Looking after children: The Report of an Independent Working Party, established by the Department of Health* (London: HMSO).

Parry, G., Moyser, G. and Walsh, K. (1992) *Citizenship: Rights, community and participation* (London: Pitman).

Parry, N. and Parry, J. (1976) *The rise of the medical profession: A study of collective mobility* (London: Croom Helm).

PAT 17 (2000) *Joining it up locally, Report of Policy Action Team 17, National Strategy for Neighbourhood Renewal* (London: DETR).

Pearce, J. (2003) *Social enterprise in anytown* (London: Calouste Gulbenkian Foundation).

Penna, S. and O'Brien, M. (1996) 'Postmodernism and social policy: A small step forwards?', *Journal of Social Policy* (January), **25** (1): 39–62.

Performance and Innovation Unit (2000) *Wiring it up. Whitehall's Management of cross-cutting policies and services* (London: Cabinet Office).

Peters, J. (1992) *Liberation management: Necessary disorganisation for the nanosecond nineties* (New York: Alfred Knopf).

Peters, J. and Waterman, R. (1982) *In search of excellence: Lessons from America's best run companies* (New York: Harper & Row).

Pfeffer, N. and Coote, A. (1991) 'Is quality good for you? A critical review of quality assurance in welfare services', *Social Policy Paper No. 5* (London: Institute for Public Policy Research (IPPR)).

Plant, R. (1992) 'Citizenship, rights and welfare', in Coote, A. (ed.) *The welfare of citizens: Developing new social rights* (London: IPPR/Rivers Oram Press).

Polanyi, M. (1970) *Personal Knowledge* (London: Prentice Hall).

Pollert, A. (1988) 'The "flexible firm": Fixation or fact?', *Work, Employment and Society*, **2** (3): 281–316.

Pollitt, C. (1995) 'Justification by works or by faith? Evaluating the new public management', *Evaluation*, **1**(2): 133–54.

Pollitt, C. (1993) *Managerialism and the public services*, 2nd Edition (Oxford: Blackwell).

Pollock, A., Shaoul, J., Rowland, D. and Player, S. (2001) 'Public services and the private sector: A response to the IPPR', *A Catalyst Working Paper* (November) (London: Catalyst).

Popple, K. (1995) *Analysing community work: Its theory and pratice* (Buckingham: Open University Press).

Popple, K. and Redmond, M. (2001) 'Community development and the voluntary sector in the new millennium: The implications of the Third Way in the UK', *Community Development Journal* (October), **35** (4): 391–400.

Powell, M. (2000) 'New Labour and the third way in the British welfare state: a new and distinctive approach?', *Critical Social Policy* (February), **20** (1): 39–59.

Powell, M. and Hewitt, M. (1998) 'The end of welfare?', *Social Policy and Administration* (March), **32** (1): 1–13.

Price, R. (1983) 'White-collar unions: Growth, character and attitudes in the 1970s', in Hyman, R. and Price, R. (eds) *The new working class? White-collar workers and their organisations* (Basingstoke: Macmillan).

Prince, L. (1998) 'The neglected rules: on leadership and dissent', in Coulson, A. (ed.) *Trust and contracts: relationships in local government, health and public services* (Bristol: The Policy Press).

Propper, C. and Green, K. (2001) 'A larger role for the private sector in financing UK health care: The arguments and the evidence', *Journal of Social Policy* (October), **30** (4): 685–704.

Pugh, G. (ed.) (1997) *Partnerships in action* (London: NCB).

Purdue, D., Razzaque, K., Hambleton, R., Stewart, M., with Huxham, C. and Vangen, S. (2000) *Community leadership in area regeneration* (Bristol: The Policy Press).

Putnam, R. (1993a) *Making democracy work* (Princetown NJ: Princetown University Press).

Putnam, R. (1993b) 'The prosperous community: Social capital and public life', *The American Prospect*, No. 13.

Putnam, R. (1995) 'Bowling alone: America's declining social capital', *Journal of Democracy* **6** (1): 65–78.

Putnam, R. (2000) *Bowling alone – The collapse and revival of American community* (New York: Simon Schuster).

Quarter, J. (1992) *Canada's social economy: Co-operatives, non-profits, and other community enterprises* (Toronto: James Lorimer and Company).

Rawnsley, A. (2000) *Servants of the people: The inside story of New Labour* (London: Penguin).

Rex, J. and Moore, R. (1967) *Race, community and conflict: A study of Sparkbrook* (London: Oxford University Press).

Robson, P., Locke, M. and Dawson, J. (1997) *Consumerism or democracy? User involvement in the control of voluntary organisations* (Bristol: Policy Press).

Rodwell, C. (1996) 'An analysis of the concept of empowerment', *Journal of Advanced Nursing*, **23**: 305–13.

Salaman, G. (1995) *Managing* (Buckingham: Open University Press).

Salamon, L. and Anheier, H. (1997) *Defining the nonprofit sector: A cross-national analysis* (Manchester: Manchester University Press).

Sampson, R., Raudenbush, S. and Earls, F. (1997) 'Neighbourhoods and violent crime: A multilevel study of collective efficacy' quoted in Halpern, D. (1999) *Social capital: The new golden goose* (Faculty of Social and Political Sciences, Cambridge University, unpublished).

Sanderson, I. (1996) 'Needs and public services', in Percy-Smith, J. (ed.) *Needs assessment in public policy* (Buckingham: Open University Press).

Saraga, E. (ed.) (1998) *Embodying the social: Constructions of difference* (London: Open University/Routledge).

Satyamurti, C. (1981) *Occupational survival* (Oxford: Blackwell).

Schein, E. (1993) 'On dialogue, culture, and organisational learning', *Organisational Dynamics* (Autumn), **22** (3): 40–51.

Schein, V. (1993) 'How can organisations learn faster?', *Sloan Management Review* (Winter), 85–92.

Schuller, T. (2000) 'Exploiting social capital: Learning about learning' (Inaugural lecture at Birkbeck College, 9 February).

Seabrook, J. (1984) *The idea of neighbourhood: What local politics should be about* (London: Pluto).

Seebohm, F. (Lord) (1968) *Report of the Committee on Local Authority and Allied Personal Social Services Cmnd 3703* (London: HMSO).

Senge, P. (1990) *The fifth discipline: The art and practice of the learning organisation* (New York: Doubleday).

Senge, P. (1999) *The dance of change: The challenge of sustaining momentum in learning organisations* (London: Nicholas Brealey).

Sennett, R. (1996) *The uses of disorder: Personal identity and city life* (London: Faber).

Sharron, H. (1980) 'NALGO: State of the union', *Social Work Today*, **11**, p. 38.

Shaw, I. (1997) 'Engaging the user: Participation, empowerment, and the rhetoric of quality', in Pithouse, A. and Williamson, H. (eds) *Engaging the user in welfare services* (Birmingham: Venture Press).

Showstack Sassoon, A. (1996) 'Beyond pessimism of the intellect: Agendas for social justice and change', in Perryman, M. (ed.) *The Blair agenda* (London: Lawrence & Wishart).

Shragge, E. (1997) 'Community economic development: Conflicts and vision', in Shragge, E. (ed.) *Community economic development: In search of empowerment* (Montreal: Black Rose Books).

Silverman, D. (1970) *The theory of organisations* (London: Heinemann).

Simon, B. (1990) 'Rethinking empowerment', *Journal of Progressive Human Services*, **1** (1): 27–39.

Snape, D. and Stewart, M. (1996) *Keeping up the momentum: partnership working in Bristol and the west of England* (Bristol: Bristol Chamber of Commerce and Initiative (unpublished)).

Social Exclusion Unit (SEU) (1998) *Bringing Britain together: A national strategy for neighbourhood renewal* (London: Cabinet Office) Cm 4045.

Social Exclusion Unit (SEU) (2000) *National strategy for neighbourhood renewal: A framework for consultation* (London: Cabinet Office).

Social Exclusion Unit (SEU) (2001) *A new commitment to neighbourhood renewal: National strategy action plan* (London: Cabinet Office).

Southall Black Sisters (1989) *Against the grain: A celebration of survival and struggle* (London: Southall Black Sisters).

Stacey, M. (1969) 'The myth of community studies', *British Journal of Sociology*, **20** (2): 134–47.

Standing Conference on Community Development [SSCD] (2000) Dialogue about the strategic framework for community development (Sheffield: SCCD).

Steele, J. (2000) 'Wasted Values, Public Management Foundation' [http://www.pmfoundation.org.uk/wasted.htm].

Stewart, J. (1995) 'Accountability and empowerment in welfare services', in Gladstone, D. (ed.) *British social welfare: past, present and future* (London: UCL Press).

Stewart, J. (1996) Local government today (London: Local Government Management Board).

Stewart, J. and Walsh, K. (1989) The search for quality (Luton, England: Local Government Management Board).

Stewart, M. (1994) 'Between Whitehall and town hall: the realignment of urban regeneration policy in England', *Policy and Politics*, **22** (2): 133–45.

Stewart, M. *et al.* (1999) *Cross cutting issues affecting local government* (London: DETR).

Stogdill, R. (1974) *Handbook of leadership: A survey of theory and research* (New York, NY: Free Press).

Stoker, G. (1995) 'Regime theory and urban politics', in Judge, D., Stoker, G. and Wolman, H. (eds) *Theories of urban politics* (London: Sage Publications).

Stone, C. (1986) 'Power and social complexity', in Waste, R. (ed.) *Community power: Directions for future research* (Newbury Park, CA: Sage Publications).

Stone, C. (1989) Paradigms, power and urban leadership, in Jones, B. (ed.) Leadership and politics (Lawrence KA: University of Kansas Press).

Stone, C. (1993) 'Urban regimes and the capacity to govern: A political economy approach', *Journal of Urban Affairs*, **15** (1): 1–28.

Tam, H. (1998) *Communitarianism: A new agenda for politics and citizenship* (Basingstoke: Macmillan).

Taylor, M. (1995) Unleashing the potential: Bringing residents to the centre of regeneration (York: Joseph Rowntree Foundation).

Taylor, M. (1996) 'Between public and private: accountability in voluntary organisations', *Policy and Politics*, **24** (1): 57–72.

Taylor, M. (1996) 'What are the key influences on the work of voluntary agencies', in Billis, D. and Harris, M. (eds) *Voluntary agencies* (Basingstoke: Macmillan).

Taylor, M. (1997) *The best of both worlds: The voluntary sector and local government* (York: Joseph Rowntree Foundation).

Taylor, M. and Hogget, P. (1994) 'Trusting in networks? The third sector and welfare change' in 6 p. and Vidal, I. (eds) *Delivering welfare: Repositioning non-profit and Co-operative action in Western European States* (Barcelona: Centre d' Initiatives de l' Economia Social).

Temkin, K. and Rohe, W. (1998) 'Social capital and neighbourhood stability: An empirical investigation', *Housing Policy Debate*, **9**: 1.

Thomas, D. (1995) *Community development at work: A case of obscurity in accomplishment* (London: Community Development Foundation).

Thomas, S. (1997) 'Tenant participation in the social rented sector', in Pithouse, A. and Williamson, H. (eds) *Engaging the user in welfare services* (Birmingham: Venture Press).

Thomson, P. (1999) 'Public Sector management in a period of radical change: 1979–92', *Public Money and Management*, **12** (3): 33–41.

Timmins, N. (1995) *The five giants: A biography of the welfare state* (London: Fontana).

Townsend, P. (1979) *Poverty in the United Kingdom* (London: Penguin).

Tyler, C. (2002) 'Breaking articles of faith' in Smulian, M. *New Start*, 11 October, p. 12.

Vaill, P. (1996) *Learning as a way of being* (San Francisco: Jossey-Bass).

Vaill, P. (1999) *Spirited leading and learning: Process wisdom for a new age* (Englewood Cliffs: Prentice Hall).

Vanclay, L. (1996) *Sustaining collaboration between general practitioners and social workers* (London: CAIPE).

Wallace, M. (2001) 'Putting local people in charge is central to the neighbourhood renewal action plan', *New Start*, 26 January, p. 13.

Walker, P., Lewis, J., Lingayah, S. and Sommer, F. (2000) *Measuring the effect of neighbourhood renewal on local people* (London: Groundwork, New Economics Foundation).

Walsh, K., Hinings, B., Greenwood, R. and Ranson, S. (1981) 'Power and advantage in organizations', *Organization Studies*, 2/2: 131–52.

Ward, D. and Mullender, A. (1991) 'Empowerment and oppression: An indissoluble pairing for contemporary social work', *Critical Social Policy*, **11** (2): 21–30.

Weber, M. (1947) *The theory of social and economic organisation*, trans. Henderson, A. and Parsons, T. (New York, Free Press).

Weber, M. (1948) 'Politics as a vocation (1921)', in Gerth, H. and Mills, C. (eds), From *Max Weber: Essays in sociology* (London: Routledge & Kegan Paul).

West (1994) *Effective Teamwork*, British Psychological Society.

White, L. (2000) 'Changing the "whole system" in the public sector', *Journal of Organisational Change Management*, **13** (2): 162–77.

Whitfield, D. (1983) *Making it public: Evidence and action against privatisation* (London: Pluto Press).

Wilding, P. (1982) *Professional power and social welfare* (London: Routledge).

Wilkinson, D. (1997) 'Whole system development – rethinking public service management', *International Journal of Public Sector Management*, **10** (7): 505–33.

Wilkinson, D. and Applebee, E. (1999) *Implementing holistic government: Joined up action on the ground* (Bristol: The Policy Press).

Williams, F. (1993) 'Women and community', in Bornat, J. *et al. Community care: A reader* (Basingstoke: Macmillan in association with the Open University).

Williams, F. (2000) 'Principles of recognition and respect in welfare', in Lewis, G., Gewirtz, S. and Clarke, J. (eds) *Rethinking social policy* (London: Sage Publication/Open University Press).

Williams, F. (2001) 'In and beyond New Labour: Towards a new political ethics of care', *Critical Social Policy* (November), **21** (4) Issue 69: 467–93.

Williams, F., Popay, J. and Oakley, A. (1999) 'Changing paradigms of welfare', in Williams, F., Popay, J. and Oakley, A. (eds) *Welfare research: A critical review* (London: UCL Press).

Williams, R. (1983) *Keywords: A vocabulary of culture and society* (London: Fontana).

Willmott, P. and Young, M. (1960) *Family and class in a London suburb* (London: Routledge Kegan Paul).

Wilson, G. (1998) 'Staff and users in the postmodern organisation: Modernity, postmodernity and user marginalisation', in Barry, M. and Hallett, C. (eds) (Lyme Regis: Russell House).

Wistow, G., Knapp, M., Hardy, B. and Allen, C. (1994) Social care in a mixed economy (Buckingham: Open University Press).

Wolch, J. (1990) *The shadow state: Government and the voluntary sector in transition* (New York: The Foundation Center).

Woodward, K. (1997) 'Feminist critiques of social policy' in Lavalette, M. and Pratt, A. (eds) *Social policy: A conceptual and theoretical introduction* (London: Sage Publications).

Woolcock, M. (2001) 'The place of social capital in understanding social and economic outcomes', *ISUMA Canadian Journal of Policy Research*, 2 (1): 11–17.

World Bank (1999) Social capital web site: [www.worldbank.org/poverty/scapital/index.htm].

Young, I. (1990) *Justice and the politics of difference* (Oxford: Princetown University Press).

Young, I. M. (1990) 'The ideal of community and the politics of difference', in Nicholson, L. (ed.) *Feminism/Post-Modernism* (London: Routledge).

Young, M. and Willmott, P. (1957) *Family and kinship in East London* (London: Pelican).

Yukl, G. (1989) 'Managerial leadership: A review of theory and research', *Journal of Management*, 15 (2): 251–89.

Index